Traditional Food from Scotland

The Edinburgh Book of Plain Cookery Recipes

Traditional Food from

SCOTLAND

The Edinburgh Book of Plain Cookery Recipes

HIPPOCRENE BOOKS
New York

Originally published by Thomas Nelson and Sons, Ltd., London.

Hippocrene paperback edition, 1996.
Second printing, 1999.

For information, address:
HIPPOCRENE BOOKS, INC.
171 Madison Avenue
New York, NY 10016

Library of Congress Cataloging-in-Publication Data
Traditional food from Scotland. -- Hippocrene pbk. ed.
    p. cm.
    Originally published: London : Thomas Nelson, 1932.
    Includes index.
    ISBN 0-7818-0514-7
    1. Cookery, Scottish.
TX717.3.T73   1996
641.59411--dc20   96-21628
                                                      CIP

Printed in the United States of America.

Front cover artwork by John Fulleylove, R.I.: Princess Street from the Steps of the New Club.

CONTENTS

PLAIN COOKERY RECIPES

PRELIMINARY NOTES

PANTRY AND SCULLERY WORK

Table Glass.

1. Rinse milky glasses with cold water.

2. Wash in a pulp bowl half filled with warm water, washing only one glass at a time. A soft nail brush can be used for cut glass.

3. If a decanter or water-bottle is stained, put into it one tablespoonful of salt, one tablespoonful of vinegar, one tablespoonful of tea leaves, and half fill with water. Leave it to soak, and shake occasionally till the stain is removed. Rinse and drain upside down in a jug.

4. Rinse in cold water and dry with a linen glass towel.

China.

1. Scrape away all bits of food and pour the dregs from the cups.

2. Wipe very greasy plates with newspaper, and put into neat piles.

3. Rinse articles which have been used for milk or starchy foods with cold water.

4. Half fill a large bowl with hot water, wash cleanest

articles first, using a small mop or net cloth. Use soap or soda if necessary, and remove stains with a little dry salt. Avoid soda when washing gilt china. Use a papier maché bowl when washing valuable china, and wash each article separately.

5. Scald milk jugs with boiling water after washing.

6. If soap has been used, rinse all china in hot water. Allow to drain upside down for a few minutes before drying with a dish towel.

7. Plates dried in a plate rack should be rinsed with almost boiling water. They will then dry quickly, and will have a good gloss.

8. Wash dish cloth after use. Dish cloths and towels should be boiled once a week.

Table Silver.

1. Wash in warm soapy water.

2. Rinse in hot water.

3. Dry well with a soft cloth.

4. Polish with a chamois leather and keep in a lined silver basket, tray, or drawer.

5. Treat stainless silver as above. No further polishing is necessary.

6. Rub silver egg-spoons with a little salt to remove egg stain.

7. Silver teapots should be occasionally filled with boiling water and soda. After soaking for several hours, clean the inside with Brooke's soap and rinse well.

8. Cruets ; wash and refill mustard pot each day. Empty, wash, dry, and polish salt-cellars and pepper pots each week.

9. Polish silver weekly. If silver is solid, use pre-

cipitated whiting moistened with methylated spirit. If silver is plated, use precipitated whiting moistened with ammonia or water.

10. Allow the polish to dry on, then rub off with a soft duster.

11. Brush engraved silver.

12. Use a double fold of felt for cleaning between prongs of forks.

13. Scald, dry, and finally polish with chamois leather.

Note.—Electro-plate, Britannia metal, and pewter are cleaned in the same way.

Cutlery.

1. Place blades in a jug of hot water and soda. Do not let the water touch the handles.

2. Wash and dry.

3. Rub knives from side to side on a knife-board sprinkled with bathbrick. Then rub back of knife and clean shoulders of knife with a cork dipped in bathbrick.

4. Clean prongs of steel forks with a grooved cork dipped in bathbrick.

5. Dust well.

6. Stainless knives: After washing, rub up with a duster and sharpen occasionally with a rotary knife sharpener.

Saucepans.

Recipe for Scouring Mixture

One pound Hudson's soap. | Mix the ingredients to-
One pound whiting. | gether, and pass them
One pound silver sand. | through an old sieve.

Iron Saucepans with or without silicate lining, baking sheets, and roasting tins.

1. If food or grease is burned into the utensil, boil with water and soda, and then scour with a wire brush or pot brush.

2. Wash inside and outside with hot water, using soap and silver sand or scouring mixture.

3. Rinse in hot and cold water and wipe with a net cloth.

4. Allow to dry upside down on plate rack of stove.

5. Frying-pans used for omelettes, pancakes, etc., should simply be rubbed with kitchen paper, and not washed.

6. Girdles should be rubbed with coarse salt and paper while hot, and not washed.

Aluminium and Enamel Saucepans.

1. If food or grease has stuck to the pan, fill with hot water and keep warm on the stove.

2. If used for starchy foods, rinse with cold water before washing.

3. Wash with Abraizo steel wool, avoiding the use of soda or of soap with much soda in it.

4. Rinse in hot water and dry with a kitchen towel.

5. Aluminium pans and lids may be polished on the outside with a paste of whiting and water.

Tin-Lids, Moulds, Measures, etc.

1. Wash in hot soapy water.   Rinse in hot water and dry well.

2. Polish the outside of tin-lids, the rim of strainers, etc., with precipitated whiting.

3. Never polish cake tins, and it should not be necessary to wash them after use.   Merely wipe off the grease while hot with kitchen paper, then rub with a dry cloth.

Copper.

Moulds, Pans, etc.

1. Wash in hot soapy water. Rinse in hot water.
2. Remove stains by rubbing with a cut lemon, and immediately rinse off acid with hot water.
3. Dry and polish the outside with a little dry whiting.
4. Be careful never to use anything that would remove the tinning from the inside of kettle or pan. This tinning should be kept perfectly whole, so that verdigris may not form on the copper.

Brass.

Brass Taps, Door Handles, Knockers, etc.

1. Clean daily with brass polish, and wash the inside of taps as far up as possible. Nickel taps may be cleaned occasionally with brass or furniture polish.
2. If brass is lacquered, only rub up with dusters.

Benares Trays, etc.

1. If greasy, wash with hot soapy water, and rinse in hot water.
2. Rub all over with a cut lemon, and rinse immediately in very hot water.
3. Dry and rub up with dusters and a leather.

Brass Jam Pans and Cooking Utensils.

1. Wash with hot water.
2. Clean with Brooke's soap, rinse with very hot water, and dry well.
3. Brighten the inside with a little dry whiting, and rub with a soft cloth.
4. Before use rub the inside with vinegar and salt, and rinse immediately.

Chromium.

Chromium is applied to brass, iron, or aluminium. It is used for fittings as well as for domestic utensils. Wash and dry, and rub up with a duster.

Zinc and Galvanized Iron.

1. Scrub with hot water, soap, and sand.
2. Rub off stains with paraffin and powdered bath-brick.
3. Rub with newspaper.
4. Polish with dry powdered bathbrick, using a pointed stick covered with a cloth for all rims and corners.
5. Rub well with a duster.

Sinks.

1. Wash and scrub iron sinks, using hot water and soda.
2. Wash porcelain sinks with soap and sand, or scouring mixture, using a little bathbrick for obstinate stains.
3. Clean overflow holes with a cloth on a pointed stick.
4. Dissolve a piece of soda in boiling water, and pour solution down outlet pipe to remove any grease from bend of pipe.
5. Each week put a little disinfectant into the outlet pipe, and allow it to remain there for half an hour before flushing it away.
6. Burn the contents of the sink basket every day.
7. Do not allow solid particles or fluff from cloths to go down the pipe.
8. Flush the pipe with cold water after emptying away the water in which greens have been cooked.

White Wood.

Tables, Pastry Boards, Rolling Pins.

1. Wash with a piece of flannel dipped in warm water.

2. Rub a little soap and sand, or scouring mixture, on the brush, and scrub in straight lines the way of the grain.

3. Wipe soap off with cloth dipped in clean warm water.

4. Give a final wipe all over article with cloth wrung out of cold water, as this improves colour of wood.

Wire and Hair Sieves.

1. Rush cold water through by putting sieve under tap.

2. Wash in hot water and soda.

3. Scrub wooden part with soap and sand.

4. Scrub wire part, but only wash a hair sieve. Use a pointed stick or skewer to get into corners.

5. Rinse in cold water and dry quickly, avoiding great heat, as it is apt to warp the wood.

Brushes.

1. Scrubbing brushes : rinse and shake after use. Remove fluff with a pointed stick, and scald occasionally with hot water and soda.

2. Pastry brushes and brushes used for egg and clarified fat : clean by whirling rapidly in hot water and soda. Rinse, shake, and dry in a moderate temperature.

3. Plate brushes should be rubbed in a soapy lather.

The Kitchen Range.

1. Remove ashes, keeping cinders for future use.

2. Sweep and rake underneath boiler.

3. Clean flues once a week.

4. Wash oven shelves and inside of oven with hot water and soda.

5. Wash grease from stove and blacklead it.

6. Clean steel with bathbrick and turpentine, or brass polish, or emery paper, rubbing in one direction only.

7. Wash and dry tiles.

8. Lay fire.

9. Wash hearth.

Combination Grates.

1. Sweep and rake underneath boiler.

2. Brush the fiue round side oven, under top boiling plate, and behind boiler, once a week.

3. Rub up stainless steel and enamelled black with dusters.

4. Wash tiles.

Interior Fires Heating Water.

1. Rake under the boiler.   There are no flues to clean.

2. Brush the back of fire as far up as possible.

3. Wash and dry tiles.

Gas Stoves.

1. Wipe off all surface stains with newspaper ; wipe inside of oven while hot with a damp cloth.

2. Remove dirt from black parts with a paraffin cloth. Clean the steel.   Wash the enamel slab and tin griller. Polish the taps.

3. Each week wash oven shelves and inside of oven with hot water and soap.   Remove all bars and burners, and scrub them with hot water and soda.   Dry and blacklead them, being careful to omit the holes of the burners. Replace.   Blacklead the rest of the stove. Attend to steel, enamel, taps, etc.

Electric Stoves.

1. Switch off current.

2. Wipe off surface stains from stove and oven.

3. Wash enamel, being careful not to let any water run into the heating elements.

4. When washing the inside of the oven, avoid wetting the heating arrangement.

Note.—Modern finish and outline entail no laborious cleaning.

Oil Stoves.

1. Trim the wicks. To do this, remove funnel and spreader, dusting both, and rub round the wick with soft tissue paper. Do not cut the wick unless this is unavoidable. Replace funnel and spreader.

2. Half fill the container with oil.

3. Wash and dry the japanning and enamel, and the inside of the oven when necessary.

Note.—Some makes have asbestos wicks that need no trimming.

Primus Stoves.

1. Remove silent spreader, and dust the burner.

2. Prick hole with pricker supplied.

3. Three-quarters fill container with oil.

4. Clean metal part of stove.

Disposal of Refuse.

1. Use dustbin for ashes, tins, and breakages only.

2. Burn dust.

3. Use waste paper for lighting fires.

4. Collect animal and vegetable refuse for pig feeding. If this is impossible, it should be burnt.

METHODS OF COOKING

The methods used in the following recipes are : boiling, stewing, braising, roasting and baking, frying, grilling, and steaming.

Boiling.

Boiling is cooking the food by immersion for a given time in boiling or simmering liquid.

Note.—Boiling-point of water is 212° F. Simmering-point of water is 180°–190° F.

Stewing.

Stewing is cooking in a small quantity of liquid at a low temperature (180° F.) in a tightly covered vessel.

Note.—Food cooked by this method is rendered tender, and the salts of vegetables, though not the vitamins, are preserved.

Braising.

Braising is a combination of stewing and roasting.

Roasting.

Roasting proper is cooking by radiation in front of the fire.   Roasting in an oven by hot air is synonymous with baking.

Note.—Instead of an oven, a strong pan with lid may be used for small joints.

Simple Tests for Oven Heat

280° F.   Comfortably hot to hand ; paper colours in five minutes.

340° F. Uncomfortably hot to hand ; flour quickly turns light brown ; paper browns almost immediately.

380°–400° F. Unbearably hot to hand ; flour sprinkled on oven shelf burns readily ; paper placed on shelf burns at once.

Note.—When testing a girdle the flour should take a few seconds to brown.

Frying.

Frying is cooking in hot fat. There are two kinds of frying. Shallow, or dry frying—*i.e.* frying with just enough fat to prevent the food sticking to the pan, or with enough fat to come half-way up the food being fried. Deep, or wet frying—*i.e.* frying in sufficient fat to cover the food.

Simple Tests for Heat of Fat

350° F. Blue haze begins to rise.

360° F. Slight blue haze all over ; bread turns light brown.

375° F. Decided haze ; bread burns at once.

Grilling or Broiling or Brandering.

These are synonymous terms for cooking by the direct rays from fire or grill. The gridiron may be placed over, or in front of, the fire, or under a gas or electric grill.

Steaming.

Steaming is cooking by moist heat in the steam that rises from boiling water.

Note.—It is a simple and economical method, and renders the food light and digestible.

WEIGHTS AND MEASURES

Avoirdupois Weight.

16 ounces = 1 pound.
14 pounds = 1 stone.

Liquid Measure.

4 gills .   . = 1 pint.
2 pints   . = 1 quart.
4 quarts . = 1 gallon.

Homely Measures.

"A spoonful" means as much above the bowl of the spoon as in the spoon.

"Half a spoonful" means a level spoonful. Divide this in two, lengthwise, to obtain a quarter spoonful.

One tablespoonful of solids = one ounce.

One teacupful of solids = four ounces.

TERMS USED IN COOKERY

1. To break flour is to mix in very gradually a small quantity of cold liquid, stirring it until it is smooth.

2. To bind a mixture is to add milk or egg to make it hold together.

3. To brown meat, etc., is to place it in a small quantity of hot fat, not turning it until the part is brown.

4. To burst rice is to put it on in cold water and bring it to boiling-point. This bursts the grains of starch.

5. To blanch is to cover with cold water and bring to boiling-point. Skim well, and pour off the water.

6. To parboil is to boil anything until partly cooked.

7. To scald vegetables, etc., is to pour boiling water over them for a few minutes, and then throw away the water.

8. To scald milk is to bring it almost, but not quite, to boiling-point.

9. To shred suet is to cut it with a sharp knife so thinly as to be almost scraping ; the suet should be so thin as to curl up.

10. To reduce is to boil quickly for five to ten minutes to concentrate the flavour.

11. To toss in fat is to shake or stir lightly in melted fat until fat is absorbed.

12. To poach is to cook in a small quantity of simmering liquid in an uncovered vessel.

13. To fold in a beaten white of egg is to mix it lightly and thoroughly with the heavier ingredients.

AVERAGE QUANTITIES PER HEAD

Soup :

Allow half-pint per head and half-pint extra.

Fish : IF FILLETED.

Allow one or two fillets per head, *i.e.* three to four ounces per head (weight before cooking).

BOILED CUT OF FISH.

Allow six ounces per head (weight before cooking).

Meat : LARGE JOINTS.

Half-pound per head (weight before cooking).

STEWS.

Four ounces per head (weight before cooking).

CUTLETS.

Three for every two persons.

Pastry : FOR PIES, etc.

One and a half to two ounces of flour, etc., per head.

Puddings : STEAMED.

One ounce flour, etc., per head.

MILK PUDDING.

One gill milk, etc., per head and half-pint extra.

NOTE ON SHELLFISH

Crabs and lobsters are marketed alive, and must be killed by the cook, and the usual method of doing this has been to plunge the live animal into boiling water. Scientific experiments have shown, however, that only a small degree of heat is necessary to paralyse the nerve centres of the animal, and thus to cause its painless death ; hence the following humane method is now adopted.

Place the crab or lobster in cold water, previously salted with a quarter-pound of salt to the gallon.   Raise the temperature very slowly to the boiling-point—the temperature of 70° Fahrenheit should not be reached in less than three minutes—and then cook by boiling from twenty to thirty minutes.   (See Recipe 69, page 57.)

SOUPS

STOCKS

Stock is the liquid obtained when the juices of meat, bones, and vegetables have been extracted by slow simmering.

1. Household Stock

Wash the bones (a nap bone makes very good stock) and cut the meat into small pieces, and free cooked bones and meat from fat and sauce. Put the bones and meat into the stockpot. Cover with cold water; add one teaspoonful of salt; bring to boiling-point and remove white scum. Add pieces of fresh carrot, onion, turnip, and celery, and let the stock simmer.

If a light-coloured stock is desired use trimmings and bones from chicken, veal, or rabbit, cooked or uncooked, and if a brown colour is wished use trimmings and bones from beef and mutton, cooked or uncooked, and fry them in marrow or dripping to give colour and flavour.

Simmer household stock for several hours, adding more water when necessary. Strain into an earthenware vessel. Keep the stock uncovered. When cold remove the fat and use the stock for soup, sauces, gravies, etc.

Note.—(1) Into the household stock may be put strainings from unthickened soups and sauces, meat and vegetable boilings, and trimmings of fresh vegetables.

(2) Bread, green vegetables, or starchy materials should not be put into the stockpot.

2. Bone Stock

Two pounds bones, cooked or uncooked.
Carrot.
Turnip.
One onion.
Twelve peppercorns, and salt.
One ounce dripping.

Two quarts cold water.

Wash and break the bones. Melt the dripping; when hot fry the bones brown, then cover with the water; add the salt, bring to the boil, and skim. Add the vegetables and peppercorns. Boil gently for four or five hours. Strain through a fine sieve.

The bones may be boiled a second or third time, with the addition of fresh vegetables.

3. Fish Stock

Fish bones and trimmings.
One onion.
A stick of celery.
Six white peppercorns.
One blade of mace.
Salt.

Cold water to cover.

Thoroughly cleanse the trimmings, and put them into a saucepan with the water and salt. Bring slowly to the boil, and skim thoroughly. Add celery, peppercorns, and mace, and allow all to simmer for forty minutes. If fish stock is cooked too long a bitter flavour is extracted from the bones. Strain off the stock. This stock can be used for fish soup or sauce.

Note.—A cod's head or a haddock can be used instead of fish trimmings.

4. Vegetable Stock

Two ounces haricot beans.	One or two onions.
Two ounces lentils or peas.	Blade of mace.
One or two sticks of celery	Few white peppercorns.
or quarter teaspoonful	Two quarts water.
celery seed.	Salt.

Wash beans and soak overnight. Put all ingredients into a well-lined pan. Simmer for three or four hours. Strain and use as required.

SOUPS

These are of four principal kinds—clear soup, broths, purées, thickened soups. Clear soup or Consommé belongs to Advanced Cookery rather than Plain. Broth is unclarified stock with garnish of rice, barley, and cut-up vegetable. Purées are soups thickened by the pulping of their own ingredients. Thickened soups owe their thickening to some binding or thickening.

Note.—Herbs improve the flavour of many soups. Any of the following herbs may be used, either separately or one sprig of several of them may be tied together in a small bunch and put in the soup and removed before serving : sorrel, parsley, sage, mint, thyme, marjoram, and bay leaf. Celery seed is also a pleasant flavouring. About half a teaspoonful may be used, tied loosely in a piece of muslin, and removed before serving.

BROTHS

5. Sheep's Head Broth

One sheep's head.
Two ounces barley or rice.
Turnip cut in dice. ⎫
Carrot cut in dice. ⎬ One pint cut vegetables.
One or two leeks. ⎭

One carrot grated.
Dessertspoonful chopped parsley.
Three to four quarts cold water.

To Prepare the Head.—Order a sheep's head already divided by the butcher; remove the brain, and soak it in cold water and vinegar to whiten it. (For the cooking and use of the brain see Recipes 82 and 83.) Soak the head in tepid water and salt for half an hour. Scrape the small bones, from the nostrils; cleanse the head thoroughly, then blanch (see Cookery Terms, p. 20) and rinse it.

To Make the Soup.—Put the head (after blanching) into a large pan and cover it with the water. Add the barley (thoroughly washed). Bring the water to boiling-point, skim well, and add the carrot and turnip in dice, and the leeks in small pieces. Season it well with pepper and salt, and simmer gently three or four hours, skimming when necessary. Half an hour before serving add the grated carrot. (When the head is tender lift it out.) At the last, add the parsley, just bring the soup to boiling-point, and then serve it in a hot tureen.

For method of serving the head see Recipes 82 and 83.

6. Scotch Broth

Half to one pound runner of beef (or neck of mutton).
One ounce barley.
Turnip cut in dice. ⎱
Carrot cut in dice. ⎰ Half-pint cut vegetables.
One leek sliced.

One carrot grated.
Pepper and salt.
One quart cold water.
One large teaspoonful chopped parsley.

Wipe the meat, put it into a pan with sufficient cold water to cover it, add the salt and the barley (thoroughly washed), bring the water to boiling-point, and skim. Add the pepper and the vegetables. Simmer for three or four hours. Half an hour before dishing add the grated carrot. When ready lift the meat out, skim the broth, add the chopped parsley, boil up, and serve.

Note.—If meat is to be served as a separate course, cook blocks of carrot and turnip in the broth. Serve meat and vegetables, pouring a little of the liquor over.

7. Hotch-Potch

One pound neck of lamb.
One pint vegetables (young carrots and turnips cut in dice and sprigs of cauliflower.)
Half a lettuce.

Half-pint green peas.
Half-pint broad beans.
A few spring onions.
Two quarts water.
Two teaspoonfuls salt.
Half teaspoonful pepper.

One teaspoonful sugar.

Scrape, wipe, and joint the lamb. Put into a pan with cold water, add salt, bring to the boil, and skim. Add pepper. Prepare the vegetables ; shell the peas, and skin the beans ; slice the onions, and cut lettuce in shreds. Add all the vegetables except peas, lettuce, and cauliflower, and simmer till meat is tender. Add remainder of vegetables twenty to thirty minutes before dishing (according to age). When ready, remove the lamb. Add the sugar to the soup, and dish. Serve the lamb separately.

Note —Hotch-Potch should be quite thick.

8. Soupe Maigre

One small carrot, turnip, and leek.
One onion.
One stick of celery.
Small cauliflower.

Half-pint vegetables.

Two or three leaves of lettuce.
One ounce butter.
One pint boiling water.
Pepper and salt.
Pinch of sugar.

Prepare the vegetables carefully. Break the cauliflower into small pieces, and cut all the other vegetables in fine shreds. Melt the butter, and toss (see Cookery Terms, p. 20) all together in it for five minutes. Add the boiling water, and boil gently for about half an hour till the vegetables are tender. Season and serve.

PURÉES

9. Lentil Soup

Half-pound lentils (Egyptian).
Half a carrot.
Half a turnip.
One stick celery.
One onion.

One ounce dripping.
Two quarts water, meat boilings, or household stock.
Pepper and salt.
About half-pint milk.

Wash the lentils. Prepare the other vegetables, and cut them in slices. Melt the dripping in a saucepan ; add the lentils and other vegetables, and toss them in the melted dripping until it is absorbed. Add the liquid, the salt and pepper, and bring to the boil. Simmer the soup two and a half to three hours, stirring frequently. When cooked, pass the soup through a sieve. Add the milk, and reheat.

Note.—With vegetable purées, dice of fried bread should be served.

10. Curried Lentil Soup

Make as for Lentil Soup, but sprinkle lentils with curry powder before tossing them in fat. Allow one tablespoonful curry powder to half a pound of lentils. Add one teaspoonful of curry paste.

11. Lentil and Tomato Soup

Four or five tomatoes to half-pound lentils.

Make in same way as Lentil Soup. Thicken, if necessary, with half an ounce of flour or cornflour, mixed with a little milk.

12. Haricot Bean Soup

Wash the beans and soak them overnight in cold water. Pour away the water and rinse the beans. Proceed in the same way as for Lentil Soup, but use only white vegetables such as onion and celery.

13. Pea Soup

Wash the split peas and soak them overnight in cold water. Strain off the water, reserving it for the soup. Proceed in the same way as for Lentil Soup. Cook from three to four hours.

14. Red Pottage

Half-pound haricot beans.
Four fresh or tinned to-
matoes.
One beetroot.
Small piece of celery.
One onion.
Pepper and salt.
One ounce dripping.
Three pints water or household stock.

Prepare the beans as for Haricot Bean Soup. Prepare and slice the vegetables. Melt the dripping, and toss the vegetables and beans in it. Add the liquid and seasonings, and boil gently from three to four hours. Remove the beetroot, and then pass the rest through a sieve. Reheat and serve.

15. Potato Soup

Two pounds of potatoes.
Two or three sticks celery.
One onion.
Two ounces butter.
One quart water, meat boil-
ings, or household stock.
Half-pint milk.
Pepper and salt.

Wash and slice the vegetables, and toss them in the butter. Add the meat boilings, pepper and salt, bring to the boil, and simmer one and a half hours. Bruise down or rub through a hair sieve. Return to rinsed saucepan. Add the milk, boil, and serve with dice of fried bread.

16. Potato and Tomato Soup.

One and a half pounds of
potatoes.
Half a pound of tomatoes.
One or two sticks of celery.
One onion.
One ounce butter.
One quart water, meat boil-
ings, or household stock.
One gill milk.
Pepper and salt.

The method is the same as for Potato Soup.

17. Purée of Carrot and Turnip

Proceed as for Potato Soup. Reheat after sieving, and thicken as for Tomato Soup. (Recipe 20.)

18. Milk Soup

One pound potatoes.
Two onions.
One quart of water or light-coloured stock.

One pint milk.
One ounce small sago.
Pepper and salt.

Wash, pare, and slice potatoes ; skin, scald, and chop the onions. Put potatoes, onions, pepper and salt, and the quart of cold water into a lined pan. Bring to the boil, and boil till quite soft. Crush the potatoes and onions with a spoon until smooth. Add the milk and sago, and boil for ten minutes until the sago is quite clear and cooked. This soup may be made richer by tossing the vegetables in one ounce of butter.

19. Brown Onion Soup

Four Spanish onions.
Two ounces butter.
Half-ounce flour.

One quart brown stock.
Pepper and salt.

Skin, scald, dry, and slice the onions. Fry them very slowly in the melted butter until a golden brown colour ; add the stock, pepper and salt, and cook till tender (about two hours). Rub the soup through a hair sieve, return it to rinsed pan, and add the flour broken smooth with stock. Stir till the soup boils, and cook for five minutes.

20. Tomato Soup

Two pounds fresh or tinned tomatoes.	One quart tomato liquor and household stock mixed.
One ounce butter.	Pepper and salt.
Half-ounce bacon.	Pinch of sugar.
One carrot, one onion, a stick of celery.	One tablespoonful of cream.

Thickening.—To one pint soup, half-ounce cornflour and half-gill milk.

Cut the bacon into small pieces, and fry in the butter. Cut vegetables in slices and fry lightly. Add the tomatoes and reduce (see Cookery Terms, p. 20) for five minutes. Add the stock and seasoning, bring to the boil, and simmer from one and a half to two hours. Rub through a hair sieve, measure, return to rinsed pan, bring to the boil, add thickening, and cook from four to five minutes. Add the cream.

21. Celery Soup

Two pounds celery.	Two pints white stock or meat boilings.
One onion.	
One ounce butter.	Two gills milk.
One ounce cornflour.	Pepper and salt.

Wash, scrape, and rinse the celery, and cut in pieces. Skin and scald the onion, and cut in slices. Melt the butter in a pan, and toss the vegetables in it for five minutes. Add the liquid and salt, and boil up. Simmer slowly till the celery is soft (about two hours), then rub it through a hair sieve. Reheat, add the cornflour broken smooth in the milk. Stir and boil for five minutes.

22. Vegetable Marrow Soup

One pound vegetable marrow.
One onion.
Two sticks of celery.
One ounce butter.

One pint light-coloured stock or meat boilings.
One gill milk.
Half-ounce cornflour.
Pepper and salt.

Wash the marrow, cut it in pieces, peel and remove seeds. Wash and scrape the celery, and cut it in pieces. Skin and scald the onion, and cut it in rings. Melt the butter in a pan, and toss the vegetables in it for five minutes. Add the stock and the salt, boil up, and simmer slowly from one to one and a half hours till the marrow is soft, then rub the soup through a hair sieve. Put the soup back into the rinsed pan, and add the cornflour broken smooth in the milk. Stir till it boils and thickens (about five minutes).

23. Green Pea Soup

Half-pound green peas.
Sprigs of mint and parsley.
Pepper and salt.

One pint light stock.
One teaspoonful cornflour.
Half-gill milk.

Put the peas, mint, parsley, and pepper and salt into the boiling stock, and cook till tender (about half an hour). Remove the mint and parsley, and rub the soup through a hair sieve. Return to rinsed pan and reheat. Add thickening, and cook from four to five minutes.

Note.—A handful of washed peapods may be put into the stock with the peas.

THICKENED SOUPS

24. White Vegetable Soup

Light half-ounce butter.
One and a half gills vegetables cut in strips (carrot, turnip, leek, celery).
One and a half pints boiling water, or light-coloured stock.

Three-quarters ounce of flour.
One gill milk.
One yolk of egg.
One tablespoonful cream.
Pepper and salt.
Pinch of sugar.

Prepare vegetables, and toss in melted butter for five minutes. Add boiling liquid and seasoning. Boil gently till vegetables are tender. Add flour broken smooth with milk, and cook for five minutes. Cool, strain in yolk and cream mixed together. Thicken without boiling, and serve at once.

25. Brown Vegetable Soup

Quarter-ounce butter.
One and a half gills mixed vegetables.

One and a half pints brown stock.
Pepper and salt.

To thicken.—Three-quarters of an ounce flour, a little stock, browning, or bovril as required.

Prepare vegetables. Toss in melted butter for five minutes. Add boiling stock. Season. Boil gently until vegetables are tender. Add flour broken smooth with stock, and cook five minutes.

26. Cabbage Soup

One small cabbage (finely shredded).
One dessertspoonful chopped onion.
Half-teaspoonful chopped parsley.
One and a half pints boiling water.
Half-ounce butter.
Half-pint milk.
One ounce small sago or tapioca for thickening.
Pepper and salt.

Cover shredded cabbage with boiling water. Bring to boil and strain. Return cabbage to saucepan. Add the one and a half pints of boiling water and all other ingredients except thickening. Simmer fifteen minutes. Sprinkle in thickening and cook until transparent.

27. Shin of Beef Soup

Two pounds shin of beef.
One ounce dripping.
Piece of carrot and turnip.
Pepper and salt.
One onion.
Stick of celery.
Herbs.
Two quarts cold water.

Wipe the meat, and cut it in small pieces. Remove the marrow (which can be used instead of dripping). Melt the dripping, and fry the meat and bone in it. Add the water and salt, bring slowly to the boil, and skim ; then add the vegetables, herbs, etc., and simmer from four to five hours. Skim ; strain and thicken.

To thicken.—(1) Add one ounce sago or tapioca to each quart of soup, and boil until the grain looks clear (about ten minutes). (2) To every quart of soup break one ounce cornflour to a smooth paste with a little stock. Strain into the boiling soup, cook for five minutes, and serve.

Note.—It is easier to remove all fat from soup if the soup is allowed to become cold first.

28. Kidney Soup

One pound ox-kidney, or six sheep's kidneys.
Two ounces dripping.
One onion.
One quart household stock.
One quart water.
Half a turnip.
One carrot.

One bunch of herbs (comprising a sprig of thyme, marjoram, and parsley, and one bay leaf).
One blade of mace.
Half a teaspoonful of black peppercorns.
Salt.

Two ounces flour.

Remove the skin, split and remove core, wash and dry the kidney, cut it in slices. Skin, scald, dry, and slice the onion. Make the dripping smoking hot in a large deep pan, and fry the kidney to a good brown colour. Fry the onion, add the stock, water, and salt; bring slowly to the boil, and skim carefully. Prepare the carrot and turnip; cut them in blocks; add to the soup with the herbs and the peppercorns; simmer for four or five hours. Skim; strain through a fine sieve; return the soup to the pan; rinse the pieces of kidney, cut in dice, and add them to the soup. Break the flour to a smooth paste with stock or water, add to soup, and cook for ten minutes.

Note.—This soup may also be made with liver or with half liver and half kidney.

Many people prefer to soak ox-kidney to remove strong flavour.

29. Ox-Tail Soup

Ox-Tail Soup is made in the same way, but the tail must be cut through at the joints, freed from superfluous fat, blanched, and dried before frying. Serve pieces of tail and rounds of cooked carrot in the soup.

30. Mulligatawny Soup

Half a rabbit or one pound lean mutton.
Two ounces butter.
One onion.
One apple.
About one ounce curry powder (amount depending on its strength).

Two ounces flour.
One quart second stock.
One quart water.
Half a teaspoonful curry paste.
Salt, and lemon juice.
Small carrot.
Small turnip.
A bunch of herbs.

Wash and cleanse the rabbit ; cut into small joints, or cut the mutton into small pieces. Chop the apple and onion finely. Melt the butter, and when hot fry the meat lightly. Lift joints from the pan, then fry the onion and apple ; fry the curry powder very thoroughly and the flour. Add the meat, the liquid, salt, and curry paste. Bring to the boil, and skim. Put in the prepared vegetables and herbs. Simmer from three to four hours. Skim ; strain through a fine sieve, and reheat the soup. If rabbit is used, add small pieces as garnish. Serve with two ounces boiled rice.

31. Vegetable Mulligatawny Soup

Half-ounce butter.
One dessertspoonful chopped onion.
One dessertspoonful chopped apple.
About half-ounce curry powder (amount depending on its strength).
One ounce flour.

One ounce desiccated coco-nut.
One quart vegetable stock.
Pepper and salt.
Few drops lemon juice.

GARNISH

One tablespoonful Valencia raisins.

To serve with Soup.—Two ounces dry boiled rice.

Heat the fat, fry the onion, the apple, and then the curry powder very thoroughly to mellow the flavour; add flour. Put in coconut, stock, and seasonings. Bring to the boil and skim if necessary. Allow to simmer for one and a half hours. Strain. Add a squeeze of lemon juice, and pour over prepared raisins. Serve with boiled rice. Raisins: stone, cut up, and cook in water for twenty minutes.

32. Rabbit Soup

One rabbit.	One and a half ounces of flour.
Two quarts water.	
One onion, one stick celery.	One gill of milk.
A blade of mace.	One tablespoonful cream.
Half-teaspoonful pepper-corns.	One yolk of egg.
Salt.	
THICKENING	GARNISH
One and a half ounces butter.	One dessertspoonful of chopped parsley.

Wash, dry, joint, and blanch the rabbit (see Cookery Terms, p. 20) ; put it into a saucepan, with the water and salt. (The best pieces may be reserved for another dish.) Bring slowly to the boil, and skim. Add the vegetables, peppercorns, and mace. Simmer for two or three hours. Strain. Melt the butter, add the flour, and cook for a few minutes ; add stock gradually, and boil for five minutes. Add the parsley. Beat up the yolk of egg, add to it the milk and cream, strain into the soup. Stir over a gentle heat until the egg is cooked.

33. Hare Soup

One hare.
Four quarts water.
Two ounces of dripping.
Four ounces of medium oatmeal.
Two onions.
One turnip.
One carrot.

One parsnip.
Two sticks celery.
One teaspoonful peppercorns.
Salt.
Two bay leaves.
Quarter-teaspoonful herbs.

Skin and clean the hare, taking care not to lose any of the blood. Rinse the hare before breaking through the diaphragm. Hold the hare over a basin when taking out the lungs, in order that the blood may be collected. Cut up the hare into suitable joints. Split the head. Put joints and head with the blood into a basin. Add the cold water. Then strain the liquid through a fine sieve. Dry and fry the joints in a little dripping. Add the strained liquid and the oatmeal. Stir until it comes to boiling-point. Add vegetables, cut in blocks, and seasonings. Cook for three to four hours. Strain through a fine sieve. Reheat, and add small pieces of the flesh of the cooked hare as a garnish.

Note.—Cutlets from the back may be reserved for Jugged Hare (Recipe 99).

34. Gravy Soup

One pound lean juicy beef.
One quart cold water.
One stick of celery.
One onion.

Half-teaspoonful peppercorns and salt.
Half-ounce macaroni.
One teaspoonful ketchup.

Wipe the meat, and cut it into small pieces ; put it into a saucepan with the water and salt ; bring it slowly to the boil, and skim. Add the vegetables and pepper-corns, and simmer slowly from two to three hours. Skim ; strain through a hair sieve ; reheat, and add the ketchup.

Boil the macaroni till tender, cut in rings and add to soup.

35. Giblet Soup

Three sets of giblets.
One carrot, turnip, and onion.
Two sticks of celery.
A bunch of herbs, half-

teaspoonful peppercorns and salt.
One quart water.
One ounce butter.
One ounce flour.

Soak and wash the giblets, and cut them up in pieces. Put them into a pan, with the water and salt. Bring slowly to the boil, and skim well. Then add the vege-tables cut in blocks, the herbs and peppercorns, and simmer steadily for three or four hours. Skim and strain through a fine sieve. Melt the butter and brown the flour, then add the stock by degrees ; boil well, and serve with small pieces of giblet in the soup.

36. Macaroni Soup

One quart good white stock.
Two ounces butter.
Two ounces flour.

One half-ounce macaroni.
Half-pint milk.
Pepper and salt.

Melt the butter, add the flour, and cook for two or three minutes, but do not brown it. Add the stock gradually. When boiling, cook for five minutes, add the milk, and season. Have the macaroni boiled, rinsed, and cut into small rings. Add it to the soup. Serve with a little grated cheese handed separately.

37. Rice Soup

One quart chicken or mutton boilings.
Two ounces rice.

One tablespoonful chopped parsley.
Pepper and salt.

Remove all fat from the meat boilings, put into a deep pan, and bring to boiling-point. Skim well. Wash the rice, and add it to the stock. Simmer the soup till the rice is cooked (about half an hour), then add the chopped parsley. Boil for a minute or two to remove the raw taste from the parsley. Season and serve.

Note.—Thinly sliced leeks (about four) may be cooked in this soup ; in which case omit parsley and add half-pint milk before serving.

38. Fish Soup

One quart fish stock. (Recipe 3.)
Two ounces butter.
Two ounces flour.

One half-pint milk.
One tablespoonful chopped parsley.
Pepper and salt.

Melt the butter, add the flour, and cook for two or three minutes. Add the stock gradually, and boil well. Add the milk, parsley, and seasonings. Boil up and serve.

Note.—If a richer soup is desired, add one yolk of egg mixed with one tablespoonful of cream, and stir over a gentle heat until the egg is cooked.

FISH

WHEN choosing fish see that they are fresh in smell, and are stiff, with prominent eyes, red gills, and, as a rule, plenty of scales and slime.

White Fish are considered most digestible. The following are classed as white fish :—

EXAMPLES	SEASON
1. Cod, Hake, Ling .	September to April.
2. Flounder . . .	All the year.
3. Haddock . . .	All the year.
4. Halibut . . .	All the year.
5. John Dory . .	Best from January to March.
6. Plaice	May to January.
7. Skate	November to August.
8. Sole	All the year.
9. Turbot	All the year.
10. Whiting . . .	May to February.

Oily Fish are more nourishing, but less digestible than white fish. The following are classed as oily fish :—

EXAMPLES	SEASON
1. Herring . . .	May to February.
2. Mackerel . . .	April to November.
3. Mullet, Red . .	All year, especially summer.

42

EXAMPLES		SEASON
4. Mullet, Grey . . .	July to February.
5. Salmon	February to August.
6. Smelts	September to March.
7. Sprats and Pilchards .	November to March.
8. Trout	February to August.
9. Whitebait	All the year.

Shellfish, with the exception of the oyster when eaten raw, are the least digestible of all fish, because of their close texture.

EXAMPLES		SEASON
1. Crab	April to December.
2. Crayfish	All the year.
3. Lobster	April to December.
4. Oysters	September to April.
5. Prawns	March to August.
6. Shrimps	All the year.

39. To boil Fish

Wash the fish in cold water, removing scales, fins, tail, eyes, black skin from the inside, and any blood near backbone. Handle it as little and as quickly as possible. Cuts of fish, skinned fish, and fillets, should not be put into water, but should only be wiped. Have sufficient water in a fish kettle to cover the fish ; add salt and vinegar to it in the proportion of one table-spoonful of salt and one teaspoonful of vinegar to one quart of water. When this is boiling draw the pan to the side of the fire, put in the fish, and cook very gently without boiling. For a large fish, or a large cut of fish, allow ten minutes to each pound and ten minutes over. Cook a small fish till the flesh is firm and will leave the bone quite clean. Drain the fish on a draining-tray or on a fish slice, dish on a folded napkin, and decorate with half-slices of lemon and sprigs of parsley. Serve with a sauce.

Note.—White fish is of a delicate texture, and breaks up if cooked at boiling temperature. It is best to cook it just under simmering point. When baking white fish use a moderate oven. When frying white fish protect with a coating.

40. To boil Salt Fish

Wash and scrape the salt fish. Soak it overnight, and if very salt change the water once or twice. Place in cold water. Bring slowly to the boil. Skim well, and simmer till tender. Serve with melted butter, or mustard or egg sauce. (See Sauces.)

41. Stuffed and Baked Cod

One pound slice of cod.

STUFFING

One ounce bread crumbs.
Half an ounce chopped suet or one dessertspoonful clarified margarine.
Half a teaspoonful of chopped parsley.
Pinch of powdered herbs.
A little grated lemon rind.
Pepper and salt.
Beaten egg to bind.

COATING

Beaten egg and dried bread crumbs.
Two tablespoonfuls of dripping.

Prepare the stuffing by mixing the crumbs, suet, parsley, herbs, and seasonings together, and binding with beaten egg to a soft consistency. Wipe the cod with a wet cloth and remove the bone, keeping the cut in a good shape. Place the stuffing in the centre of the fish.

pressing it into place and keeping it piled up in the centre. If necessary tie into shape with string. Dust over with a little flour, brush with beaten egg, and coat well with dried crumbs. Melt the dripping in a Yorkshire pudding tin, put in the fish, and baste with the dripping. Bake in a moderate oven for about twenty minutes, basting from time to time. Drain, remove the string, and dish on a deep ashet. Serve with anchovy sauce round. (See Recipe 223.)

42. Stuffed and Baked Haddock

The same ingredients as for Stuffed Cod. Clean, rinse, and dry the fish. Place the stuffing inside, and sew up the opening, always inserting the needle in the under side of the fish so that the thread may be withdrawn without breaking the fish. Truss with a skewer into the shape of the letter S. Finish in the same way as Baked Cod.

43. Stuffed Plaice

The same ingredients as for Stuffed Cod.
To prepare the Plaice.—After cleaning, cut a slit from head to tail on the white side, and form pockets on either side by partially filleting the fish from the bone. Place the stuffing in the opening thus made, and finish in the same way as Baked Cod.

44. Fried Haddock in Batter

One haddock.

BATTER
One dessertspoonful flour.
Pepper and salt.
One tablespoonful milk.

Dried bread crumbs.
Parsley to garnish.
One tablespoonful dripping for frying.

Mix the flour and seasonings with milk. Clean and dry the haddock, removing the head. Put a skewer through the tail of the fish and coat with the batter. Then toss in paper of crumbs. Make the dripping smoking hot in a frying-pan. Put in the fish. Brown on one side. Then turn and brown on the other. Fry more slowly till cooked (five to seven minutes). Drain, dish, and garnish.

Note.—Skinned haddock or filleted haddock or John Dory or cod steaks may be cooked in the same way.

45. Fried Whitings

Two skinned whitings.	FOR FRYING
One dessertspoonful flour.	Pan of deep fat.
Pepper and salt.	
Beaten egg.	FOR GARNISHING
Dried bread crumbs.	Parsley and lemon.

Wipe and toss in seasoned flour. Place tail through eye-holes. Coat with beaten egg and bread crumbs. Fry in faintly smoking fat. Drain and dish on an ashet with dish paper, and garnish with fried parsley and fans of lemon.

To fry Parsley.—Wash the parsley, pick each sprig from the stalk, and dry carefully. Put the parsley in a frying basket, and cool the fat till there is no smoke rising from it. Put the basket gently into the pan, and fry till the hissing noise stops. Drain well.

46. To skin and fillet Haddock or other Round Fish

Cut the skin along the back and across the neck. Begin at the flap part, and skin from head to tail. When filleting begin at open side and loosen the flesh from the bone, working from the head towards the tail, then turn the fish and loosen the other side from the tail towards the head. Do not separate the two sides from each other.

47. Fried Filleted Haddock

One filleted haddock.	Beaten egg.
Half a teaspoonful flour.	Dried bread crumbs.
Pinch of pepper and salt.	Pan of deep fat.

Sprigs of parsley to garnish.

Wipe the fillets and cut in suitable pieces, cutting on the slant. Dip these in the seasoned flour, then brush with beaten egg, and coat with dried crumbs. Press the crumbs evenly on with a broad-pointed knife. Heat a pan of deep fat till a faint haze rises from it, then drop in the pieces of fish, and fry till a golden brown colour, lift out with a draining-spoon and drain on kitchen paper. Dish on an ashet with dish paper, and garnish with fried parsley.

48. To skin and fillet Flat Fish

Lay the fish with dark side uppermost. Cut across the skin at the tail. Loosen from sides to centre, then pull the skin off from tail towards head. The white skin on the other side may or may not be removed, according to taste. When filleting, cut through the flesh along the back line and raise the fillet from the middle of the back, working out toward the side and from the head to the tail. Then turn the fish and raise the other fillet from tail to head. There are two fillets from each side of the fish.

Note.—Plaice is filleted first, and then the skin is removed from each fillet, beginning at tail end.

49. Fried Filleted Fish (in Batter)

One filleted fish.	One white of egg.
	Salt and pepper.
BATTER	Dessertspoonful salad oil.
Two ounces flour.	Half a gill tepid water.

Put the flour, pepper, and salt into a bowl, and add the oil and water gradually. Beat well, then mix in lightly the stiffly-beaten white of egg. Cut the fillets in neat pieces, coat them with the batter, and fry in deep fat till of a golden brown colour. Drain thoroughly, then dish and garnish with fried parsley.

Note.—This batter may be used for kromeskies, and, with the pepper omitted, for fruit fritters, etc.

50. Baked Fillets of Fish

Four fillets of haddock or whiting.	Two tablespoonfuls milk or fish stock.
Half a teaspoonful of lemon juice.	One and a half gills of white sauce. (See
Pepper and salt.	Recipe 215.)

Wipe the fillets, sprinkle with a little pepper, salt, and lemon juice, and fold in two, skinned side in. Place on a greased tin and cover with a greased paper. Add the milk or fish stock. Cook in a moderate oven from ten to fifteen minutes, till the fish is firm and white. Dish neatly on a hot ashet, and coat with the sauce.

Note.—Fillets or slices of John Dory may be similarly baked.

51. Fried Herrings

Two herrings.	One ounce seasoned oat-
One ounce dripping.	meal.

Wash and clean the herrings thoroughly and trim. Cut across the flesh slantwise in two or three places to prevent the skin curling up. Toss in the oatmeal. Heat the dripping in a frying-pan ; fry the herrings from ten to fifteen minutes. Drain and serve very hot.

Note.—(1) Trout may be similarly prepared and fried. (2) If desired, herrings and large trout may be boned (see Baked Herring, Recipe 53) and fried.

52. Grilled or Broiled Herring, Mackerel, or Trout

One herring or mackerel.	Quarter-ounce maître d'hôtel
Half an ounce butter.	butter (Recipe 145).

Wash and clean the fish thoroughly, and dry it with a cloth. Brush with melted butter. Heat gridiron over a clear fire, grease well, and lay the fish on it. When brown on one side turn over on the other. When the fish is cooked, dish and place the maître d'hôtel butter on top.

Note.—(1) Any other oily fish may be cooked in the same way with or without the maître d'hôtel butter, *e.g.* kippers, bloaters, and red herring. If the fish is very salt soak it in hot water first. (2) Mackerel may also be boiled and served cold with salad.

53. Potted or Baked Herring

Two fresh herrings.	One blade of mace.
One half-gill water.	Two cloves.
One half-gill vinegar.	Quarter-teaspoonful salt.
Six peppercorns.	

Wash and clean the herrings, and trim. Cut from the opening already made for cleaning down to the tail end ; lay them on their backs ; remove the bones ;

sprinkle the salt over them ; roll them up, beginning at the tail end.   Place them in a small pie-dish, with the peppercorns and mace ; pour over them enough vinegar and water to cover them ; bake in the oven from half to three-quarters of an hour.

Note.—Mackerel and small trout may be similarly baked.

54. Stewed Finnan Haddock

One medium-sized finnan haddock or smoked fillet.	Half an ounce flour.
	Half-pint milk.
	Pepper.
One ounce butter.	Sippets of toast.

Scald or heat in front of fire and remove the skin. Cut the fish into neat pieces and place them in a saucepan with the butter and two-thirds of the milk.   Bring very slowly to the boil, and simmer slowly with the lid on the pan for five to ten minutes until fish is cooked. Dish the fish on a hot deep ashet.   Thicken the liquid in the pan with the flour broken with the rest of the milk.   Season with pepper.   Pour the sauce over the fish and garnish with the sippets of toast.

Note.—Finnan haddocks may be similarly cooked in the oven.

Smokies may be baked in a fireproof dish, or poached (see Cookery Terms, p. 20) and served with melted butter.

55. Fish Soufflé

Four ounces of filleted un-cooked fish (whiting or haddock).	Half a gill of milk.
	Two small eggs.
	One tablespoonful cream.
One ounce flour.	Pepper and salt.
Half an ounce butter.	Squeeze of lemon juice.

Wipe the fish and shred it finely. Heat and sieve the flour, melt the butter in a pan, add the milk, and when boiling add the flour, and cook until the sauce is thick. Pound the fish, sauce, one egg and one yolk of egg, and seasonings in a mortar ; then rub through a fine sieve. Add the cream and the whipped white of one of the eggs. Pour the mixture into a buttered soufflé tin. Cover with a buttered paper, and steam very gently for about three-quarters of an hour. When firm, turn the soufflé on to a hot dish, and coat it with a white sauce (Recipe 215).

56. Fish Pudding

Half a pound cooked or un-
    cooked fish.
Two ounces bread crumbs.
One ounce butter.

One egg.
Half-gill fish stock or milk.
One teaspoonful of finely
    chopped parsley.

Pepper and salt.

Heat milk and butter, and pour on to bread crumbs. Remove the skin and scrape the flesh from the bones of the fish, mix with the bread crumbs, add parsley and beaten egg, and season well. Turn into a greased pudding bowl ; cover with greased paper ; steam from twenty to thirty minutes. Serve coated with egg or fish sauce. (See Sauces.)

57. Gâteau of Fish

Half-pound cooked fish.
One pound cooked sieved
    potatoes.
One teaspoonful chopped
    parsley.
A little milk or fish stock.

Two tablespoonfuls thick
    white sauce.
One egg.
A few dried bread crumbs
    for the tin.
Pepper and salt.

Grease a plain tin, and coat with brown crumbs. Remove all skin and bone from the fish, and divide in flakes. Mix all ingredients in a pan and heat thoroughly. The mixture should be of a stiff consistency. Season well ; turn mixture into the prepared tin ; cover with greased paper ; bake in moderately hot oven from thirty to forty minutes. Turn out, and pour either anchovy or melted butter sauce round. (See Sauces.)

58. Fish Pie

Half-pound cooked fish. | One pound cooked potatoes.
One gill fish sauce (Recipe 221). | Pepper and salt.
| Half-ounce butter.
Little milk.

Carefully remove all skin and bone from the fish, mix with the sauce, and season well. Put into a greased pie-dish. Sieve the cooked potatoes ; melt the butter in a pan, add potatoes, seasonings, and milk, and beat to a soft creamy consistency. Pile on the top of the fish, smooth with a knife and mark neatly. Brush over with egg or milk, and put in a moderate oven till nicely browned.

59. American Fish Pie

Half-pound cooked fish. | One hard-boiled egg.
Half-pint white sauce. | One or two tomatoes.
One teaspoonful finely chopped parsley. | One pound cooked potatoes.
| One ounce butter.
Squeeze of lemon juice. | Beaten egg and milk.
Pepper and salt. | One ounce of cheese.

Remove all skin and bone from the fish, mix with the sauce ; add parsley and seasonings. Cut the egg in slices. Scald, skin, and slice tomatoes. Sieve the potatoes ; melt the butter in a pan, add potatoes, seasonings, egg and milk, and beat until soft and creamy. Put a layer of potato into a greased fireproof dish and fill the dish with alternate layers of fish mixture, sliced eggs, and sliced tomatoes. Pipe creamy potato on top. Sprinkle with cheese. Bake until thoroughly hot and brown on top.

60. Macaroni and Fish Pie

Two ounces macaroni.
One filleted haddock.
Half-ounce butter.
Half-ounce flour.
Half-pint milk.
Pepper and salt.
One tablespoonful white crumbs.
Melted butter.

Cook the macaroni in boiling salted water till tender. Drain and cut in half-inch lengths. Wipe the fish and cut it in small pieces. Make the sauce with the butter, flour, and milk. Add the macaroni and the fish, and season with pepper and salt. Turn into a greased pie-dish and scatter lightly with bread crumbs. Put a little melted butter on top, and cook in a moderately hot oven for twenty-five to thirty minutes until the fish is cooked and the pie a pale brown colour. Serve hot.

61. Baked Fish in Custard

One filleted haddock or quarter - pound white fish.

THE CUSTARD
One egg.
Half-pint milk.
Salt. Lemon juice.

Wipe the fish and cut it in small pieces. Lay in a greased pie-dish. Beat the egg ; add the milk, heated, and the seasonings. Pour the custard over the fish ; place the pie-dish in a tin of cold water and bake in a moderate oven from three-quarters to one hour.

62. Kedgeree

Half-pound cooked finnan haddock or white fish.
Quarter-pound of cooked rice.

Two ounces butter.
One hard-boiled egg.
Cayenne pepper, nutmeg, salt.

Wash, boil, and dry the rice. Remove all skin and bones from the fish, and chop roughly. Separate the white from the yolk of the egg ; chop the white roughly ; rub the yolk through a wire sieve.

Melt the butter in a stewpan ; add the rice, fish, and white of egg. When thoroughly heated, season with cayenne pepper, nutmeg, and salt. Pile on a hot dish, and decorate with the sieved yolk.

Note.—One teaspoonful of curry powder may be added to the fish, rice, etc.

63. Curry of Fish

Half-pound filleted haddock, plaice, lemon sole, or cod.
Half-ounce butter.
Half onion.
Half apple or small piece of rhubarb.

Quarter-ounce curry powder.
Quarter-ounce flour.
Half-pint fish stock.
Salt.
A little lemon juice.
One tablespoonful cream.

Chop the onion and fruit finely. Melt the butter in a saucepan ; fry the onion lightly, but do not brown ; fry the fruit, then the curry powder thoroughly, and lastly the flour. Stir in the stock gradually, add pinch of salt and few drops of lemon juice, bring to the boil and skim. Simmer half an hour, strain, return to the rinsed saucepan. Put the fish, cut into pieces, into the sauce, and cook gently about ten minutes. Add the cream. Serve with two ounces of well-boiled rice.

64. Curried Prawns

Wash and shell the prawns, and prepare the dish in the same way as Curry of Fish.

65. Fish Cakes

Half a pound cooked fish.	One ounce butter.
Half a pound cooked pota-	Beaten egg to bind.
toes.	Pepper and salt.

To COAT

Beaten egg, dried bread crumbs.

Remove all skin and bones from the fish, and break it into small flakes. Sieve or mash the potatoes. Melt the butter in a small pan ; add the fish and potatoes. Season, mix well together, and add sufficient egg to bind. Cold fish sauce may be used in place of egg. Turn the mixture on to a slightly floured board and form into small cakes. Coat with egg and bread crumbs, place in a frying basket, and fry in deep fat till of a golden brown colour. Drain carefully, and dish on an ashet with a dish paper. Garnish with fried parsley. (See under Recipe 45.)

66. Scalloped Fish

Half a pound cooked fish of any kind.	Three gills thick white sauce.

Some bread crumbs, and a little melted butter.

Butter some scallop shells, and sprinkle with white bread crumbs.

Remove skin and bones from the fish, and divide into flakes. Put a little sauce in the scallop shells. Half fill with fish, cover with sauce, and sprinkle with bread crumbs. Put a little melted butter on the top of each shell. Bake in a hot oven about fifteen minutes, and serve.

67. Scalloped Oysters

One dozen oysters.
One gill oyster liquor and milk mixed together.
Half-ounce butter.
Half-ounce flour.
Pinch of mace.

Lemon juice.
One tablespoonful of cream.
Salt.
One tablespoonful bread crumbs.
A little melted butter.

Blanch the oysters in their own liquor ; strain them, and remove the beards. Mix the liquor and milk together, melt the butter in a saucepan, add the flour, cook a few seconds. Add liquor by degrees ; bring to the boil. Add the seasonings ; cook five minutes. Add the cream. Finish as for Scalloped Fish.

68. Potted Shrimps

Half-pint shrimps.
Two ounces fresh butter.
Salt and white pepper.

Pinch of powdered mace.
Pinch of nutmeg.

Pick and wash the shrimps, and put them with the other ingredients into a stewpan. Let them heat gradually in the butter, but do not let them boil. Turn into small jars ; cover with clarified butter to exclude the air.

Note.—Shrimps, after being cooked in the butter, may be pounded, rubbed through a sieve, and then potted.

Other varieties of cold fish may be potted.

To half-pound cold fish—

Three to four ounces butter clarified.

Pepper, salt, and pinch of nutmeg.

69. Dressed Crab

One crab.
White bread crumbs.
One to two tablespoonfuls
   salad oil or cream.

One tablespoonful vinegar.
Seasonings of pepper and
   salt.

To Boil.—For the most humane method of killing shellfish, see note on page 22. Take off the claws, break them, and remove the white meat. Remove the body from the shell. Throw away the bag near the mouth, and the feathery gills. Chop up the creamy meat from the inside with the meat from the claws. Mix with bread crumbs, one or two tablespoonfuls of oil, and one tablespoonful of vinegar. Season. Wash, dry, and rub the shell with a little salad oil, and fill it with the mixture. Decorate in sections with chopped white of egg, chopped parsley, sieved yolk, and the small claws.

Note.—Choose a medium-sized heavy crab. It should not be watery inside. The shell should be rough.

70. Fish Salad

Half-pound cooked white
   fish.
Half-gill Mayonnaise sauce
   or cooked salad dress-
   ing (see Sauces).
One lettuce or endive.

Two tomatoes.
Small piece of cucumber or
   one small sliced beet-
   root.
One chopped gherkin.
One dessertspoonful capers.

Cress.

Remove fish from skin and bone and leave in large flakes. Season. Prepare the salad vegetables. Mix the ingredients with the salad dressing. Arrange in a salad bowl or in individual dishes, and decorate with dainty pieces of lettuce, etc.

Note.—Cooked shell-fish may be added.

MEAT

Beef

WHEN choosing beef see that it is fresh in smell. The lean should be of a bright red colour, and should be firm and elastic in texture. Some fat should be intergrained with the lean, and the outside fat should be firm and creamy in colour. The best cuts are always on the back of the animal. The under cuts are tougher. The longer meat is hung before being purchased the more tender it becomes.

Note.—Chilled beef is sent to England chiefly from the Argentine. The meat is duller in colour than freshly killed meat, and if pressed will feel cold and hard. It should be thawed by leaving it in an airy place until softened before cooking.

Cuts suitable for Stock and Soups.—Neck, marrow bone, hough or shin, ox-tail.

For Boiling.—Thick and thin flank, runners, shin.

Pickling.—Nineholes, silverside of round, tongue.

For Stewing.—Brisket, nineholes, thick flank, round, skirting steak (*i.e.* diaphragm).

For Roasting.—Fillet undercut of sirloin, ribs, and sirloin.

For Grilling or Frying.—Fillet, heuck bone, rump.

Mutton

When choosing mutton see that it is fresh in smell. The lean should be of a dull red colour, and should be

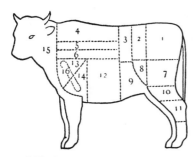

DIFFERENT CUTS OF BEEF

1. Buttock or Rump
2. Heuck Bone
3. Sirloin
4. Spare Ribs and Ribs
5 and 6. Large and Small Runners
7. Round (Top-side and Silverside)
8. Thick Flank
9. Thin Flank
10. Small Round
11. Hough, or Shin, or Leg (Nap-bone)
12. Nine Holes
13. Brisket
14. Shoulder
15. Neck and Cheek
16. Marrow Bone

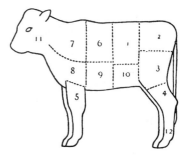

DIFFERENT CUTS OF VEAL

1. Loin
2. Chump End of Loin
3. Fillet
4. Hind Knuckle
5. Fore Knuckle
6. Neck (Best End)
7. Shoulder
8. Blade Bone
9. Breast
10. Flank
11. Head
12. Calf's Foot

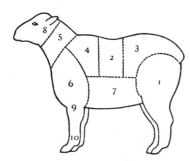

DIFFERENT CUTS OF MUTTON

1. Leg or Gigot
2. Loin
3. Chump End of Loin
4. Neck (Best End or Back Ribs)
5. Scrag
6. Shoulder
7. Breast
8. Head
9. Shank
10. Trotter

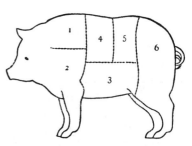

DIFFERENT CUTS OF PORK

1. Spare Rib
2. Hand or Shoulder
3. Spring
4. Fore-loin
5. Loin
6. Leg

firm and elastic in texture. The fat should be white
and hard.   In lamb the flesh is paler.

Cuts suitable for Stock and Soups.—Scrag-end of neck,
head, shank, trotters.

For Boiling.—Gigot or leg, shoulder.

For Stewing.—Brisket or breast, back ribs and neck.

For Roasting.—Gigot or leg, loin, also chump-end,
shoulder.

For Frying or Grilling.—Loin and gigot chops. (Two
loins make a saddle.)

Note.—Frozen mutton—from Australia and New
Zealand—is frozen whole, and the skin protects the meat
from becoming too hard. It is cold to the touch. The
meat is not so red as freshly killed meat, and the fat
is harder and very white. It should be thawed by
leaving it in an airy place until softened before cooking.
It is cheaper than home-fed mutton, but is a little
less nourishing, and loses more weight in the cooking.

Veal

When choosing veal see that the lean is pink, dry,
and closely grained.   The fat should be firm and white.
Veal should always be cooked as soon as possible.

Cuts suitable for Stock and Soups.—Knuckle, feet.

For Boiling.—Shoulder, breast, feet.

For Stewing.—Shoulder, breast, fillet.

For Roasting.—Shoulder, best end neck, loin, fillet.

For Frying.—Chops from loin, fillet.

Note.—Fillet is the most economical joint, as it has no
bones and little fat.

Pork

When choosing pork see that the lean is pink and even
in colour, the skin thin, and the fat white.   It is in season

BEEF

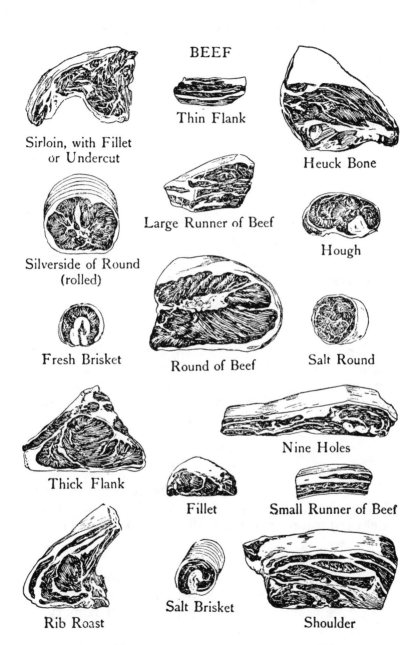

Sirloin, with Fillet or Undercut

Thin Flank

Heuck Bone

Silverside of Round (rolled)

Large Runner of Beef

Hough

Fresh Brisket

Round of Beef

Salt Round

Thick Flank

Nine Holes

Fillet

Small Runner of Beef

Rib Roast

Salt Brisket

Shoulder

from October to April, and should not be used in warm weather.

Cuts suitable for Boiling and Roasting.—Loin, leg, shoulder.

For Frying.—Chops from loin.

Bacon

Bacon is the name given to the back and sides of a pig when salted and dried. The lean should be pink, the fat white and firm, and the rind thin.

Cuts suitable for Frying.—Streaky, loin, shoulder or collar.

For Boiling.—Gammon, back, flank, knuckle.

Ham

When choosing ham see that the lean is pink, the fat white, and the rind thin. A small ham is best, and on running a knife close to the bone it should come out without any unpleasant smell, and should not be greasy. A whole ham should be covered with muslin and hung up.

Young Fowls

Young fowls should have smooth skin and legs, pliable joints and breastbones, plump breasts and necks, bright red combs, and the flesh should be finely grained.

POULTRY	SEASON
Fowls	All year round.
Turkey	September to March.
Geese	September to January.
Duck	All year round.
Pigeons	April to January.

MUTTON

Back Ribs

Part of Shoulder

Loin of Mutton

Saddle

Best End of Neck,
for Cutlet Mutton

Chump End
of Loin

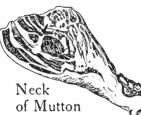
Neck
of Mutton

Fore Shank

Leg or Gigot

Shoulder

SIDE OF BACON

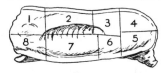

| 1. Collar | 3. Loin | 5. Gammon | 7. Streaky |
| 2. Back. | 4. Corner | 6. Flank | 8. Fore-end |

Game

Choose birds with smooth legs, soft beaks, clear eyes. As a rule, game should hang for some time before being cooked. Hang from neck with feathers on.

GAME	SEASON
Grouse . .	12th August to 18th December.
Partridge .	1st September to end o1 January.
Pheasant .	1st October to end of January.

Rabbits

When choosing rabbits see that the flesh is of a good colour, not bluish, and that it is dry and has a fresh smell. The body should be firm and stiff. Rabbits are paunched at once, but should be hung for one or two days with the fur on. They are in season from May to the end of January.

Hares

The same tests for freshness apply to hares as to rabbits. Hares may be hung for several days with fur on and not paunched. Hares are in season from 1st August to 1st March.

Internal Meats

When choosing any internal meat see that it has a fresh smell, is of a good even colour, and is firm to the touch.

Suet

Suet is the fat that is round the kidneys of the ox and the sheep.

BOILING

71. Boiled Mutton

Three or four pounds of leg or shoulder of mutton.	Boiling water to cover. One teaspoonful salt. Carrot, turnip, onion.

Weigh, trim, wipe, and if necessary joint the meat. Plunge it into boiling salted water, boil for five minutes, skim thoroughly, then only allow the meat to simmer. Allow twenty minutes to the pound and twenty minutes over, and a longer time in proportion for a small joint. Prepare the vegetables and cut them in neat pieces, and add them to the meat. If old, they will take from about one to one and a half hours to cook ; if young, they may be added about thirty to forty minutes before the mutton is done. When the meat is cooked, lift it on to a hot dish. Pour over either parsley or caper sauce (see Sauces), and garnish with the pieces of vegetable.

Note.—The boiling hardens the albumin on outside of meat so that juices are sealed in. Simmering—*i.e.* bubbling at one side of pan only—is the method used for the rest of the time so that meat may be tender when cooked.

72. Boiled Salt Beef

Three or four pounds of salt beef. Sufficient tepid water to cover.	Carrot, turnip, onion. Dumplings. (See **Suet** Pastry, Recipe 250.) Boiled greens (Recipe 181).

Wash the meat thoroughly in cold water to draw out the salt. If very salt, soak for several hours. Put it into a pan, cover with tepid water (or, if the meat has been long in pickle, with cold water), bring slowly to the boil, skim, and then allow to simmer. Allow thirty minutes per pound and thirty minutes over. While cooking put in the prepared vegetables, allowing for old vegetables about one to one and a half hours ; for spring vegetables, about forty minutes. About half an hour before the meat is cooked add the dumplings. Serve the beef on a hot ashet. Pour over some of the beef liquor. Garnish with the pieces of carrot and turnip, boiled greens, and the dumplings. Send to table a sauceboat of the liquor in which the meat was boiled.

Note.—The gradual application of heat softens the fibres of the meat which have become hardened by the pickle.

73. Dry Pickle for Spiced Beef

Five to six pounds brisket or flank of beef.
Two pounds common salt.
One pound moist brown sugar.
One ounce saltpetre.
One shallot or small onion.
Two bay leaves.
One small teaspoonful of crushed peppercorns.
One small teaspoonful of herbs.
One small teaspoonful spice (allspice, mace, and cloves).

Remove any discoloured parts from the meat, and wipe very thoroughly with a damp cloth. Pound the saltpetre, and mix all the ingredients in the pickle jar. Put in the meat, and rub well with the salt mixture. Cover and keep in a cool larder from ten to fourteen days ; rub, and turn the meat daily. Remove from pickle, wash and scrape, and cook as for Salt Beef (Recipe 72). When quite tender, take out the meat, remove bones, and press between two dishes with a weight on top. When cold, trim and brush over with liquid meat glaze. (See Recipe 78.)

74. Wet Pickle for Beef or Ox Tongue

Four to six pounds silver-side of beef.	Six ounces moist brown sugar.
One pound salt.	Half-ounce saltpetre.

One gallon water.

Put all the ingredients for the pickle into a large pan, bring to the boil, and boil for five minutes. Skim well. Strain into a large basin or pickling jar, and leave until quite cold. Remove any discoloured parts from the meat, and wipe very thoroughly with a damp cloth. Put into the cold pickle, cover, and keep in a cool larder from ten to fourteen days. Turn the meat every day.

To cook. See Boiled Salt Beef (Recipe 72). Serve hot or cold.

75. Boiled Salt Pork and Pease Pudding

Three or four pounds of leg or spring of pork.

Wash the joint, put into a pan, and cover with tepid water. Bring to the boil, skim, then simmer. Allow twenty-five minutes per pound and twenty-five minutes over.

Place the joint on a hot dish, and pour over it a little of the liquor in which it was boiled, and serve with pease pudding and parsnips.

PEASE PUDDING

Half a pint of split peas.	Half an ounce of butter.
One small egg.	Salt, pepper, and sugar.

Wash the peas and soak all night in water. Next day tie them loosely (to allow for swelling) in a pudding-cloth ; put them into a pan of boiling water ; boil for three or four hours till the peas are quite soft. Drain very well, and pass them through a wire sieve. Beat in the egg, pepper, salt, and sugar. Return all to the cloth, tie up tightly, and boil for twenty minutes. Turn out on a dish, or serve round the pork.

76. Boiled Ham

If the ham is very salt and dry, soak in warm water from twelve to twenty-four hours. Put it into a large pan, cover it well with cold water, bring slowly to the boil, skim well, and simmer gently till tender. A ham weighing ten pounds will take from four to five hours to cook. When ready, peel off the rind carefully, and dredge over with fine bread crumbs which have been browned in the oven. If the ham is wanted cold, after removing the rind return the ham to the water in which it has cooked, and leave till cool. Then lift out, and finish with browned bread crumbs (see Recipe 601).

Note.—Ham may be baked : Soak overnight. Make a paste of flour and water, roll it out and encase the ham in it ; seal the edges well. Bake steadily in a moderate oven from three to four hours. When ready remove crust ; then remove rind, and finish according to directions for Boiled Ham.

77. Boiled Tongue

Wash thoroughly, and soak from one to two hours : if pickled, soak from three to four hours. Put into a large pan of tepid water. Bring slowly to the boil, skim, add carrot, turnip, onion, peppercorns, and a bunch of herbs.

Cook gently from four to five hours, allowing thirty minutes to each pound, and thirty minutes over. When ready remove skin very carefully, and shape on a board. Leave till cold, then trim and glaze. Put a frill round the root of the tongue and garnish with parsley, or turn into a tin or bowl, fill up with stock, cover, and press with a weight on top. Leave till cold, then turn out.

78. Glaze

Reduce household stock (Recipe 1) to the required consistency by boiling. Skim while boiling. When stock has been reduced to about half a pint, change to a smaller pan and continue.

Two quarts of stock may give about half a gill of glaze.

A more economical glaze may be made by dissolving gelatine in cold water, using an ounce of powdered gelatine to one gill water. Colour with bovril. Use when it has become of a coating consistency.

79. Boiled Rabbit

Wash the rabbit in tepid water with a little salt. Remove the eyes, liver, kidneys, heart, and lungs. Soak in cold water for half an hour. Divide the rabbit into nice joints, split the head, and soak until free from blood. Put all into a saucepan, cover with cold water, add a little salt, and boil. This whitens and cleanses the rabbit. Pour away the water, rinse the rabbit, and just cover it with boiling water ; add a pinch of salt, bring to the boil, and skim. Then simmer from one to one and a half hours. Place the joints on a hot dish. Do not serve the head or the flaps ; these may be put into the stockpot. Cover the rabbit with onion or

parsley sauce (see Sauces).   Garnish with rolls of bacon,
and serve.

Note.—The onions for the sauce should be cooked in
the pan with the rabbit.

Rolls of Bacon.—Cut three or four slices of bacon
thinly, remove the rust and the rind, cut each slice in
half.   Roll up the pieces neatly, place on a skewer, and
bake in a moderate oven from seven to ten minutes.

80. Boiled Fowl

To truss a Fowl for Boiling.—The fowl is trussed as for
roasting (see Recipe 119), except as follows: Draw the
sinews at the *first* joint, and cut off the legs.   Put the
fingers into the bird, and loosen all the skin round the
legs, until they can be pushed back within the skin.
Push back the legs under the skin of the bird.   Fold the
skin of the breast over the ends of the legs which appear
at the opening, and tie firmly with a double string.

To boil a Fowl.—Put into a large pan of boiling
salted water with giblets added, or put into boiling
stock.   Cook gently till tender, from one to one and a
half hours or longer according to age and size of bird.
When ready, lift out, and remove string, place on a hot
dish, coat with a white sauce or egg sauce (see Sauces),
and garnish with bacon rolls.   (See Recipe 79.)

The bird may be stuffed with one of the following
stuffings :

VEAL STUFFING

See Roast Veal (Recipe 114).

OATMEAL STUFFING

Half-pound medium oat- meal.	Quarter-pound beef suet. Two onions (medium size).

Salt and pepper.

Chop the suet. Scald and chop the onions. Mix all ingredients and work together.

81. Beefsteak and Kidney Pudding

One pound stewing steak.
One sheep's kidney.
One dessertspoonful flour.
A small teaspoonful salt.

Quarter - teaspoonful pep·per.
About a gill stock or water.
Suet pastry (Recipe 250).

Prepare the steak and kidney as for Beefsteak Pie (Recipe 124).

Make the pastry ; turn on to floured board, and roll out to about one-third of an inch in thickness, keeping the pastry round. Line a greased bowl with the pastry, and trim ; put in half of the rolls of steak, then the stock, and fill up with the rest of the steak. Knead up trimmings of pastry and roll into a round. Wet the edge of the pudding ; lay the round of pastry over the top ; press the edges together. Cover with a floured pudding-cloth. Put the pudding into a pan of boiling water, and cook steadily from two to three hours. Turn the pudding out of the basin on to a hot dish, and serve.

82. Dressed Sheep's Head (1)

Take the sheep's head from the broth (see Recipe 5), and place the halves on a baking-sheet, rounded side up. Sprinkle with brown crumbs, place some pieces of dripping on the top, and brown in the oven. Dish on a bed of mince prepared from cooked heart and liver. Garnish with " brain cakes " and fried liver.

The tongue may be sliced and used as a garnish or minced with the other parts.

MINCE

Three or four tablespoon-fuls of the chopped heart and liver from the pluck cooked for haggis (Recipe 84).	Liquid, from the boilings of the pluck, to moisten. Seasoning.

Mix these together and heat in a pan. Dish on an ashet.

BRAIN CAKES

Sheep's brain. Two tablespoonfuls bread crumbs.	One teaspoonful finely chopped parsley. Pepper and salt.

One tablespoonful dripping.

After soaking the brain in cold water and vinegar to whiten it, place in boiling salted water, and boil gently for from ten to fifteen minutes. Strain and chop the brain, mix with the bread crumbs, parsley, and seasoning. Form into small cakes, using a little flour to prevent the mixture sticking to the board. Make the dripping smoking hot in a frying-pan, fry the cakes, drain, and serve them round the head.

83. Dressed Sheep's Head (2)

One sheep's head. One ounce butter. One ounce flour.	Three gills milk. Sheep's brain. Pepper and salt.

Make the sauce (see Recipe 215), add the brain, previously cooked and chopped, as above, and seasonings of pepper and salt. Remove all the meat from the head (after boiling). Put it into the sauce and reheat thoroughly. Dish on a hot ashet, and garnish with chopped parsley and fried sippets of bread.

Note.—Lamb's Head is prepared in the same way, and

is a more delicate dish. The head should be cooked in boiling salted water till tender (about one and a half hours).

84. Sheep's Haggis

The stomach-bag of a sheep.

The pluck—*i.e.* the heart, liver, and lights.

Half a pound minced beef-suet.

Two teacupfuls toasted oatmeal.

Four onions (parboiled).

One pint of the pluck boilings.

Pepper and salt.

Wash the bag well in cold water, put it into hot water, and scrape it ; then let it lie in cold water all night with a little salt. Wash the pluck well ; put it into a pan, letting the windpipe hang over the side ; cover it with boiling water, add a teaspoonful of salt, and let it boil for two hours ; then take it out of the pan, and when it is cold cut away the windpipe. Grate a quarter of the liver (not using the rest for the haggis), and mince the heart and lights, the suet and the par-boiled onions. Add to all these the oatmeal, which has been dried and toasted to a golden colour before the fire or in the oven ; also the pepper and salt, and a pint of the liquor in which the pluck was boiled. Mix these all well together. Take the bag and fill it little more than half full of the mince ; if it be too full, it will burst in boiling. Sew up the hole with needle and thread, and put the haggis into a pan of boiling water. Prick the bag occasionally with a needle, to prevent it bursting. Boil this for three hours, then serve it on a hot plate.

85. Pan Haggis

Prepare the same mixture as for sheep's haggis ; but instead of putting it into a bag, put it into a pan with a little more of the liquor, and let it stew for two hours.

86. Mealy Puddings

Some long pudding skins.
One pound oatmeal.
Half-pound minced beef suet.

Three small or two large onions (parboiled).
Quarter-teaspoonful salt.
Quarter-teaspoonful pepper.

Get from the butcher some long skins for puddings; wash them well in warm water, then lay them to soak all night in cold water and salt. Rinse them well. Toast the oatmeal to a light golden colour before the fire or in the oven, stirring it to let it toast equally. Chop the suet very fine, also the cooked onions; mix all together, with the pepper and salt. Tie the end of the pudding skin with thread, then put in enough of the mixture to make it the length of a sausage; tie the skin again, but leave room for the pudding to swell. Leave about an inch of the skin, tie it again, then fill another, and so on. (The space is to allow each pudding to be cut off without letting out the mixture.) Have a pan with water in it nearly boiling, and a little salt. Prick the puddings all over with a darning needle, to prevent them bursting, and boil them for twenty minutes or half an hour. Serve hot.

87. Potted Hough

One pound hough.
Two pounds nap-bone or knuckle of veal.
Two quarts water.
One teaspoonful salt.

Half-teaspoonful mixed spice tied in double muslin.
Half-teaspoonful peppercorns.
Half-teaspoonful whole mace.

Wipe meat and cut in pieces. Wash the bone. Put water and salt into pan; add meat and bone. Bring to the boil and cook from two to three hours. Take out meat ; add the spices and boil for one and a half hours. Strain. Shred meat and put into a rinsed china mould. Pour the stock over and leave to set. While setting keep stirring up the meat.

Note.—If stock is not sufficiently jellied add gelatine —quarter ounce to the pint.

88. Brawn

Half a pig's head.	Four cloves.
Twenty peppercorns.	Twelve allspice.
One blade of mace.	Bunch of herbs.

One onion.

Cleanse, and blanch the head (see Sheep's **Head**, Recipe 5). Cover with cold water and bring to the boil, add seasonings and simmer till quite tender. Remove from the pan, and take all the meat from the bones and cut into dice. Strain the liquor in which the head was boiled, and reduce till it will form a jelly when cold. Add dice of meat, and season as required. Pour into wet moulds or basins, and set aside till cold. Turn out. Garnish with parsley, and serve.

89. Galantine of Beef or Veal

One pound stewing steak, or veal, or steak mince.	Two eggs.
	One gill stock.
Half a pound pork, or sausage meat.	Pepper and salt.
	Pinch of allspice.
Six ounces bread crumbs.	Meat glaze.

Wipe the steak and pork, and remove any skin. Cut meat into small pieces, and pass it twice through the mincing machine. Mix with the bread crumbs, beaten egg, and stock, and season thoroughly. Roll in a cloth, and tie the ends tightly. Cook in a pan of boiling water, with a few vegetables to flavour, or in the stock-pot for about two hours.

When cooked, remove the cloth, roll up the galantine in a dry cloth, tie the ends tightly. The galantine may be pressed between two plates. When cold, remove the cloth, and brush over the top with a little liquid meat glaze (see Recipe 78). Garnish it with parsley, and serve.

Note.—A hard-boiled egg may be placed in the middle of the galantine mixture before rolling in a cloth.

90. Meat Roll

Half-pound raw mince.	Chopped parsley and herbs.
Two ounces bacon, minced.	Half-gill gravy or water.
Three ounces bread crumbs.	Two ounces dripping.
One egg.	Dried bread crumbs.
Pepper and salt.	Half-pint brown sauce.

Mix the ingredients and bind with egg and gravy. Turn the mixture on to a floured board and form into a roll. Make the dripping very hot in a roasting tin. Lay the roll in this. Baste and sprinkle with dried bread crumbs. Roast in a steady oven for one and a half hours. Lift on to a hot dish. Pour the sauce, made with the dripping in the tin, round it.

STEWING

91. Irish Stew

Half a pound neck or flank of mutton.	Quarter-pound of onions.
	Pepper and salt.
One pound potatoes.	Half a pint of hot water.

Wipe and trim the meat, and cut into neat pieces. Put it into a stewpan, and just cover it with hot water. Add a good pinch of salt, bring it to the boil, and skim well. Skin the onions, and cut them into thin rings. Wash and peel the potatoes, and slice down one or two. Add the onions and sliced potatoes to the meat, season with pepper, and simmer from one and a half to two hours. About forty minutes before serving add the rest of the potatoes whole, or, if large, cut in two. When ready, arrange the whole potatoes neatly round a hot ashet, pile the meat in the centre, and pour the gravy over and round.

Note 1.—Remains of cooked meat make excellent Irish stew, but should merely be reheated after the onions and potatoes are tender.

Note 2.—To Scald Onions. Onions may be scalded before being added to any stew, etc., in order to make them more digestible. Place the onion, previously skinned, in a small basin, add a pinch of salt, and cover with boiling water. Pour off the water and dry the onion.

92. Stewed Beef

One pound stewing steak.	One pint stock.
One ounce dripping.	One onion, carrot, turnip
One ounce flour.	(small).

Pepper and salt.

1. Wipe the meat ; leave it whole, or cut into pieces. Skin the onion, and cut into rings. Make the dripping smoking hot in a stewpan, and brown the meat quickly on both sides ; then lift out on to a plate. Fry the onion until nicely browned. Add the stock or water, bring to the boil, return the meat, season with salt, and skim well. Add the vegetables, cut into neat blocks, and a little pepper. Simmer the stew gently from one

and a half to two hours. Pile the meat neatly on a hot dish, with blocks of vegetables at each end. Keep hot. Thicken the gravy with the flour broken with stock or water. Boil for ten minutes, and pour over the meat.

2. Wipe the meat ; leave it whole, or cut into pieces. Skin the onion, and cut into rings. Make the dripping smoking hot in a stewpan, and brown the meat quickly on both sides ; then lift out on to a plate. Fry the onion for a few seconds, add the flour, and fry them together until of a good brown colour. Add the stock by degrees, season with salt, bring to the boil, and skim well. Return the meat to the pan, and simmer gently from one and a half to two hours. Pile the meat neatly on a hot dish. Season the sauce well, add a few drops of cold water, boil up again, and skim thoroughly (this clarifies the sauce), then strain over the meat. Garnish neatly with boiled strips of carrot and turnip, and serve.

To prepare the Garnish.—Cut even-sized strips of carrot and turnip, and cook in boiling salted water from ten to fifteen minutes. Drain well, and use as directed above.

Note.—The trimmings of the vegetables may be cooked with the meat to flavour the sauce.

93. Sea Pie

One pound stewing steak.	Pepper and salt.
One onion.	Half an ounce flour.
Carrot and turnip.	Suet pastry (Recipe 250).

Wipe the meat, cut into thin slices, and dip in seasoned flour. Clean the vegetables, and cut into slices. Put a layer of meat into a stewpan, then a layer of vegetables ; repeat until all the meat and vegetables are in. Just cover with hot stock or water, bring to the boil, then simmer for about three-quarters of an hour. Make a round of suet pastry ; lay this on top of the meat, and cook steadily for one hour. When cooked, lift out the pastry, turn the meat and vegetables on to a hot dish, pour the gravy over, cut the pastry in pieces, and place on the top.

94. Hot-Pot

Half-pound lean mutton or stewing steak.	Slices of carrot.
One large onion.	One pound potatoes.
	Half-pint hot water.

Pepper and salt.

Cut meat in neat slices. Lay them in Hot-Pot dish with onion cut in rings and sliced potato and carrot in alternate layers. Place thickly sliced or halved potatoes on the top. Cover with greased paper. Bake in a moderate oven for two hours till quite tender. Remove the paper fifteen minutes before dishing. Fill up with gravy or hot water.

95. Brazilian Stew

Half-pound shin of beef or skirting steak.	Three tablespoonfuls vinegar.
Slices of carrot and turnip.	Quarter teaspoonful salt.
One onion.	Pinch of pepper.

Cleanse, prepare, and slice the carrot and turnip; skin, scald, and slice the onion. Cut the meat into neat pieces and dip them in the vinegar ; place them in a fireproof dish with the vegetables on the top of the meat ; add the pepper and salt and the rest of the vinegar. Cover the dish and bake in a moderate oven from two to three hours.

The stew may also be cooked by steaming. Put the ingredients into a jar or basin. Cover the basin and place in a pan with cold water. Bring to boiling-point, and steam for four hours.

96. Haricot Mutton

One pound lean mutton. | One pint stock.
One ounce of dripping. | Onion, carrot, and turnip.
One ounce of flour. | Half a gill haricot beans.
Pepper and salt.

Wipe and cut the mutton in pieces, not too small. (For the method of cooking and dishing, see Stewed Beef, Recipe 92.)

Note.—Wash the haricot beans and soak overnight; then put them in a stewpan with plenty of cold water and a pinch of salt, bring to the boil, and cook for about two hours. Drain well, and use with the other vegetables.

97. Stewed Liver and Beans

Half-pound liver. | One small onion.
Half-ounce dripping. | Pepper and salt.
Half-ounce flour. | One teaspoonful ketchup.
Half-pint water. | Half a gill haricot beans.

Rinse and dry the liver, or, if preferred, merely wipe it. Cut it in slices about one-third of an inch in thickness. Proceed as for Stewed Beef (Recipe 92, 1st Method), omitting carrot and turnip. Cook the beans as directed in Recipe 96, and place at each end of the dish.

For extra liver recipes see pp. 307–314.

98. Ragoût of Veal

One pound of fillet or | One pint of stock.
shoulder of veal. | Pepper and salt.
One ounce of dripping. | Rolls of bacon.
One ounce of flour. | Onion, carrot, and turnip.

Wipe the veal, remove all fat, cut in neat pieces. Make the dripping smoking hot in a stewpan, and quickly brown the meat on both sides. Lift on to a plate. Cut the onion in rings, and fry for a few seconds. Add the flour and fry till a light brown colour. Add the stock by degrees, season with salt, bring to the boil, and skim. Return the meat to the pan, add the trimmings of carrot and turnip, and simmer for from one and a half to two hours. Pile the meat neatly on a hot ashet. Boil up the sauce, and skim thoroughly. Season well, and strain over the meat. Garnish with rolls of bacon (Recipe 79), and with strips of carrot and turnip cooked in boiling salted water.

RAGOÛT OF RABBIT

Wash, cleanse, and joint rabbit, then cook as for Ragoût of Veal.

99. Jugged Hare

Cutlets from the back of a hare.
One ounce of butter.
One pint of brown sauce (Recipe 228).

One small tablespoonful of red-currant jelly.
FOR GARNISHING
Forcemeat Balls (Recipe 101).

Remove the cutlets from the back of the hare when preparing the remainder for hare soup (see Recipe 33). Fry the cutlets in butter in a pan. Add the brown sauce and cook for half an hour. Then add the red-currant jelly. Dish on a hot ashet and garnish with forcemeat balls (see Recipe 101). These should be previously poached (see Cookery Terms, p. 20) for ten minutes and drained on a cloth.

100. Beef or Veal Olives

Half-pound stewing steak (thinly cut) or veal fillet.
One onion.

Half-ounce flour.
Half-ounce dripping.
Half-pint stock.

STUFFING

Two small tablespoonfuls bread crumbs.
One small tablespoonful chopped suet.
One teaspoonful chopped parsley.
Pepper and salt.
Beaten egg.
Pinch of powdered herbs.

Stuffing.—Mix the crumbs, suet, parsley, herbs, pepper and salt in a basin, and add enough beaten egg to bind them together.

Wipe the meat, and cut it into pieces about two by two and a half inches. Place a little of the stuffing in each piece, roll up neatly, and tie into shape with a piece of thread. Make the dripping smoking hot in a stewpan and brown the olives in it ; then lift them on to a plate. Fry the onion for a few seconds, add the flour, and fry these together till well browned. Add the stock by degrees and a pinch of salt ; bring to the boil, and skim well. Season with pepper, return the olives to the pan, and simmer from one and a half to two hours. When the olives are tender, remove the thread, and arrange them neatly on a hot ashet. Pour the sauce over, and, if wished, garnish with green peas.

Note.—For veal olives, add the grated rind of a lemon to the stuffing.

101. Exeter Stew

The ingredients used are the same as for Beef Olives. Make a stew according to the method in Recipe 92, and add forcemeat balls made as follows :

Forcemeat Balls.—Mix the crumbs, suet, parsley, herbs, pepper and salt ; and add enough beaten egg or milk to bind together. Flour the hands and form the mixture into small balls ; add these to the stew and cook for twenty or thirty minutes. Pile the meat on a hot ashet, place the balls round, and pour the sauce over.

102. Stewed Breast of Veal

Two pounds breast of veal.	Onion, carrot, and turnip.
Stuffing as for roast veal.	Pepper and salt.
One ounce dripping.	One pint stock.
One ounce flour.	Rolls of bacon.

Wipe, bone, and stuff the veal as for Roast Veal (Recipe 114). Cut the onion in rings, make the dripping smoking hot in a stewpan ; brown the veal quickly ; lift on to a plate ; fry the onion for a few seconds, add the flour, and fry these together until of a light brown colour. Add the stock by degrees and a pinch of salt ; bring to the boil, and skim. Return the veal to the pan ; simmer gently from two to two and a half hours. Place the veal on a hot dish. Add a few drops of cold water to the sauce, boil up briskly, and skim thoroughly. This is to remove any fat. Season the sauce well, and strain it over the veal. Garnish with strips of carrot and turnip cooked for about fifteen minutes in boiling salted water, and with rolls of bacon (Recipe 79).

Note.—The veal may be braised. Cut the vegetables in slices and brown them in the hot dripping. Cover with the stock, and lay the stuffed veal on the bed of vegetables. Then simmer for two hours. Lift out the meat and brown it in the oven. Place on a hot dish and pour round it gravy made from the stock in which the veal has been cooked, thickened with a little flour.

103. Stewed Ox-tail

One ox-tail.	Pieces of carrot and turnip.
Half an ounce dripping.	One pint of second stock.
One onion.	Pepper and salt.
Bunch of herbs.	One ounce flour.
Twelve peppercorns.	One dessertspoonful of
Blade of mace.	ketchup.

Wipe and joint the tail, removing any superfluous fat ; then blanch the tail to cleanse it. Dry the pieces of tail, fry in hot dripping till brown, add the stock, and salt ; bring to the boil, and skim. Then add the vegetables and seasonings, and simmer from three to four hours. To thicken the sauce, add the flour, broken with stock or water, cook for ten minutes, skim well. Add the ketchup, and serve in a suitable dish.

Note.—The stew may be garnished with strips of carrot and turnip.

104. Stewed Kidney

One pound ox-kidney or sheep-kidneys.	One ounce flour.
	One ounce dripping.
One onion.	One pint stock.

Pepper and salt.

Remove the skin from the kidney, split and remove the core, wash and dry it, and cut into pieces. Skin the onion and cut into rings. Make the dripping hot in a stewpan and fry the kidney till brown, then lift it on to a plate. Fry the onion till nicely browned. Add the stock and a pinch of salt. Bring to the boil, skim well, and season with pepper. Return the kidney to the pan and simmer gently till tender. It will probably take from two and a half to three hours. Thicken with flour broken with stock or water. Arrange a border of mashed potatoes or boiled rice (Recipe 201) round a hot ashet. Dish the kidney in the centre and pour the sauce over.

Note.—When using sheep-kidneys prepare them as for Grilling (see Recipe 147), cutting them in halves. Many people prefer to soak ox-kidney to remove strong flavour.

105. Tripe

Wash and scrape the tripe thoroughly in several warm waters, removing all discoloured parts. Put it into a deep pan, cover with cold water, bring it almost to boiling-point, and rinse thoroughly. Repeat this process till the tripe smells sweet ; then cover with cold water, and simmer very slowly for eight to ten hours, till the tripe is tender.

106. Stewed Tripe

Half a pound well-boiled tripe.
Half an ounce butter.
Half an ounce flour.

One gill tripe liquor.
One gill milk.
One boiled onion.
Pepper and salt.

Sippets of toast.

Make a white sauce with the flour, butter, milk, and tripe liquor (see Recipe 215). Cut the tripe into neat pieces and chop the onion. Add these to the sauce, season well, and simmer very gently about twenty minutes. Serve on a hot ashet, with the sippets of toast round. One or two teaspoonfuls of cream added to the sauce makes it more nourishing.

107. Baked Tripe

Cut slices of bread and butter into squares. Cut cooked tripe into squares. Fill up pie-dish with alternate layers, finishing with bread and butter. Pour a custard over (see Recipe 61), and bake till set and browned.

108. Stewed Sweetbread

One sweetbread or half a pound lambs' sweetbreads.
Half a pint white stock or milk.

One tablespoonful cream.
One teaspoonful flour.
Pepper and salt.
Few drops of lemon juice.

Soak the sweetbread in cold water and a little salt for one hour, then blanch it. Lift the sweetbread into a bowl of cold water, and with the fingers pull away any fat or gristle. Place in a stewpan, and cover with hot stock or milk. Simmer gently for one hour. When the sweetbread feels tender, lift it out and keep it hot. Break the flour to a smooth paste with a little cold milk, strain it into the stock in the pan, bring to the boil, and cook from five to seven minutes. Add the cream, season, and pour the sauce over the sweetbread.

109. Stewed Pigeon

One pigeon trussed for roasting.
Half an ounce butter.

Half a pint hot brown stock.
One teaspoonful flour.
Pepper and salt.

Make the butter smoking hot and brown the pigeon in it, then add the hot stock. Cook very gently till tender (from one to one and a half hours). When cooked, serve the pigeon on hot dish and keep hot. Break the flour to a smooth paste with a little cold water or stock ; add it to the stock. Stir till boiling, and cook thoroughly. Season well, and strain the sauce over the pigeon.

Note.—Partridge can be prepared in the same way.

110. Mince Collops (1)

Half-pound minced steak. | One gill of stock.
One small onion. | Pepper and salt.
Quarter an ounce dripping. | Sippets of toast or fried
One teaspoonful of flour. | bread.

Prepare and chop the onion finely. Make the dripping hot in a stewpan, and fry the onion in it for a few seconds. Put in the mince and brown it carefully, beating it well with a wooden spoon or a fork to keep it free from lumps. Sprinkle in the flour, and mix it well with the meat. Add the hot stock and a pinch of salt, bring it to the boil, and season with pepper. Simmer about one hour, stirring it frequently. Serve it on a hot ashet, garnished with sippets of toast.

111. Mince Collops (2)

Half-pound minced steak. | One gill stock.
One small onion. | Pepper and salt.
One teaspoonful flour. | Sippets of toast or fried
 | bread.

Put the mince into a stewpan and brown it carefully, beating it well with a wooden spoon or a fork to keep it free from lumps. Sprinkle in the flour, and mix it well with the meat. Add the hot stock and a pinch of salt. Bring to boiling-point, and season with pepper.

Add the onion, skinned, but left whole. Simmer about one hour, stirring it frequently. Lift out the onion. Serve the mince on a hot ashet. Garnish with sippets of toast.

112. Curried Veal

Half-pound fillet or shoulder of veal.
One ounce butter.
One tablespoonful chopped onion.
One tablespoonful chopped apple.
Quarter to half-ounce curry powder (depending on strength of powder).
Half an ounce rice flour.
About half a pint of light-coloured stock.
Quarter of a teaspoonful curry paste.
One dessertspoonful of chutney or plum or gooseberry jam.
Half-teaspoonful salt.
Few drops lemon juice.

Trim the veal, wipe, and cut in cubes. Melt the butter in a stewpan, and when hot fry the meat. Lift out on to a plate. Fry the onion lightly; fry the apple, then the curry powder thoroughly to mellow the flavour, and the flour. Add the stock gradually, and the salt. Bring to the boil and skim; then add the lemon juice, the curry paste, and the chutney or jam. Return the meat to the sauce and simmer one and a half hours, stirring frequently. Dish on a hot dish, and serve with it two ounces well-boiled Patna rice (Recipe 201).

Note.—A good substitute for stock for curry is coconut milk. To prepare this, pour half a pint of boiling water over one tablespoonful of desiccated coco-nut, and allow it to infuse for fifteen minutes. Strain off the liquid, and use instead of stock.

Curry of Cold Meat (see Recipe 160)

ROASTING

113. Roast Beef or Mutton

Beef or mutton for roasting should be well hung.

Weigh, trim, and wipe the meat, and place it best side down on a double roasting-tin with water underneath. Place two or three tablespoonfuls of dripping on the meat. Put the meat into a hot oven at first, and after it begins to brown reduce the heat slightly. Baste every fifteen to twenty minutes ; and after the meat is half-cooked turn it, with the best side up. The time for cooking depends on the weight of the meat, twenty minutes for each pound and twenty minutes over being usually allowed. For a small roast of two or three pounds longer time in proportion is given. A roast of this size takes from one and a half to two hours. Dish on a suitable ashet, and serve with the usual accompaniments : with roast beef—gravy, Yorkshire pudding, horse-radish sauce ; with roast mutton—gravy, baked potatoes, red-currant jelly.

To make Gravy.—After dishing the roast, pour all the clear dripping from the tin, keeping back all the brown sediment. Add pinches of salt and pepper, and half a pint of good brown stock or water. Stir it over the fire till boiling, then strain it into a gravy dish.

Note 1.—*Time for different meats :* (1) Beef or mutton —twenty minutes to the pound and twenty minutes over. (2) Veal and pork—twenty-five minutes to the pound and twenty-five minutes over. (3) Lamb—twenty to twenty-five minutes to the pound, according to the thickness of the joint.

Note 2.—It is essential to keep the meat moist when baking, therefore if a double roasting-tin is not available place a jar of water in the oven beside the roast. The meat must be frequently basted, and the oven ventilator should be open.

Note 3.—In gas ovens the meat may be placed on a grid shelf and the drip tin supplied with the oven will catch the dripping, or a large joint may be hung from the hook fixed to the crown plate.

Note 4.—A covered roaster conserves the moisture of the meat, and renders the placing of water in the oven and basting unnecessary. The cover should be removed or the ventilating hole opened for fifteen minutes before removing the meat from the oven to allow the meat to brown.

Note 5.—Roasting in electric ovens is the same in principle as roasting in a covered roaster. Electric ovens are almost air-tight, therefore the placing of water beside the meat and basting are unnecessary. The small steam ventilator should be opened during the last fifteen minutes to allow the food to brown.

For fuller notes on the use of range, gas, and electric ovens see pp. 236–237.

Note 6. *Roasting in the Pan.*—Melt and heat one ounce of dripping in an iron pan. Brown all sides of the meat in this, so as to harden the outside and keep in the juices. Then draw the pan aside, and let the meat cook slowly with the lid on. For the length of time required, see preceding directions. This way of roasting is especially suitable for small pieces of meat, and is economical because of the small quantity of fuel required.

Note 7. *Rolled Ribs of Beef.*—With a sharp-pointed knife remove the bones (using them for stock or gravy). Roll the beef, beginning at the thin end. Fasten it with string and skewers. Cook according to general directions above. Remove the string and skewers before serving.

114. Veal : Stuffed and Roasted

Two pounds breast of veal. | Two tablespoonfuls drip-
Rolls of bacon. | ping for basting.

STUFFING

Three ounces bread crumbs. | Quarter-teaspoonful of pow-
One and a half ounces suet. | dered herbs.
One and a half teaspoonfuls | Pepper and salt.
of chopped parsley. | A beaten egg and milk to
Little grated lemon rind. | bind.

Prepare the stuffing by mixing the dry ingredients and binding with the egg and milk. Wipe, bone, and trim the veal ; spread with the stuffing ; roll up ; sew firmly all round. Place on a roasting-tin with the dripping, and follow the ordinary rules for roasting. When cooked, remove the thread ; place the veal on a hot dish ; pour off the fat from the roasting-tin, keeping back any brown sediment. Add about one teaspoonful of flour ; mix well, and brown it over the fire ; add the half-pint of stock or water and a pinch of pepper and salt ; boil up and skim, then strain round the veal. Garnish with bacon rolls (see Recipe 79), and serve.

115. Roast Heart

One ox heart. | Two onions (previously
Quarter-pound bread | boiled).
crumbs. | Half-teaspoonful powdered
Two ounces dripping or | sage.
suet. | Quarter-teaspoonful pepper.
Two tablespoonfuls milk. | Half-teaspoonful salt.

Soak the heart in cold water and salt from fifteen to twenty minutes to draw out the blood. Clean it well, taking care to remove all the clots of blood. Cut off all the loose flaps and the coarse fat ; dry thoroughly. Put the bread crumbs and dripping into a basin, rub thoroughly together. Chop the onions finely, add them, the sage, pepper, salt, and milk. Mix well ; stuff the heart with this mixture and sew it up. Roast according to general directions, and serve very hot. Instead of sage and onions, minced parsley and mixed herbs may be used.

Note.—A Sheep's Heart may be cooked in the same way. As it is small, it should be roasted either in the oven or in a pan.

116. Roast Pork

Loin of pork is the most suitable part for roasting. Weigh, trim, joint, and wipe the pork. Scrape the rind, and score in narrow lines from the top to the bottom of the roast. Cook according to rules. Make the gravy as for Roast Beef, and strain round. Serve with apple sauce (Recipe 233) and Savoury Batter. The joint may be stuffed.

Stuffing.—To half a teacupful of bread crumbs allow two parboiled chopped onions, half a teaspoonful of powdered sage, pepper and salt. Mix all together.

Savoury Batter.—Use recipe for Yorkshire Pudding, 135, and add one cooked chopped onion, one teaspoonful chopped parsley, a pinch of powdered herbs and pepper.

117. Roast Rabbit

One young rabbit.
Stuffing (see Roast Veal, Recipe 114).

Two tablespoonfuls of dripping for basting.

Wash the rabbit in tepid water with a little salt. Remove the eyes, liver, kidneys, lungs, and heart.

Rinse it, and leave to soak in cold water while preparing stuffing. Make the stuffing, rinse and dry the rabbit, fill up the inside with the stuffing, sew it up, truss into shape, place it on a roasting-tin with two table-spoonfuls dripping, and cover it with a piece of greased paper to keep the rabbit moist while cooking. Bake about one hour, basting frequently. When nearly done, remove the paper, baste the rabbit well, and let it brown nicely. When cooked, remove the trussing string, place on a hot dish, pour round it the gravy (see Roast Beef, Recipe 113), or half a pint of brown sauce. Garnish with bacon rolls (Recipe 79) and serve.

118. Roast Hare

Prepare and cook in the same way as Rabbit. Serve with red-currant jelly.

119. Roast Chicken

To draw a Fowl or Chicken.—Pluck the feathers, then singe the fowl to remove the small hairy feathers. Draw the sinews, and cut off feet. Cut off head, make an incision along the back of the neck, separate the skin from the neck and fold the skin back over the breast, then cut off the neck close to the body. Draw out the crop carefully and then the windpipe. Wipe the piece of skin to remove the blood. With a sharp knife enlarge the opening at the other end of the bird, about an inch upwards, from the middle. Draw out all the inside of the bird, taking care not to break the gall bladder, which is attached to the liver. Clean the inside of the bird thoroughly, using a damp cloth. Preserve the neck and the giblets for soup or gravy.

To truss a Fowl for Roasting.—Put the legs in a basin

of boiling water for a few minutes ; the scales can then be easily peeled off. Place the fowl on its breast ; fold the skin over the opening at the neck on to the back ; turn in the wings, with the ends inside, in the shape of triangles : the points will then keep the loose skin in its place.

Push back the legs close to the sides of the bird. Take a trussing-needle and long piece of string ; pass the needle through the joint of the wing, then through the second joint of the leg, then through the body and other leg and wing. Draw the string through. Turn the bird breast-side down and cross the string over the back, then bring down and tie the legs with the tail or " parson's nose " firmly together. Tie a greased paper over the legs to prevent charring, and roast. (See Roast Beef.)

Remove the gall bladder from the liver carefully. Remove the fat from the gizzard ; cut it open, and remove the inside and coarse skin. Wash liver, gizzard, neck, and feet, which may be put on to make stock for gravy. If the fowl is lean, put a small piece of butter or dripping inside. The fowl may be stuffed. (See Roast Veal, Recipe 114.) Serve with bread sauce (Recipe 235), gravy, and rolls of bacon.

120. Roast Turkey

Draw and truss as for Chicken, stuffing the breast with Veal Stuffing (Recipe 114), or with Oatmeal Stuffing (Recipe 80). Cover the breast with fat bacon and spread the top with dripping or butter. Place in a hot oven for first quarter of an hour. Then reduce the heat. Baste frequently. A small turkey takes from one to one and a half hours. For a large turkey allow twelve minutes to the pound and twelve minutes over.

Dish and garnish with forcemeat balls (Recipe 101) or sausages, which may be fried or cooked with the turkey in the oven. Serve with bread sauce and thickened gravy. (See Roast Veal, Recipe 114.)

121. Roast Goose

Draw and truss as for Chicken, but cut off the wings at the first joint, and do not cross them over at the back. The legs are stuck down close by the side of the body. Stuff the body of the bird with sage and onion stuffing (see Roast Pork, Recipe 116). Follow the directions for the roasting of turkey. Dish and garnish with watercress, and serve with apple sauce (Recipe 233) and thickened gravy.

122. Roast Duck

Truss as for Goose, but leave the feet on and turn them close to the legs. Stuff with sage and onion stuffing, or season the inside of the bird with pepper and salt and put in a piece of butter. Cover with greased paper while roasting. Dish and garnish with watercress, and serve with brown sauce flavoured with orange juice or clear brown gravy, apple sauce, green peas, and potato chips.

123. Roast Pigeon

Draw and truss as for Chicken. Wash and dry. Place one ounce of butter and seasonings inside the bird. Cover with rasher of bacon. Follow the directions for the roasting of chicken. Dish on toast. Garnish with watercress. Serve with brown gravy and bread sauce.

BAKING

124. Beefsteak and Kidney Pie

One pound stewing steak. | A quarter-teaspoonful of
One sheep's kidney. | pepper.
One dessertspoonful flour. | One hard-boiled egg.
A small teaspoonful salt. | About a gill stock or water.
Rough puff pastry (Recipe 257).

Soak the kidney, wash, cut in small pieces, removing core. Wipe the steak with a damp cloth, cut in thin slices, and dip into the seasoned flour. Put a piece of kidney on each slice of steak, and a small piece of fat, if liked, and roll up the steak. Half fill a pie-dish with the rolls of steak and kidney ; put in a little stock, and the hard-boiled egg cut in slices ; put the rest of the rolls of steak on the top. Roll out the pastry to about one-third of an inch in thickness, rather larger than the pie-dish to be covered. Cut off a strip round three sides of the pastry. Wet the edges of the dish and place the strip round. Wet the edge again and place the remaining piece of pastry over the pie. Trim off the rough edges of the pastry and decorate. Cut a hole in the middle of the pie to allow the steam to escape whilst baking. Brush the pastry with beaten egg. Roll out the trimmings and cut some leaves. Place these round the hole in the middle of the pie, and brush with egg. Place the pie in a hot oven until the pastry is set ; then reduce the heat, and cook until the meat is tender. The pie will take about two hours to cook. When cooked, fill up with hot, well-seasoned stock. Garnish with parsley, and serve.

125. Veal and Ham Pie

One pound fillet or shoulder of veal.
Quarter-pound raw ham or bacon.
Half-teaspoonful salt.
Quarter-teaspoonful pepper.

One teaspoonful chopped parsley.
Pinch of herbs.
Grated lemon rind.
About a gill stock.
Rough puff pastry (Recipe 257).

One hard-boiled egg.

Chop the parsley, and mix all the seasonings together. Remove rind from the bacon, and cut in neat pieces. Wipe the veal, remove the skin, and cut into pieces about two inches in length. Dip the veal into the seasonings. Place a layer of veal at the bottom of the pie-dish, then a layer of bacon. When the dish is half full put in a little stock and the slices of hard-boiled egg, then fill the dish with the rest of the bacon and veal. Cover with the pastry, and bake. (For directions, see Beefsteak Pie, Recipe 124.) When cooked, fill up with stock, and serve hot or cold.

126. Rabbit Pie

One rabbit.
Quarter-pound bacon.
A small teaspoonful salt.
Quarter-teaspoonful pepper.
One hard-boiled egg.

One teaspoonful chopped parsley.
Pinch of herbs.
Grated lemon rind.
Rough puff pastry (Recipe 257).

About a gill stock.

Chop the parsley, and mix all the seasonings together. Prepare and blanch the rabbit (see Recipe 79), then rinse and dry the joints. Dip the pieces of rabbit into the seasonings. Place a layer of rabbit at the bottom of a pie-dish, then a layer of bacon cut in neat pieces. Add the hard-boiled egg cut in slices and a little of the stock. Fill up the dish with the rest of the bacon and rabbit, cover with the pastry, and bake. (For directions, see Beefsteak Pie, Recipe 124.)

127. Sausage Rolls

Half-pound sausages. | ounces flour, etc., Recipe
Rough puff pastry (four | 257).

Wipe, prick, and blanch the sausages, remove the skin, and, if too large, cut in half. Roll the pastry to about one-eighth of an inch in thickness. Cut it in pieces. Place a sausage on each piece of pastry; wet round the edges, fold the paste over, press the edges together, and knock up with the back of a knife. Place the sausage rolls on a baking sheet, brush them with beaten egg, and bake in a hot oven for about thirty minutes. Pile the sausage rolls neatly on a dish, and garnish with parsley.

128. Cold Meat Patties

Quarter-pound cocked | ounces flour, etc., Recipe
   meat. | 257).
Rough puff pastry (four | One gill well-seasoned sauce.

Remove all skin, fat, and gristle from the meat, and cut in dice or chop. Roll out the pastry to about one-eighth of an inch in thickness, and cut into rounds. Line six or eight patty-pans with pastry, put a spoonful of the meat in each tin with a tablespoonful of sauce, wet round the edge of the pastry, and place a round on the top. Press the edges together, and knock up and flute them with the back of a knife. Make a small hole in the middle of the patty. Decorate with small leaves of pastry. Brush with beaten egg, and bake in a steady oven for about thirty minutes.

129. Cornish Pasties

Two ounces cooked meat.
One potato.
One onion.
Pepper and salt.

One tablespoonful gravy.
Short-crust pastry (four ounces flour, etc., Recipe 254).

Remove skin and fat from the meat. Parboil potato and onion. Chop the ingredients roughly, mix with the gravy and season. Roll the pastry thinly, and cut into rounds. Place a portion of the mixture on each round of pastry. Damp the edge. Double the round and press the edges together. Raise the pastry, letting it rest on the middle of the round, and bend the edges into deep curves. Brush with a little milk. Place on a greased tin. Bake for about thirty minutes.

130. Raised Pie

Half-pound veal.
Two ounces bacon.
One gill good stock.
Pepper and salt.
Pinch of powdered herbs.

One teaspoonful of chopped parsley.
Raised pie crust (see Recipe 251).

Trim the veal, wipe and cut in small square pieces. Remove rind from bacon and cut in pieces. Mix with seasonings. Make the pastry. Cut off one-third, and keep it warm for the top of the pie. Roll out the remaining two-thirds and line a suitable tin. Fill up with the meat. Add one tablespoonful of stock. Roll out remaining pastry into a round ; place on top of the pie, pressing the edges together. Make a hole in the middle.

Decorate the pie neatly, brush with beaten egg, and bake in a hot oven for about one hour. When cooked, fill up with good jellied stock.

Mutton or pork can be substituted for veal.

Note.—When shaping small mutton pies, cut the pastry into strips. Damp the strip along one edge and one end. Join the ends and gather the damped side together so as to form a shallow cup. It is also possible to shape a small pie on a tumbler. Fill up with meat and stock, leaving at least half an inch of pastry above the level of the meat. Fix a lid of pastry to this projecting rim. Trim and decorate by snipping the rim with scissors quarter of an inch apart so that it may be bent alternately up and down. Make a round hole in the middle. Trimmings of pastry may be made into small leaves and used to decorate. Brush all over with beaten egg. Place on a greased tin. Bake and finish as for Raised Pie.

131. Plate Pies

Line a greased plate with potato pastry (see Recipe 252 or 253). Fill with prepared mince (see Recipe 110 or 152). Cover with the other half of pastry. Mark edge. Brush with milk. Bake in a good steady oven for half an hour.

132. Stuffed and Baked Liver

One pound calf's liver.
Three ounces bread crumbs.
One small onion, chopped.
Quarter-teaspoonful herbs.
Pepper and salt.
A little beaten egg.

One teaspoonful chopped parsley.
Three ounces fat bacon.
One gill stock or water.
One dessert-spoonful ketchup.

Prepare the liver and bacon as directed in Recipe 139. Lay the slices in a greased dripping-tin. Make a forcemeat with the bread crumbs, onion, parsley, and seasonings, binding with beaten egg. Cover each strip of liver with this, and place strips of fat bacon on the top. Pour the stock round, and bake slowly for three-quarters of an hour. Dish neatly, and strain the gravy round the liver.

133. Poor Man's Goose

Sheep's liver and heart.
Half-pound fat bacon.
About one teaspoonful powdered sage.
Two onions (previously boiled).

One ounce flour.
One gill cold water.
Quarter-teaspoonful salt.
Quarter-teaspoonful pepper.
Two pounds potatoes.

Rinse the liver, or, if preferred, merely wipe. Soak the heart from fifteen to twenty minutes and wash thoroughly; cut them into thin slices; dip each slice into the flour. Chop the onions; cut the bacon into thin slices and remove the rind. Place a layer of heart and liver in the bottom of a greased pie dish; sprinkle over it a little of the chopped onion, sage, pepper and salt; place a layer of bacon, then a layer of potatoes; repeat this till the materials are all in the dish. Add the cold water. Cover the dish with a greased paper; bake in a moderate oven for about an hour.

134. Toad-in-the-Hole

Quarter-pound sausages.
Quarter-pound flour.
One egg.
Half-pint milk.
Quarter-teaspoonful salt.

Sieve the flour and salt into a bowl. Make a well in the centre; drop in the egg, and stir in half the milk. Stir till smooth, then beat the batter well until air bubbles rise. Stir in the rest of the milk, cover the

batter, and let it stand for an hour. Wipe, prick, and
blanch the sausages, remove the skin, and put them
into a greased pie-dish ; pour the batter over them, and
bake in the oven for about three-quarters of an hour.
Instead of sausages, kidneys or very small pieces of
uncooked meat may be used.

135. Yorkshire Pudding

Quantity and preparation of batter as for Toad-in-
the-Hole. After the batter has been allowed to stand
for an hour, put about two tablespoonfuls of hot dripping
from the roast of meat into a Yorkshire tin. Pour in
the batter. Bake in a quick oven for about twenty
minutes. When brown, well risen, and sufficiently
cooked, cut the pudding into about eight pieces, and
serve neatly on a hot dish.

Note.—Batter may be made richer by using :

Two ounces flour.	One gill milk.
One egg.	Salt.

FRYING

136. Fried Steak

Half-pound best steak (about one inch thick).	Half a gill hot water. Pepper and salt.

Wipe the meat, remove the outside skin, and beat
it slightly with a heavy iron spoon dipped in cold water
to make it more tender. Make an iron frying-pan
thoroughly hot, and rub it well over with the fat side
of the skin trimmed from the steak. Place the steak
in the pan, and brown it quickly on both sides, then
cook it more slowly, from seven to ten minutes accord-

ing to thickness. Lift it on to a hot ashet. Add a pinch of pepper and salt, and the hot water to the pan. Boil it up, and put it round the steak.

Note.—A scalded onion may be sliced and fried with the steak. For this, make about one ounce of dripping smoking hot in the frying-pan. Brown the steak on both sides and then reduce the heat. Add the thinly sliced onion, and stir carefully while frying it at one side of the pan. Cover the onion with a lid while it is cooking further. It may take about fifteen minutes. When ready, dish it on top of the steak.

137. Fried Sausages

Half-pound sausages. | Half an ounce dripping.

Melt the dripping in a frying-pan. Wipe and prick the sausages well with a darning-needle to prevent them bursting. Put them into the pan and fry rather slowly (about fifteen minutes) turning them frequently. Keep hot while frying pieces of bread in the fat left in frying-pan. Dish the sausages on the fried bread and serve very hot.

Note.—Sausages may also be grilled or baked in the oven.

138. Fried Chop and Potatoes

One chop from loin, or best | Two or three potatoes.
end neck of mutton. |

Wipe the chop, and trim off any superfluous fat. Beat it slightly with cutlet bat or spoon dipped in cold water to soften the fibres of the meat. Put the fat trimmed from the chop into a frying-pan and melt it. Put in the chop and brown it quickly and thoroughly on both sides, then cook it more slowly for five or seven

minutes according to thickness.   Have the potatoes parboiled and dried in a cloth.   Cut them into slices about
a quarter-inch thick, and fry them beside the chop to
a light brown colour on both sides, then sprinkle them
with pepper and salt.   Lift the chop on to a hot plate,
and round it arrange the potatoes neatly.

Note.—Any cold cooked potatoes can be reheated in
this way.

139. Liver and Bacon

One pound calf's or sheep's | Four ounces sliced bacon.
    liver. | One ounce flour.
Pepper and salt.

Rinse and dry the liver, or, if preferred, merely wipe,
and cut in slices about one-third of an inch in thickness.
Remove the rind and the rust from the bacon ; place
in a frying-pan, and fry slowly on both sides till slightly
crisp.   Lift on to a hot dish and keep it hot.   Mix the
flour, pepper and salt together.   Dip the slices of liver
into the seasoned flour.   Make the bacon fat hot, and
fry the liver on both sides, adding more fat if necessary.
When cooked it should be firm to the touch.   Place the
liver on the hot dish, and arrange the bacon on top.

Note.—Sheep's kidneys may be used instead of liver,
and shou'd be prepared as for Grilling (Recipe 147).

140. Fried Calves' Sweetbreads

Stew until tender (see Stewed Sweetbread, Recipe 108).
Press between two plates.   Cut in slices, coat with
seasoned flour, egg and bread crumbs, and fry in deep
fat. (See Methods of Cooking, page 19.)   Dish and
garnish with fried parsley.

141. Mutton Cutlets

One and a half pounds best end neck of mutton.
One beaten egg.

Two tablespoonfuls clarified fat.
Some dried bread crumbs.

Choose small, well-hung mutton. Remove the spinal cord, and scrape and wipe the joint well. Saw the rib bones to an even length, about three inches. Remove the chine bone and divide into cutlets. Trim the cutlets, leaving a small rim of fat round the eye. Scrape the inside of the cutlet bones free from skin and fat, and leave the end of the bone clear for a cutlet frill. Brush the cutlets with beaten egg, toss in the bread crumbs, remove any crumbs from the cutlet bones, and press well into shape. Make the dripping smoking hot in a frying-pan, place the cutlets in the fat, and fry to a golden brown on one side. Turn and fry quickly until brown on the other side. Reduce the heat, and allow the cutlets to cook from seven to ten minutes, or longer. Drain well on paper, arrange in a circle on a potato border, pour round a brown or tomato sauce, and serve a seasonable vegetable in the centre. Put a cutlet frill, if desired, on each cutlet, and serve.

Note.—The potato border may be omitted and the cutlets dished overlapping one another, the first one being supported with a small piece of fried bread.

POTATO BORDER

Quarter - pound cooked, sieved potatoes.
Pepper and salt.

Quarter-ounce butter.
A little beaten egg to bind.

Melt the butter in a small pan, add the potato and lastly the egg, and make thoroughly hot. Season, and turn on to a lightly-floured board. Quickly form into a roll, and place on a hot dish. Mark the edges with a fork, and keep in a hot place till wanted.

142. Veal Cutlets

One pound veal fillet.
Marinade. — One beaten egg, one teaspoonful chopped parsley, a pinch of powdered herbs, a little grated lemon rind, pepper and salt, one teaspoonful oiled butter.
Some dried bread crumbs.
Two tablespoonfuls of clarified fat.
Bacon rolls (Recipe 79).
Thinly-cut slices of lemon.

Trim and wipe the veal, cut into suitable pieces, and beat it with a spoon or cutlet bat. Add the oiled butter and seasonings to the beaten egg. Soak the cutlets in the marinade for about one hour ; then toss them in bread crumbs, and press into shape. Make the dripping smoking hot in a frying-pan, and fry the cutlets to a golden brown on one side, then turn and brown quickly on the other side. Reduce the heat, and cook the cutlets from about ten to twelve minutes in all. Drain thoroughly. Arrange with or without potato border, and garnish with lemon and bacon rolls. Serve with a seasonable vegetable, and pour tomato sauce round.

143. Danish Meat Cakes

Four ounces steak mince.
One dessertspoonful grated onion.
One teacupful bread crumbs.
One small tablespoonful flour.
Seasonings.
Ketchup.
One gill of stock or gravy.

FOR FRYING
One ounce dripping.

Mix all together to a soft consistency. Allow to stand for twenty minutes. Make the dripping smoking hot in a frying-pan, and drop the mixture in spoonfuls into this, shaping the cakes with a knife. Fry on both sides. Dish on a potato border (see Recipe 141), and pour tomato, brown, or piquante sauce round.

144. Vienna Steaks

Four ounces veal.
Four ounces steak.
One teaspoonful chopped parsley.
One tablespoonful grated onion.
Three-quarters ounce of butter.
Three-quarters ounce of flour.
Three-quarters gill of stock.
Half-beaten egg.
Pepper and salt.

FOR COATING

Egg and dried bread crumbs.

FOR FRYING

Pan of deep fat.

FOR GARNISHING

Rings of onion, white of egg and flour.

FOR SERVING

Half a pint brown sauce.

Mince veal and steak, and steam for fifteen minutes. Make the panada (see p. 137) with the butter, flour, and stock. Add to it the meat, parsley, onion, and seasonings, and turn the mixture on to a plate to cool. Form into cakes; coat with egg and bread crumbs, and fry in deep fat. Dip onion rings in white of egg and flour, and fry to a golden colour. Dish steaks neatly. Garnish with onion rings. Serve with sauce.

GRILLING

145. Grilled Steak

Three-quarters of a pound of rump or fillet steak.

Two baked tomatoes (Recipe 205).

Half an ounce maître d'hôtel butter.

Potato chips (Recipe 198).

Trim the steak and wipe with a damp cloth. Beat with a cutlet bat or with an iron spoon. The steak may be brushed with oil or clarified margarine. Have a clear red fire, and make the grill hot. Rub the bars of the grill well with a little suet, place the steak on the grill, and after two or three minutes turn it. Cook altogether from ten to fifteen minutes, according to the thickness of the meat, and turn frequently while it is cooking. Lift the steak with the grilling tongs on to a hot dish, place maître d'hôtel butter on top, and serve potato chips and baked tomatoes round.

Maître d'Hôtel Butter

Half an ounce butter.

One dessertspoonful chopped parsley.

A few grains of cayenne pepper.

Few drops lemon juice.

Mix all these ingredients together on a plate. Spread the butter into a neat pat, put in a cool place until firm, then use as directed.

146. Grilled Chop

Choose a leg or loin chop, remove spinal cord, trim off the skin, and scrape the loin bone clean. Wipe chop with a damp cloth. Grill as for steak, allowing from ten to fifteen minutes. Serve as above.

Note.—The gridiron should be placed three to six inches above a clear fire. A folding broiler may also be used in front of a fire. The gas or electric grill should be glowing before the food is put on to the greased bars of the toaster beneath the grill.

147. Grilled Kidneys and Bacon

Three sheep-kidneys. | Half-ounce maître d'hôtel
Three rashers of bacon. | butter (Recipe 145).
Three rounds of fried bread.

Make the maître d'hôtel butter, and set it aside to harden. Remove the skin from the kidneys. Split each almost in two, and remove the core. Wash and dry well. Run a skewer through each kidney, and place them on the greased bars of a hot gridiron, cut side down. Place this over a clear fire, and brown quickly, then turn the kidneys and continue cooking for about seven to ten minutes, turning frequently. Grill the bacon for two or three minutes. Dish each kidney on a round of fried bread, and place a pat of the butter on each. Serve the bacon piled in the centre of the dish.

148. Mixed Grill

This consists of loin chop, sausage, and kidney, with usual accompaniments as described above.

FAT AND DRIPPING

149. To Render down Fat

Take about two pounds of scraps of fat from beef, mutton, or veal. Remove skin, flesh, glands, or discoloured parts, and cut the fat into small equal-sized pieces. Place it in a strong, unlined iron pan ; cover it with cold water and add half a teaspoonful of salt. Bring it slowly to the boil, and remove all scum. Simmer without the lid for five or six hours till the water has evaporated, the fat is shrivelled and crisp, and a clear, yellow liquid remains. Allow it to become slightly cool, then strain it through a cloth into a strong basin. When cold it should form a firm, white cake. This fat may now be used for pastry or cakes, and for frying, etc. When using deep fat for frying do not put more fat into the pan than will make it half or three-quarters full.

The fat after being used for frying, should be strained, and kept for that purpose only.

Note.—Cooked fat may be clarified in the same manner.

150. Clarified Dripping

Take any clarified fat that has become discoloured by frequent use, or fat from the top of meat boilings, etc. Put it into a strong, unlined pan, and cover it with cold water, adding a good pinch of baking soda to whiten the fat. Bring it to the boil, skim, and boil about twenty minutes. Allow it to cool slightly and strain it through a cloth into a bowl. When cold, lift off the cake of fat, scrape away the sediment underneath, melt it down, and pour it into a clean bowl.

COLD MEAT COOKERY

151. Hash

One pound cooked meat (mutton or beef).

Two to three gills brown sauce (Recipe 228).

FOR GARNISHING

Sippets of toasted or fried bread.

Remove all fat, gristle, and skin from the meat, and cut into neat thin slices.   Add to the hot sauce, and re-heat thoroughly without boiling.   Place the meat in the centre of a hot dish, pour the sauce over, and garnish with the fried bread.

152. Mince

Half-pound cooked meat.	One teaspoonful ketchup or
Pepper and salt.	Harvey's sauce.
About one gill heated stock.	Fried sippets of bread.

Remove skin and fat from the meat, and chop it finely.   Put it into a saucepan with the stock and seasonings, and allow it to reheat very thoroughly. Dish, and garnish with the fried bread.

Note.—Poached eggs may be served on the top.

153. Croquettes

Half-pound cooked meat.	One teaspoonful of chopped
Half-ounce dripping.	parsley.
Half-ounce flour.	One teaspoonful ketchup or
One gill second stock.	Harvey's sauce.

Pepper and salt.

To Coat the Croquettes

One beaten egg.	Dried bread crumbs.

Free the meat from fat and skin, and chop or mince it finely.   Make a sauce of the dripping, flour, and stock ; add to it the meat, parsley, and seasonings, and spread the mixture on a plate to cool.   When cold and firm divide into equal-sized sections, and form into cro-quettes.   Brush with beaten egg.   Toss in the bread crumbs, and fry to a golden brown in smoking-hot fat.

Dish, and garnish with fried parsley (see under Recipe 45).
Serve with a suitable sauce.

154. Cold Meat Cutlets

Prepare the same mixture as for Croquettes, but form
into the shape of cutlets before coating.

155. Rissoles

Mixture as for Croquettes.	To Coat
Short crust pastry (see Recipe 254).	Beaten egg. Dried bread crumbs.

Make the meat mixture, then roll out the pastry
thinly, and cut into rounds. Place a teaspoonful of
meat on each round of pastry. Damp the edges, fold
over, and seal well. Coat with egg and bread crumbs,
and fry in smoking-hot fat. Garnish with fried parsley.

156. Gâteau of Meat

Half-pound cooked meat.	One teaspoonful of chopped parsley.
Two ounces bread crumbs.	
One and a quarter gills stock or meat gravy.	A small cooked onion.
	One egg.
	Pepper and salt.

Grease a plain round tin, and coat it well with brown
crumbs. Remove all skin and gristle from the meat,
and chop or mince it finely. Chop the onion. Mix all
the ingredients together in a basin, and season well.
Turn the mixture into the prepared tin ; cover with a
greased paper ; bake in a steady oven for about thirty
minutes, or steam till firm (about forty-five minutes).
Turn the gâteau on to a hot dish, and pour round
brown or tomato sauce. (See Sauces.)

157. Macaroni and Meat Shape

Two ounces cooked maca- | Pinch of powdered herbs.
roni. (See Recipe 60.) | Pepper and salt.
Four ounces cooked meat. | One small egg.
One ounce bread crumbs. | One gill stock.

Chop the macaroni and the meat. Mix all the dry ingredients, and add the beaten egg and the stock. Turn the mixture into a greased basin, cover it with greased paper, and steam from thirty to forty minutes. Turn on to a hot dish.

Note.—Rice may be used instead of macaroni.

158. Meat Roly-Poly

Three or four tablespoon- | A little ketchup.
fuls of chopped cold | Half-gill of gravy.
meat. | Suet pastry (six ounces
Any cold cooked vegetables. | flour, etc., see Recipe
Pepper and salt. | 250).

Chop the meat and vegetables, and mix all ingredients together. Make the pastry and roll into an oblong. Spread the meat mixture on the pastry and roll up. Tie in a floured cloth and boil from one and a half to two hours. Remove the cloth; turn on to a hot dish, and serve with brown sauce (Recipe 228).

159. Shepherd's Pie

Half a pound cold cooked | One gill stock or water.
meat, or cooked mince. | Pepper and salt.
One small cooked onion. | To Cover
Quarter an ounce drip- | Five or six cooked potatoes.
ping. | One tablespoonful milk.
Quarter an ounce flour. | Pepper and salt.

(1,293)   8

Make the dripping hot in a small pan, and fry the flour till brown. Add the stock by degrees. Season well, and boil three or four minutes. Remove all skin and gristle from the meat and chop it. Add the meat and chopped onion to the sauce, season well, and pour it into a pie-dish. Mash the potatoes, and add the milk, pepper, and salt. Beat this over the fire till hot and smooth. Place it evenly over the meat, brush with milk or beaten egg, and mark it with a fork or knife. Reheat the pie in the oven until brown on top.

160. Curry of Cold Meat

One pound of cooked meat. | Two to three gills curry sauce (see Recipe 231).

Remove all skin and gristle from the meat, and cut into half-inch cubes. Reheat in the sauce, without boiling, for about fifteen minutes. Put the curry on a hot dish, and on a separate dish serve some well-boiled rice (Recipe 201).

161. Cold Meat Shape

Quarter-pound cold chicken, veal, rabbit, or beef. | One teaspoonful chopped parsley.
One hard-boiled egg. | One white of egg.
Pepper and salt. | Gelatine, if required (quarter to half-ounce).
Three gills of good stock. |

Put the stock and white of egg into a pan. If the stock is not jellied, add a quarter to half an ounce of gelatine. Stir over the fire until the gelatine is dissolved, then whisk until nearly boiling. Stop whisking and boil up the stock well. Let it settle a few minutes, then strain through muslin, and let it cool. Cut the hard-boiled egg in slices. Remove any skin, fat, or gristle from the meat, and cut it into small dice. Rinse a plain tin with cold water, then cover the bottom of the tin with a little of the cold stock. When this is set, decorate with egg and parsley. Cover the decoration with some stock, and let it set. Put the rest of the ingredients into the stock, and when beginning to set fill up the tin. Put in a cool place until set. Pass the tin through warm water ; turn the shape on to a dish. Garnish with parsley, and serve.

162. Potted Meat

Six ounces cooked meat, chicken, veal, ham, etc. Three to four ounces clarified butter.

Salt and pepper. Powdered allspice or aromatic spice. Nutmeg.

Melt the butter in a pan ; when hot, skim and strain through muslin, to keep back any sediment. (The butter is clarified to remove the salt.) Remove all skin and gristle from the meat, and pass it twice through the mincing machine. Then pound the meat, seasoning, and two-thirds of the butter in a mortar, and sieve if necessary. Place in jars ; make it smooth on the top. Run the rest of the clarified butter over the meat : this excludes the air. It will keep for some time.

VEGETABLES AND SALADS

CONSERVATIVE COOKING OF VEGETABLES

Green Vegetables.

Cleanse vegetables ; shred them or divide them in small pieces. Parboil (see Cookery Terms, p. 20) from one to five minutes, according to the age and nature of the vegetable. Drain. Then cook by either of the two following methods :

Method 1. *To Steam.*

Place in a jar or basin with a piece of butter. Cover the jar and place it in a pan of boiling water. Small pieces of vegetable will probably be cooked in about thirty minutes. When tender, dish with the juices.

Note.—On no account throw away the juices, as they contain the natural salts.

Method 2. *To Cook in Butter.*

Cook very gently in a small quantity of butter in a tightly covered saucepan until tender. Shake frequently while cooking. Dish.

Root Vegetables.

Cook by either of the above methods. Young vegetables may be left whole, but old vegetables should be sliced. They will probably be cooked in about half an hour. Root vegetables may also be cooked by either of the two following methods :

Method 3. To Bake.

Place the prepared vegetables in a casserole or pyrex dish with a piece of butter. Cover the dish. Cook in a moderate oven. Serve in the dish.

Method 4. To Stew.

Place the prepared vegetables in a pan with a little milk and water. Butter may also be added. Stew until tender. Dish the vegetables. Thicken the liquid and use as a sauce.

When Boiling Vegetables.

If cooking vegetables by boiling, cook them as rapidly as possible, because long, slow cooking destroys vitamins. Do not use too much water, and, when possible, use the water in sauce or soup making.

163. Artichokes (Globe)

Cut off stalks and remove outer leaves. Wash and rinse in cold water to which lemon juice and salt have been added. Plunge into boiling salted water, and cook rapidly until the leaves can be easily detached. This will take thirty minutes to one hour, according to the size and quality of the artichokes. Drain well. Serve on a folded napkin placed on a hot dish. Serve melted butter in a separate dish.

164. Artichokes (Jerusalem)

Scrub and wash the artichokes, scrape or peel thinly, and put at once into cold water, adding a few drops of

Vegetable.	Season.	Desirable Condition.
Artichokes :		
Globe.	July–Sept.	Crisp and green.
Jerusalem.	Sept.–June.	Of good shape, not too much soil.
Asparagus.	May–July.	Fresh green tops, stalks thick, turgid, and not too long.
Beans :		
Broad.	July–Aug.	Full pods, fresh and young, skin of beans tender.
French or Kidney.	July–Sept.	Fresh green and young, pods break easily.
Scarlet Runner.	July–Sept.	Fresh green and young, break easily. Much larger and appear coarser than French Beans.
Beetroot.	July–May.	Unbroken and of good colour. Globe varieties of moderate size popular.
Cabbage :		
Spring and Summer.	April–Sept.	Fresh and green.
Savoys.	Sept.–April.	Large, firm, and crisp.
Reds.	Oct.–March.	Large, very firm, and of good colour.

Vegetable.	Season.	Desirable Condition.
Brussels Sprouts.	Oct.–March.	Fresh, green, and firm.
Carrots :		
Old.	Aug.–June.	Of medium size and firm. No worm holes. Core crisp.
New.	June–Aug.	Of good shape, bright, firm, and easy to break.
Cauliflower :	Late June–Nov.	White, firm, with close flower.
Broccoli (heading).	Dec.–June.	White, firm, with close flower.
Broccoli (sprouting).	Dec.–March.	Fresh, firm stems.
Celery :	Sept.–April.	Fresh, white, and crisp.
Celeriac.	Nov.–April.	Firm and clean.
Chicory.	Jan.–March.	Fresh, white, and turgid.
Cress :		
Small Cress or Mustard and Cress.	All the year.	Fresh, crisp, and green.
Water-cress.	All the year.	Fresh, crisp, and green.
Cucumber.	June–Nov.	Fresh, turgid, and green, thin skin, of good shape.

Vegetable.	Season.	Desirable Condition.
Egg Plant.	July–Oct.	Of good shape, firm, skin tender.
Endive.	Winter.	Fresh and green.
Greens or Curly Kale.	Oct.–March.	Fresh and green.
Horse Radish.	Oct.–March.	Hard, and not too much earth.
Leeks.	Late Aug.–May.	Fresh and green, with firm white stem.
Lettuce.	March–Nov.	Fresh, crisp, and green.
Mushrooms.	Aug. and Sept.	Some mushrooms are edible ; many are poisonous. The commonest edible mushrooms are generally found in meadows and on open ground. The top should be smooth ; the underside is pink in young mushrooms and brown in older ones. The stalk is firm and fleshy.
Onions :	All the year.	Firm, with no blemishes or decay.
Spring Onions.	April–early July.	Fresh and firm, with white stem.

Vegetable.	Season.	Desirable Condition.
Parsley.	All the year.	Fresh and green.
Parsnips.	Oct.–May.	Firm, of good shape and colour, with no worm holes.
Peas.	June–Sept.	Full crisp pods, fresh and young.
Peppers (Chillies) : Green (unripe). Red (ripe). }	July–Oct.	Clear colour, smooth skin.
Potatoes :	All the year.	Of good shape, even size, not too much soil.
Do. New	June and July.	Freshly lifted.
Radishes.	May–Oct.	Fresh and firm.
Rhubarb.	Jan.–Sept.	Fresh, turgid stems, not too large.
Salsify.	Dec.–March.	Clean roots, fresh and white.
Sea Kale.	Jan.–May.	Fresh, crisp, and white.
Spinach.	All the year.	Fresh, green, and young.
Tomatoes.	All the year.	Firm, good colour, even size, unblemished.
Turnips :	Sept.–May.	Firm and unblemished.
Do. New.	June–Aug.	Fresh and firm, unblemished.
Vegetable Marrows.	July–Oct.	Of good shape, firm and heavy, skin tender.

vinegar to preserve the colour. Cook for about thirty minutes in a lined pan in boiling salted water, adding vinegar or lemon juice. Drain, dish, and coat with white sauce.

165. Asparagus and Sprue

Trim and scrape the stalks. Place an inverted pie-dish in a fish-kettle. Lay the drainer on the top of the pie-dish. Have water boiling under the drainer. Lay the asparagus on the drainer and steam till tender (from thirty to forty minutes). Lift on to a hot dish, and serve with melted butter.

166. Beans (Broad or Windsor)

Shell and wash. Remove the skin that covers the bean. This is easily done after scalding. Cook for about thirty minutes in boiling salted water till tender. Remove any scum as it rises. Drain. Toss in a little melted butter with seasonings. Dish and sprinkle with finely chopped parsley.

167. Beans (French or Kidney)

Wash and string the beans; leave whole or cut them into strips or diamond shapes. Cook in boiling salted water till tender (about fifteen minutes). Drain. Toss in a little melted butter with seasonings. Pile in a vegetable dish.

Note.—Beans may be steamed instead of being boiled. Scarlet Runner Beans are treated in the same way, but will take longer to cook.

168. Beans (Haricot)

Half-pound beans. | Cold water.
                           Salt.

Wash the beans, and soak overnight in cold water.
Put into a pan with the water, add salt, and boil gently
for two hours, till the beans are quite soft but not
broken.   Drain, dish, and coat with a suitable sauce,
e.g. white, parsley, cheese, tomato, or curry sauce.
   Fried bacon may be added to this dish.
   Note.—Butter Beans are cooked in the same way,
but do not need such long soaking or cooking.

169. Beetroot

Wash the beetroot very carefully to remove earth.
Avoid breaking the skin.   Put it into a large pan with
cold water to cover.   Add salt.   Bring quickly to the
boil, and boil gently till it feels soft when pressed with
the finger.   Do not prick with a fork, or the colour will
be lost.   Lift the beetroot from the pan, and leave it
to cool slightly, then remove the skin.   Leave till cold,
and cut into thin slices.   Arrange these on a dish, and
put a little vinegar over.
   To keep.—Put the slices into a jar and cover with
boiling vinegar, cork tightly, and keep in a cold place.
   To serve hot.—Cut in thick slices, dish neatly, and coat
with parsley sauce.

170. Brussels Sprouts

Remove coarse stalk and discoloured leaves.   Cut a
cross at the stalk end, and soak the sprouts in cold water
with salt for half an hour.   Wash and rinse.   Boil till

tender, but not broken (see Cabbage).   Drain well, toss
in a little butter, season, and serve.

171. Boiled Cabbage

Remove root and coarse outer leaves, cut in four and
remove hard stalk.   Soak for half an hour in cold
water, with salt added to remove insects and earth ;
then wash and rinse very thoroughly.   Plunge into
boiling salted water, and boil briskly without a lid till
tender, skimming frequently.   Drain in a colander, and
press out all the water.   Lift on to a hot dish and score
across several times.

172. Dressed Cabbage

After draining, chop roughly, and reheat with seasonings of pepper and salt, and a small pat of butter or
dripping.

173. Colcannon

Equal quantities of cold potatoes and cold cabbage.
One ounce dripping to one pound vegetables.

Quarter-teaspoonful salt.
Quarter - teaspoonful pep-
per.
Dripping to grease the basin.

Crush the potatoes with a fork ; chop the cabbage
small ; mix both together and place in a saucepan with
the dripping, pepper, and salt.   Stir over the fire till
the dripping has melted, and mix with the vegetables.
Grease a basin or pie-dish ; place the mixture in it ;
put it in a hot oven for about half an hour.   Turn out
on a dish ; serve hot.

174. Stuffed Cabbage

One cabbage.
Four ounces cold meat,
    ham, or bacon.
Ketchup.

One ounce Patna rice or
    macaroni.
Pepper and salt.
Gravy.

Prepare the cabbage and parboil for five minutes. Boil the rice (see Recipe 201). Add the meat, chopped, and mix in seasonings and gravy.

Stuff the cabbage with this mixture and bind with tape. Place in a stewpan with a little boiling water. Add salt and pepper. Put on the lid and cook steadily for one hour. Dish on a hot vegetable dish.

Note.—Oatmeal Stuffing (Recipe 80) could be used.

175. Boiled Carrots

Wash and scrape the carrots, and, if they are large, cut them in half, lengthways and across. Put them in a pan of boiling salted water and boil for one hour till soft. Drain, dish, and coat with a white sauce ; or toss in melted butter, dish neatly, and sprinkle with finely chopped parsley.

176. Stewed Carrots

Half-pound young carrots.
Two to three gills brown
    stock.

Half a teaspoonful finely
    chopped parsley.
Pepper and salt.

Prepare the carrots, and parboil for five to ten minutes. Drain. Cook in stock till tender. Dish the carrots, reduce the stock to half glaze, and pour over. Sprinkle with finely chopped parsley.

177. Cauliflower

Cut off the coarse stalk and the coarse outer leaves, leaving enough green to hold the flower together. Scoop out part of the hard stalk. Soak the cauliflower in cold water with salt for half an hour. Wash carefully and rinse. Boil in the same way as cabbage, but cook more gently. Keep the flower downwards in the water. When quite tender, but not broken, drain very carefully, place in a vegetable dish, and coat with white sauce.

178. Stewed Celery

Wash and scrape the celery very thoroughly, cut it into four-inch lengths, and tie it in bundles. Blanch (see p. 20) to remove the strong taste and whiten the celery. Put into a lined pan sufficient milk and water almost to cover the celery, and add a pinch of salt ; when boiling, put in the celery, and stew till tender (about one hour). Drain thoroughly, remove thread, and coat with a white sauce.

Note.—The liquor in which the celery was cooked may be used for the sauce.

179. Celeriac

Wash, brush, and peel off outside skin. Cut into neat pieces. Cook in the same way as for Celery. When dished, coat with parsley or egg sauce.

180. Egg Plant

Wash the egg plants, remove the stalks, and place them in a fireproof dish with a little water. Cover the dish and put it into a moderate oven. Bake the egg plants until they are tender.

Egg plants may be served whole with butter, pepper, and salt, or they may be peeled before being sent to table and coated with a white sauce, made with the liquid in the dish.

181. Greens or Curly Kale

Remove coarse outer blades and strip the leaves off stalks. Discard the stalks; prepare and serve the greens as for Dressed Cabbage.

182. Leeks

Remove the roots and the coarse green leaves, split the leeks in two, wash them thoroughly, and cut them into lengths of about four inches. Tie them in bundles, and boil in boiling salted water till tender (about forty minutes). Drain them thoroughly, remove thread, and coat with white sauce.

183. Grilled Mushrooms

Wash the mushrooms to remove earth and sand; remove the stalks and the skin, and dry the mushrooms. Heat and grease the gridiron, and place it over a slow fire. Brush the mushrooms with melted butter. Grill for five to ten minutes, turning them when half-done. Sprinkle with pepper and salt, and serve hot. The skin and stalks should be used to flavour soups and stews.

184. Baked Mushrooms

Prepare the mushrooms as above, and place on a greased tin. Sprinkle with pepper and salt. Cover with greased paper. Cook in a moderate oven. Serve hot, and pour any liquid that is in the tin over the mushrooms before serving. If the mushrooms are cooked in a fireproof dish they should be served in the dish in which they have been cooked.

185. Mushrooms in Butter

Prepare the mushrooms as above. Melt some butter in a stewpan and fry the mushrooms in this until tender. Season with salt and pepper. Place on small rounds of buttered toast and serve hot.

186. Onions

Choose Spanish onions. Skin and parboil for one minute, and then cook in boiling salted water till tender (large onions take about one and a half to two hours, small onions about three-quarters of an hour). Drain. Dish and coat with white sauce.

187. Parsnips

Wash the parsnips, cut into neat pieces, and peel. Cook in boiling salted water until tender (about forty minutes). Drain well, dish, and coat with a white sauce.

188. Peas (Green)

Rinse the peas and shell them. Have a pan with just enough boiling salted water to cover them. Add the peas with a sprig of mint and a pinch of sugar. Boil gently till tender (from ten to twenty minutes). Drain. Toss in melted butter, and serve.

189. Peppers (Chillies)

Cut off a thin slice from the stem end of each pepper, and remove the inner fibre and seeds. Parboil (see Cookery Terms, p. 20) from two to five minutes. Drain.

Fill up each pepper with a savoury mixture. Cover the open end with bread crumbs and sprinkle with melted butter ; bake in a moderate oven, and serve with a suitable sauce.

Note.—Any cold cooked meat, such as chicken, sweetbread, etc., may be cut in neat pieces, mixed with sauce, and reheated in the peppers.

190. Potatoes boiled in their Jackets

Choose potatoes of an equal size. Scrub well; peel off thin strip round each potato; place in a pan with enough cold water to cover them, add the salt (one dessertspoonful to each quart of water). Bring quickly to boiling point, and boil for about twenty minutes. When almost cooked, pour away the water ; continue cooking in their own steam, then lift the lid partly off to allow the steam to escape. Place the pan beside the fire till the potatoes are dry, shaking it occasionally to prevent them from sticking to the pan. Serve hot.

191. Boiled Potatoes

Scrub well, and pare very thinly. Proceed as in the previous recipe.

192. Baked or Jacket Potatoes

Wash, wipe, and dry the potatoes. Place them on a grid in a moderate oven. They are ready when they feel soft, and generally take about one and a half to two hours. Serve very hot, with butter.

193. Roast Potatoes

Choose medium-sized potatoes. Scrub, pare, and parboil. Drain and place on roasting-tin beside the meat forty minutes before meat is to be ready. Baste with the roast, and turn the potatoes to equalize the colour.

194. Mashed Potatoes

One pound potatoes. | Half-gill milk.
Half-ounce butter. | Pepper and salt.

Boil, drain, and mash the potatoes. Heat the milk and butter. Add the potatoes and seasonings. Beat over the fire till creamy. Serve very hot.

195. New Potatoes

One pound new potatoes. | Half-ounce butter.
Boiling water. | Half a teaspoonful finely
One dessertspoonful salt to | chopped parsley.
  one quart water. |

Wash and scrape the potatoes. Place them in a pan and just cover with boiling water. Add the salt. Boil for fifteen to twenty minutes till soft. Drain and dry at the side of the fire, as described for old potatoes. Add the butter, serve on a hot dish, and sprinkle with parsley.

196. Steamed Potatoes

Scrub and peel the potatoes. Put them in a steamer, add salt or not according to taste, and cover with a lid. Place the steamer over a pan of boiling water, and cook the potatoes till tender. Then place a plate between the pan and the steamer so that all steam is cut off from the potatoes, and tilt the lid to allow any steam to escape.

197. Stoved Potatoes

One ounce dripping or margarine.
Two pounds potatoes.

Half-pound onions.
Half-pint hot water.
Pepper and salt.

Melt fat in a pan. Skin, slice, and fry the onions. Wash, peel, and slice the potatoes and put them also into the pan. Add seasonings and hot water. Put on the lid and cook slowly till ready, from one to one and a half hours, stirring now and then to prevent burning. Serve very hot.

198. Potato Chips

Two or three small potatoes. | Pan of deep fat.

Scrub and peel the potatoes, and cut them into very thin slices. Keep for half an hour in cold water. Drain well on a cloth and dry. Have the fat smoking hot. Put the chips into a frying basket and cook till tender (about three minutes). Lift up the basket and let the fat reheat. Put the potatoes into the fat again and fry until they are crisp and brown. Drain thoroughly on paper. Sprinkle with pepper and salt.

199. Potato Straws

Prepare the potatoes and cut into slices about one-eighth of an inch in thickness. Cut into strips, and cook as for Potato Chips.

200. Potato Ribbons

Prepare the potatoes and cut into half-inch thick slices. Then cut each slice round and round very thinly into ribbon-like strips. Cook as for Potato Chips.

201. Rice

Take the quantity of Patna rice required, wash it thoroughly, put it into a pan with plenty of boiling salted water. Boil till tender (about fifteen minutes), strain off the water, and rinse the rice well with cold water to separate the grains. Reheat the rice. Place it on a dish, cover, and dry it in a warm place.

Note.—The rice water may be used in the making of Curry Sauce, etc.

202. Salsify

Wash and scrape the salsify thoroughly, using lemon juice or vinegar in each water to preserve the colour. Place in boiling salted water, to which a few drops of lemon juice or vinegar has been added, and boil till tender (about thirty minutes). Drain. Toss in melted butter and sprinkle with chopped parsley and lemon juice. Dish.

203. Sea Kale

Wash and scrape the sea kale thoroughly, and tie it up in bundles of even thickness. Put into a saucepan sufficient water to cover the sea kale and add a pinch of salt; when boiling, put in the sea kale, and stew gently for thirty minutes till tender. Drain, undo the bundles, and coat with sauce, using the liquid in which the vegetable has been cooked.

Note.—Chicory may be cooked in the same way.

204. Spinach

Soak spinach in plenty of cold water for half an hour. Wash and rinse very thoroughly. Remove the coarse stalks; put it into a rinsed lined pan, with the water that clings to the leaves; put the lid on the pan, and cook till tender, stirring frequently. When ready, drain well, chop finely, or rub it through a sieve ; put it into a pan, with a small pat of butter and pinches of pepper and salt ; allow it to heat thoroughly, and pile neatly on a hot vegetable dish. Garnish with croutons of fried bread.

205. Baked Tomatoes

Wipe tomatoes, cut across in two, but if small keep whole. Place on a greased tin, season with salt and pepper. Cover with greased paper, and bake in a moderate oven from five to seven minutes.

206. Stuffed Tomatoes

Three medium firm tomatoes.

STUFFING

One teaspoonful butter.
Half - teaspoonful grated onion.
One dessertspoonful chopped ham.

One tablespoonful bread crumbs.
Cayenne and salt.

GARNISH FOR TOP

Dried bread crumbs and grated cheese.

FOR DISHING

Rounds of fried bread.
Parsley.

Wipe the tomatoes. Cut a small round from each at the end opposite the stalk and scoop out all the pulp. Melt the butter in a small pan and add the onion and ham ; stir in the bread crumbs, moisten with the tomato pulp, and season. The mixture should be of a soft consistency. Fill the tomatoes with this ; sprinkle with cheese and dried crumbs on the top, and bake in a moderate oven from twelve to fifteen minutes till soft. Dish on rounds of fried bread and garnish with parsley.

207. Mashed Turnips

Wash, cut in blocks, and peel thickly. Cook in boiling salted water till soft. Drain and mash or sieve ; add pepper, salt, and a little dripping or butter.

208. New Turnips

Wash and peel the turnips, and cook in boiling salted water till soft. Drain well. Dish neatly and coat with white sauce.

209. Vegetable Marrow

Wash the marrow. Cut in four from end to end, and remove the seeds. Cut in neat pieces and peel thinly. Cook in boiling salted water till tender. Drain, and coat with melted butter sauce (see Recipe 226).

Note.—The pieces of marrow may be laid on a steamer, salt being added or not according to taste, and cooked steadily by steaming. Dish and serve as above.

210. Stuffed Vegetable Marrow

One small vegetable marrow	One gill milk.
	One hard-boiled egg.
STUFFING	Two ounces grated cheese.
Three tablespoonfuls bread	One yolk of egg.
crumbs.	Pepper and salt.

Wash the marrow. Cut in two from end to end, and remove the seeds. Peel thinly. Parboil for two minutes. Drain. Boil the milk and pour over the bread crumbs. Chop the hard-boiled egg. Mix all the ingredients of the stuffing and bind with the yolk of egg. Place the pieces of marrow on a greased fireproof dish and fill the hollows with the stuffing. Cover with greased paper. Bake in a moderate oven till tender. Serve the vegetable in the dish in which it has been cooked.

211. Mixed Salad

One lettuce or endive.
Bunch of water-cress.
Bunch of mustard cress, or small cress.

One hard-boiled egg.
One tomato or a few radishes.
A small piece of cucumber.

Wash the green salads carefully, taking care not to bruise the leaves, and drain them well on a cloth. Pour boiling water over the tomato, peel it, and cut it into sections. Skin the cucumber and cut in thin slices. Wash the radishes, divide in eight half-way through, and keep in cold water until opened up. Cut the egg into neat pieces. Mix the salad with a dressing, and arrange tastefully in a salad bowl.

Note.—Any salad in season may be used.

212. Winter Salad

For this salad any cooked vegetables—namely, potato, haricot beans, dried green peas, beetroot, carrot, cauliflower, etc., may be used. The vegetables must be cut into pieces of a suitable size, and tossed in a dressing, *e.g.* boiled salad dressing.

Note 1.—This salad may be improved by the addition of raw vegetables, such as raw grated carrot, a few shreds of raw cabbage (the most tender leaves), shreds of celery, thin slices of raw onion, finely chopped parsley. A little grated cheese sprinkled over will improve the food value.

Note 2.—Firm or new cooked potatoes may be cut in slices, quarter-inch thick, and served with French dressing to which a little onion juice and chopped parsley have been added.

213. Tomato and Celery Salad

Two tomatoes. | Three sticks celery.

Scald the tomatoes, peel and slice thinly. Prepare the celery, shred into cold water, and allow it to stand for half an hour : this makes the celery curl up. Drain well.

Arrange the tomatoes in a circle, pour French dressing over and pile the celery in the centre. Decorate with a little small cress, or finely-chopped parsley.

Note.—The celery may be omitted, and finely chopped spring onion sprinkled over the slices of tomato.

214. All-the-Year-Round Salad

One lettuce.
Bunch of small cress.
One sweet apple.
One banana.
One orange.

Nuts, *e.g.* walnuts, pine kernels.
Dried fruit, *e.g.* dates, prunes, or raisins.

Wash and drain the green salads. Cut the apple into dice, the banana into slices, and squeeze a little lemon juice over them to prevent discoloration. Divide the orange into liths and remove all pith. If large, cut across in slices. Soak the prunes ; then stone the prunes and the dates. Remove seeds from raisins. Break the nuts into pieces. Mix the ingredients with a cream dressing, and decorate with tiny lettuce leaves, cress, orange, walnuts, prunes, etc.

SAUCES

Proportions for Sauces.

For a pouring sauce, use half an ounce of butter and half an ounce of flour to half a pint of liquid.

For a coating sauce, use one ounce of butter and one ounce of flour to half to three-quarters of a pint of liquid.

Note on White Sauces.

Equal quantities of fat and flour are blended together without discolouring. Then liquid is added gradually. The sauce should be boiled for ten minutes to obtain the full flavour of the flour.

Note on Brown Sauces.

Equal quantities of fat and flour are fried together till of a fawn or brown colour. Then liquid is added. The sauce should be simmered for some time to develop the flavour, and any grease should be skimmed off during cooking.

Note 1.—The mixture of fat and flour is called a " roux." A roux may be white, fawn, or brown.

Note 2.—Flour may be browned in oven previous to frying. When using increase proportion slightly.

Note on a Panada.

This is the term given to a thick binding sauce (usual proportion one ounce of fat and one ounce of flour to

one gill of liquid) used for croquette mixtures and for
the foundation of soufflés.

215. White Sauce

Half-ounce butter. | Half-pint milk.
Half-ounce flour. | Pepper and salt.

Melt the butter in a saucepan ; add the flour, and cook
for a few minutes without browning. Add about one-
third of the milk ; stir carefully till boiling. Add the
remainder of the milk gradually ; bring to the boil, and
boil for three minutes. Season with pepper and salt.

216. Parsley Sauce

Prepare in the same way as for a white sauce. When
cooked, add one teaspoonful finely chopped parsley,
and boil up once to remove the raw taste of the parsley.

217. Egg Sauce

Prepare in the same way as for a white sauce, and
add one hard-boiled egg roughly chopped.

218. Cheese Sauce

Half-ounce butter. | Cayenne and salt.
Half-ounce flour. | One gill milk or water.
        Two ounces grated cheese.

Prepare in the same way as for a white sauce, cool
and add half the cheese and seasonings. Use the remaining half of the cheese for sprinkling on top of
dish.

219. Caper Sauce for Boiled Mutton

Two ounces butter.
Two ounces flour.
Half-pint meat boilings.
Half-pint milk.

One tablespoonful capers.
One teaspoonful caper vinegar.

Prepare in the same way as for a white sauce, making it thick enough to coat the back of the spoon. When cooked, add the capers and the caper vinegar.

220. Onion Sauce

Two ounces butter.
Two ounces flour.

One pint milk.
Three onions.

Pepper and salt.

Skin the onions and boil till soft, drain, and rub through a sieve or chop finely.

Prepare sauce in the same way as for a white sauce; add the chopped onions.

221. Fish Sauce

Prepare in the same way as for white sauce, using half fish stock and half milk.

222. Shrimp Sauce

Prepare as for fish sauce, and add half a gill of picked shrimps.

223. Anchovy Sauce

One ounce butter.
Half-ounce flour.
Half-pint fish stock.

Pepper.
One to two teaspoonfuls anchovy essence.

Prepare in the same way as for white sauce, and add the anchovy essence.

224. Oyster Sauce

Six sauce oysters.
One ounce butter.
Half-ounce flour.
Half-pint of oyster liquor

and fish stock or water mixed.
Salt, cayenne, lemon juice.
One dessertspoonful cream.

Blanch the oysters in their liquor; strain them, reserving the liquor for the sauce. Remove the beard, and cut each oyster in two. Make the sauce (see White Sauce). Add the oysters, seasonings, and cream.

225. Mustard Sauce

One ounce butter.
Half-ounce flour.
One gill fish stock.

One teaspoonful of mustard.
One dessertspoonful vine-gar.

Pepper and salt.

Prepare in the same way as white sauce. Mix the mustard with the vinegar. Add to the sauce, and bring again to boiling point. Add seasonings and a little extra vinegar if necessary.

226. Melted Butter Sauce

One ounce butter.
Half-ounce flour.

Half-pint cold water.
Pinch of salt.

Prepare in the same way as for a white sauce. For a sweet melted butter, instead of salt, add one teaspoonful sugar, and flavour with lemon essence, vanilla, or lemon juice.

227. Brandy Sauce

One ounce butter.
Half-ounce flour.

Half-pint water.
One tablespoonful brandy.

Sugar to sweeten.

Prepare in the same way as for a white sauce. When cooked, add the sugar and brandy.

228. Brown Sauce

Half-ounce dripping.
Half-ounce flour.
Half-pint second stock.
One onion.

Small piece of carrot.
One dessertspoonful ketchup.
Pepper and salt.

Prepare carrot and onion, and cut in thin slices. Melt the dripping, fry the vegetables slightly, add the flour, and fry carefully over a slow fire till of a good brown colour. Add stock by degrees, also a pinch of salt. Boil up, and skim thoroughly. Add pepper. Put on the lid, and simmer the sauce steadily for thirty to forty minutes, stirring and skimming when necessary. Strain, and reheat.

229. Sauce Piquante

Half-ounce dripping.
Half-ounce flour.
Half-pint stock.
One dessertspoonful ketchup, or Harvey's sauce.

One tablespoonful vinegar.
Pepper and salt.
One onion and a small piece of carrot.

Melt the dripping, fry the vegetables slightly, add the flour, and brown carefully ; then add the vinegar, and reduce for four or five minutes. Add the stock by degrees and a pinch of salt. Boil up, skim thoroughly, and add the ketchup. Simmer steadily for thirty to forty minutes, stirring and skimming when necessary. Strain, and reheat.

230. Tomato Sauce

Half-ounce butter.	One onion.
Half-ounce rice flour.	Small piece of carrot.
Half-pint second stock or liquor from tinned tomatoes.	Half-ounce bacon.
	Four or five tomatoes.
	Pepper and salt.

Pinch of sugar.

Prepare onion and carrot, and cut into slices. Cut the bacon in pieces, put into a saucepan with the butter, and fry slightly. Add onion and carrot, then the tomatoes ; bruise down with a spoon, and reduce the sauce for four or five minutes. This improves the flavour and colour. Stir in the rice flour, add the stock. Boil up, and skim if necessary. Season with salt and pepper. Put on the lid and simmer slowly for forty to forty-five minutes, stirring occasionally. Rub through a hair sieve, reheat, and add sugar.

231. Curry Sauce

Half-ounce butter.	stock, rice water, or coco-nut infusion (see Recipe 112).
One tablespoonful chopped onion.	
One tablespoonful chopped apple.	Quarter teaspoonful curry paste.
Quarter to half-ounce curry powder (depending on strength of powder).	One dessert-spoonful chutney or plum or gooseberry jam.
Half-ounce rice flour.	Lemon juice.
Half-pint light-coloured	Salt to season.

Melt the butter in a pan. Fry the onion lightly; fry the apple; then fry the curry powder thoroughly and the flour. Add the stock gradually and the salt. Bring to the boil and skim, then add the lemon juice, the curry paste, and the chutney or jam. Put on the lid, and simmer one to one and a half hours, stirring frequently. Strain if required.

232. Horse-radish Sauce

Two tablespoonfuls grated horse-radish.	Salt and pepper. Good pinch of sugar.
One gill cream.	Vinegar and lemon juice.

Wash and scrape the horse-radish and allow it to lie in cold water. Then grate. Half-whip the cream and stir in the other ingredients.

233. Apple Sauce

One pound apples.	Half-ounce butter.
One gill water.	Half-ounce sugar.

Peel, core, and slice the apples, put into a saucepan with the water, butter, and sugar, and cook until quite soft. Beat smooth with the back of a wooden spoon, or rub through a hair sieve, and reheat.

234. Mint Sauce

Two heaped tablespoonfuls chopped mint.	Two tablespoonfuls hot water.
One dessertspoonful moist sugar.	Half-gill vinegar.

Put the mint into a sauceboat; add the sugar and hot water. When cool, add the vinegar.

235. Bread Sauce

Half-ounce butter.	Half-pint milk.
One gill freshly-made bread crumbs.	One small onion.
	Two cloves.

Six peppercorns.

Put the milk, peppercorns, and onion stuck with cloves into a saucepan, and infuse at the side of the fire for fifteen minutes, then strain.

Return the seasoned milk to the pan with the butter and bread crumbs. Stir till boiling and of a dropping consistency.

236. Caramel Sauce

Four ounces sugar (loaf). | One gill water.

Put the sugar and half the water into a small old pan. Melt the sugar and then bring to boiling point. Then boil without stirring until the desired colour is attained. Then remove the pan and add the rest of the water.

237. Cornflour Sauce

| Quarter-ounce cornflour. | One teaspoonful sugar. |
| Half-pint milk. | Strip of lemon rind. |

Break the cornflour smooth with a little of the cold milk. Put the remainder of the milk into a pan with the lemon rind and bring to the boil. Remove lemon rind, add the cornflour, stirring all the time. Boil for five minutes, then add the sugar.

Note.—A vanilla pod may be used to flavour sauces. Infuse the pod in the milk until the milk is sufficiently flavoured ; then remove the pod. It may be used over and over again.

238. Arrowroot Sauce

Quarter-ounce arrowroot. | Half-pint water or fruit juice.
Sugar or syrup to sweeten.

Break the arrowroot smooth with a little of the water
or juice. Bring the rest of the water or juice to boiling
point. Add the arrowroot, stirring all the time. Boil
for five minutes, and then sweeten with sugar or syrup.
A few drops of lemon juice or other flavouring may be
added. Cornflour may be used instead of arrowroot.
The sauce may also be coloured with a few drops of
carmine, or sap-green, etc.

239. Custard Powder Sauce

Quarter-ounce custard pow- | Half-pint milk.
der. | One teaspoonful sugar.

Break the custard powder with a little of the cold
milk. Bring the remainder of the milk to boiling-point.
Add the custard powder, stirring all the time. Boil
for three minutes. Sweeten and use.

240. Custard Sauce

One egg. | Half-pint milk.
Two teaspoonfuls castor | Vanilla or lemon essence.
sugar. |

Beat the egg and sugar together. Heat the milk and
pour it over the egg, stirring carefully. Add the flavouring. Strain back into the rinsed pan and stir till the
custard thickens, but do not let it boil. Serve at once.
If the sauce is to be served cold stir occasionally while
cooling.

241. Economical Custard Sauce

One egg.
One pint milk.

Quarter-ounce cornflour.
One teaspoonful sugar.

Break cornflour smooth with a little of the cold milk. Heat the rest of the milk ; add the cornflour, stirring all the time. Boil for three minutes ; sweeten and cool ; beat in the egg. Stir it over a gentle heat till the egg cooks and thickens, being very careful to avoid curdling.

242. Marmalade Sauce

One dessertspoonful corn-flour.
Half-pint water.

One tablespoonful sugar.
One tablespoonful marma-lade.

Rind and juice of one lemon.

Break the cornflour with the lemon juice. Boil the water with the lemon rind, remove rind and add the cornflour, stirring all the time. Boil for five minutes. Add the marmalade and sugar. Boil up.

243. Jam Sauce

Two tablespoonfuls rasp-berry jam.
ne gill water.
rour or five lumps sugar.

Rind and juice of half a lemon.
One teaspoonful cornflour.
A few drops of carmine.

Put all ingredients except the cornflour and carmine into a pan, boil up, and skim. Infuse from seven to ten minutes. Strain, return to pan, and thicken with cornflour. Add a few drops of carmine if necessary.

Note 1.—One tablespoonful of sherry may be added to the above sauce.

Note 2.—A simpler jam sauce may be made with one

tablespoonful raspberry jam, squeeze of lemon juice, one gill water, and one teaspoonful cornflour.

SAUCES FOR SALADS

244. French Dressing

Half to one tablespoonful salad oil.

One dessertspoonful vinegar.

Pepper and salt.

Mix the oil and seasonings in a bowl, then gradually work in the vinegar.

245. Mayonnaise Sauce

One yolk of egg.
Salt, pepper, and made mustard.
Salad oil (half to one gill).

Malt and tarragon vinegar (one or two teaspoonfuls).

Put the yolk of egg and seasonings into a bowl. Add the salad oil drop by drop, stirring all the time. When thick and smooth, thin down gradually with the vinegar. The Mayonnaise dressing should be about the consistency of thick cream.

246. White Dressing

Two tablespoonfuls cream.
One teaspoonful tarragon vinegar.
One teaspoonful lemon juice.

Cayenne pepper, salt, sugar and made mustard.
Beaten white of egg.

Half-whip cream with seasonings. Add vinegar and lemon juice gradually, and lastly fold in the stiffly beaten white of egg.

Note.—Sour cream may be used for this Mayonnaise.

247. Cream Salad Dressing

One hard-boiled yolk of egg.

Pepper, salt, sugar, and made mustard.

Two tablespoonfuls cream or oil.

One dessertspoonful vinegar or lemon juice.

Sieve the yolk into a bowl, add the seasonings and the cream. Then gradually work in the vinegar.

248. Cooked Salad Dressing

One egg.

Half-ounce butter.

One tablespoonful vinegar.

One tablespoonful milk or cream.

One dessertspoonful sugar.

Half-teaspoonful dry mustard.

Pepper and salt.

Beat the egg and mix all the ingredients in a basin. Stand the basin in a pan of hot water and whisk until the egg thickens, or cook in a double saucepan.

249. Boiled Dressing

One teaspoonful flour.

One teaspoonful dry mustard.

One teaspoonful salt.

One teaspoonful sugar.

Half-gill malt and tarragon vinegar.

One gill water.

One tablespoonful salad oil.

One egg.

Mix the dry ingredients with a little of the water to a smooth paste. Bring the rest of the water with the vinegar to boiling point, and add the thickening, stirring all the time. Boil for three minutes. Add the salad oil, and cool; stir in the beaten egg. Cook till the egg thickens.

PASTRY

USES, PROPORTIONS, AND METHODS

Suet Pastry.

Used for Sweet and Savoury Dishes.

Proportions.—Half suet to flour.

Method.—The suet is shredded and chopped very finely so that it may be easily absorbed by the flour during the process of cooking.

Hot-Water Crust.

Used for Savoury Dishes.

Proportions.—Quarter fat to flour.

Method.—The fat is melted and poured with the water (at boiling-point) into the dry ingredients. Such pastry is only flexible while still hot.

Potato Pastry.

Used for Savoury Dishes.

(i.) *Proportions.*—Half fat to flour, and equal quantities of flour and potatoes.

Method.—The fat is rubbed into the flour before potatoes are added.

(ii.) *Proportions.*—Equal quantities of butter, potato, and flour (approx.).

Method.—The butter is creamed before being mixed with the potatoes and flour.

Short Crust.

Used for Sweet and Savoury Dishes.
Proportions.—Half fat to flour.
Method.—The fat is rubbed into the flour. Rubbing in the fat makes pastry short and crisp, hence the name " short crust." The fat (which may be dripping, margarine, butter, or lard) is called the shortening.

Cornflour Pastry.

Used for Sweet Dishes, etc.
Proportions.—Half butter to flour and cornflour.
Method.—Same as for Short Crust.

Cheese Pastry.

Used for Savouries.
Proportions.—Half butter to flour, and half cheese to flour.
Method.—Same as for Short Crust.

Rough Puff.

Used for Sweet and Savoury Dishes.
Proportions.—Half to three-quarters fat to flour.
Method.—The butter is cut into large lumps and is rolled into the dough. The rolling and folding is repeated four times in order to mix the butter through the dough, to fold in cold air which acts as a raising agent, and to make the pastry rise in flakes.

A few rules for pastry making :

1. Keep everything as cool as possible, and mix with very cold water.
2. Mix pastry evenly.
3. Knead and roll out lightly.

4. Bake in a hot oven for the first ten minutes to set and colour the pastry. Then finish the thorough cooking of the pastry at a moderate temperature until it is crisp.

250. Suet Pastry

Eight ounces flour.
Four ounces suet.
Half-teaspoonful salt.

One teaspoonful baking-powder.
Cold water.

Sieve the flour, baking-powder, and salt into a basin. Shred down the suet, chop it very finely. and mix with the other dry ingredients. Add cold water gradually to make a fairly soft dough. Turn the pastry on to a floured board, knead it lightly, then roll it out to the size required.

251. Hot-Water Pastry, or Raised Pie Crust

Eight ounces flour.
Two ounces lard or butter.
Half-teaspoonful salt.

Three-quarters of a gill hot water or milk.

Sieve the flour and salt into a basin. Put the water and lard, or butter, into a pan, and when boiling pour into the dry ingredients. Mix with a spoon, and when cool enough turn on to a floured board and knead till smooth. Form quickly into the shape required.

252. Potato Pastry (Method 1)

Eight ounces mashed potatoes.
Four ounces flour.
Two ounces dripping or butter.

Half-teaspoonful baking-powder.
Pinch of salt.
Water.

Rub the fat into the flour. Add the baking-powder and salt, then mix in the potatoes, adding enough water to form a stiff paste. Roll out to quarter-inch in thickness.

253. Potato Pastry (Method 2)

Five ounces flour.
Three ounces butter.
Four ounces cooked, sieved potatoes.

One teaspoonful baking-powder.
Pinch of salt.

Cream the butter ; add the potatoes, flour, baking-powder, and salt. Turn on to a well-floured board. Knead and roll very lightly. Use as required.

254. Short Crust Pastry

Eight ounces flour.
Four ounces butter.
Half-teaspoonful baking-powder.
Half-teaspoonful salt.

A little cold water ; or, if a richer pastry is desired, one yolk of egg and water.

Sieve the flour, baking-powder, and salt into a dry, cool basin. Put in the butter, and rub it into the flour with the tips of the fingers till the mixture resembles fine bread crumbs. Add sufficient cold water to form a stiff paste. Turn the pastry on to a floured board. Knead lightly, then roll it out to the size required.

Note.—Half butter and half lard may be used. A richer short crust may be made with six ounces butter to eight ounces flour. The baking-powder is then unnecessary.

255. Cornflour Pastry

Three ounces cornflour.
Four ounces flour.
Three ounces butter.

One ounce castor sugar.
One yolk of egg.
A little milk.

Sieve the flour and the cornflour ; with the tips of the fingers rub in the butter until like fine bread crumbs ; add the castor sugar. Beat up the yolk of egg with a little milk, and with this mix the dry ingredients to form a stiff paste. Turn on to a floured board. Knead lightly then roll it out to the size required.

256. Cheese Pastry

Four ounces flour.
Two ounces butter.
Two ounces grated Cheddar
    cheese.

Quarter-teaspoonful salt.
Pinch of cayenne.
A little beaten yolk of egg.
A little water.

Sieve the flour, rub in the butter, add the grated cheese, and mix all the dry ingredients ; bind with the yolk of egg and water to form a stiff paste. Knead lightly, roll out thinly, and use as required.

257. Rough Puff Pastry

Eight ounces flour.
Four ounces butter.

Half-teaspoonful salt.
Few drops of lemon juice.
Cold water.

Sieve the flour and salt into a bowl ; add the lemon juice and the butter broken into pieces the size of a walnut ; add sufficient cold water to bind the ingredients together. Turn on to a floured board, and roll the pastry into a long strip. Fold it in three, and press the edges together. Half turn the pastry, rib it with the rolling pin to equalize the air in it, and again roll it into a strip. Fold in three, and repeat this until the pastry has had four rolls, folds, and half-turns. It is then ready for use.

Note.—If a richer pastry is desired, use six ounces butter to eight ounces flour. Half butter and half lard may be used.

PUDDINGS AND SWEET DISHES

SOME GENERAL PROPORTIONS

Milk Puddings.

One and a half ounces grain to one pint of milk.

Milk Shapes.

Two ounces grain to one pint of milk.

Custards.

Baked.—One egg to half a pint of milk.
Steamed.—One egg to one gill of milk.
Cup.—One yolk of egg to one gill of milk.

Steamed Suet Puddings.

Half suet to flour or to flour and bread crumbs.
Note.—Two tablespoonfuls of bread crumbs equals one ounce.

General Outline for all Suet Puddings.

Half-pound flour ; quarter-pound bread crumbs ; four to six ounces chopped suet ; one teaspoonful of any ginger or spice ; four to eight ounces currants, dates, figs, or any dried fruit, or one gill treacle, syrup, jam, or marmalade, or eight ounces chopped apples

(fresh) ; three to six ounces sugar, according to sweetness
of fruit, etc., used ; enough milk, or buttermilk, to make
a thick batter ; one and a half teaspoonfuls baking-
powder, or one teaspoonful baking-soda if there is
syrup or treacle or vinegar in recipe.

Light Steamed Puddings.

Butter and sugar in equal proportions and together
equal to flour.

Soufflés.

Four whites and three yolks of eggs to one gill of
panada.

Batter.

Pancake.—Four ounces flour to half-pint of milk and
one egg.
Fritter.—Two ounces flour to half-gill water and one
white of egg.

Gelatine.

To stiffen liquids.—Use three-quarters ounce gelatine
to one pint.
*To stiffen thicker mixtures, e.g. custards, prune shape,
etc.*—Use half-ounce gelatine to one pint.
Note.—The gelatine used in these recipes is powdered
gelatine.

Stewed Fruit.

For one pound fresh fruit.—Syrup made from half-pint
water and four ounces sugar.
For one pound dried fruit.—One pint of water and
enough sugar to sweeten.

258. Rice Pudding

One and a half ounces Caro- | One dessertspoonful granu-
lina rice. | lated sugar.
One pint milk. | A little grated nutmeg.

Grease a pie-dish.   Wash the rice well, and put it into
the dish with the sugar and milk.   Grate a little nutmeg
over the top, and bake in a moderate oven for about two
hours.   If the milk dries up too much, add a little more.
Note.—The above ingredients may be put into a jar.
The jar should be covered with greased paper and placed
in a pan of boiling water, sufficient to come half-way
up the jar.   Steam for about two hours until the rice is
thick, soft, and creamy.   Then pour into a dish.

259. Boiled Rice

One and a half ounces Caro- | One dessertspoonful granu-
lina rice. | lated sugar.
One pint milk. |

Wash the rice and put it into a double saucepan with
the milk.   Cook gently till soft and creamy.   Add sugar
to sweeten.

If an ordinary saucepan is used it is better to burst
the rice before adding the milk.   To do this put the
washed rice into the saucepan, just cover with cold water,
bring to boiling-point, and cook without stirring it until
the water is completely evaporated.   Then add the milk,
and simmer till soft and creamy.   Lastly, add sugar to
sweeten.

260. Tapioca Pudding

One and a half ounces tapioca.	Three gills milk.
One gill water.	One dessertspoonful granulated sugar.

One egg.

Wash the tapioca. Put it into a bowl, and cover with the water, and soak it about one hour until all the water is absorbed. Put the milk and tapioca into a rinsed pan, bring to the boil and simmer till the grain is soft and clear (about thirty minutes), then draw to the side of the fire and let it cool a little. Add the sugar. Beat the egg, mix well with the tapioca. Pour the mixture into a buttered pie-dish, and bake in a moderate oven for about thirty minutes.

Note.—Large sago is prepared and cooked in the same way.

261. Macaroni Pudding

Two ounces macaroni.	Two ounces sugar.
One pint milk.	One egg.

Break the macaroni into small pieces, and put into a pan of boiling water ; boil it uncovered for twenty minutes ; pour away the water ; add the milk. Simmer very slowly for about a quarter of an hour till the macaroni is quite tender. Draw the pan to the side of the fire to cool the mixture a little. Add the sugar and the beaten egg. Pour into a greased pie-dish, and bake in a moderate oven for about thirty minutes.

262. Semolina Pudding

One and a half ounces semolina.	One dessertspoonful granulated sugar.
One pint milk.	One egg.

Heat the milk in a rinsed saucepan and sprinkle in the semolina ; stir till boiling, and simmer until the grain is soft (about ten minutes). Remove the pan from the fire, add the sugar, and allow the mixture to cool a little. Break the egg and separate the yolk from the white ; add the yolk to the semolina, and mix well. Beat up the white to a stiff froth, and mix lightly with the other ingredients. Pour into a greased pie-dish, and bake in a moderate oven for about thirty minutes.

Note.—Pearl tapioca and small sago are prepared and cooked in the same way.

263. Ground Rice Pudding

One and a half ounces ground rice. | One pint milk.
One dessertspoonful sugar.
One egg.

Prepare and cook as for Semolina Pudding (above). If the ground rice is very fine, prepare as for Farola Pudding.

264. Farola Pudding

One and a half ounces farola. | One pint milk.
One dessertspoonful sugar.
One egg.

Break the farola to a smooth paste with a little of the cold milk. Heat the rest of the milk in a rinsed pan, add the farola, and finish as for Semolina Pudding (Recipe 262).

265A. Bread Crumb Pudding (1)

One and a half ounces bread crumbs.
Half-pint milk. | Half-ounce butter.
Half-ounce sugar.
One egg.
Few drops of vanilla essence.

Heat the milk and butter in a saucepan, then add the bread crumbs and allow to swell out ; add the sugar. Break the egg, add the yolk to the mixture, and mix well ; add the flavouring. Beat up the white of the egg stiffly, and mix lightly with the other ingredients. Turn the mixture into a greased pie-dish. Bake in a moderate oven for about thirty minutes.

265B. Bread Crumb Pudding (2)

(Queen of Puddings)

One and a half ounces bread crumbs.	One and a half ounces sugar.
Half-pint milk.	One egg.
Half-ounce butter.	Jam.

Heat the milk and butter in a saucepan, then add the bread crumbs and allow to swell out ; add half an ounce of sugar, or less according to taste. Break the egg, add the yolk to the mixture, turn into a greased pie-dish, and bake in a moderate oven for about twenty minutes. Then spread jam over the top. Beat up the white of egg stiffly, and add about one tablespoonful of castor sugar. Pile this over the jam and return the pudding to the oven to set, and slightly brown the white of egg.

266. Cornflour or Arrowroot Shape

One and a half ounces corn-flour or arrowroot.	One pint milk.
	One dessertspoonful sugar.

Break the cornflour to a smooth paste with a little of the cold milk. Heat the rest of the milk in a rinsed pan, stir in the cornflour, and boil from seven to ten minutes, stirring all the time. Add the sugar, and pour into a wet mould.   When cold, turn out, and serve with fruit or jam.

Note.—One ounce of powdered chocolate or cocoa may be mixed with the cornflour and broken with it to a smooth paste.

267. Farola Shape

Use two ounces of farola to one pint milk.   Proceed as for Cornflour Shape.

268. Fairy Pudding

Two ounces cornflour.
Two ounces sugar.
Three-quarters pint water.
One white of egg.
Rind and juice of one lemon.

SAUCE

One yolk of egg.
One gill milk.
Sugar to sweeten.

Bring the water to boiling-point, and infuse the lemon rind in the water for ten minutes ; break the cornflour smooth with lemon juice.   Add cornflour to the water and boil for ten minutes.   Add the sugar, cool and fold in the stiffly-beaten white of egg.   Pour into a wet mould.   Turn out when cold.   Pour round a cold custard sauce.

269. Casserole of Rice

Two ounces ground rice.
One pint milk.

Few drops of flavouring.
Two small eggs.

One ounce castor sugar.

Heat the milk, then sprinkle in the rice, and stir over the fire until the rice is cooked.   Add the sugar and flavouring, and stir in the beaten eggs ; then pour this into a well-greased border mould, and steam very gently till firm (about thirty minutes). When ready turn out, and fill the centre with stewed fruit or jam.

This casserole can be served either hot or cold.

270. Tapioca Cream

Two ounces flaked tapioca. | One egg.
One pint milk. | Half a teaspoonful vanilla.
Two ounces sugar. |

Wash the tapioca and soak in half-gill of water until the water is absorbed. Cook the tapioca in the milk for thirty minutes till quite transparent. Stir in sugar and vanilla, and, when slightly cooled, the yolk of egg. Stir over the fire until the yolk is cooked, but do not boil. Mix in lightly the stiffly-beaten white of egg. Pour into a glass dish and serve cold.

271. Bird's Nest Pudding

One ounce pearl tapioca. | Half-pint water.
Two apples. | Half-ounce sugar.

Core and pare the apples. Place in a greased pie-dish and fill the holes with sugar. Wash the tapioca. Put into a pan with the water, and boil for five minutes. Pour over the apples. Bake in a moderate oven from half to three-quarters of an hour.

272. Semolina Sponge

Two ounces semolina. | Rind and juice of one
One pint water. | good-sized lemon.
Sugar to sweeten.

Wipe lemon, and peel rind thinly. Bring the water to boiling-point, and infuse the lemon rind in the water for ten minutes ; strain, and make up with water to one pint. Put water in pan, sprinkle in semolina, and cook thoroughly. Add lemon juice and sugar. Turn into a large basin and whisk until stiff ; pile up in a glass dish or pour into a china mould, and turn out when stiff.

273. Cup Custard

One yolk of egg.	One gill milk.
Teaspoonful castor sugar.	Vanilla or lemon essence.

Beat the yolk of egg and sugar together. Heat the milk, and pour it over the egg, stirring carefully. Add the flavouring. Strain back into the rinsed pan, and stir till the custard thickens, but do not let it boil. Pour into a basin. Stir while it is cooling. Pour into custard cups. Place a ratafia biscuit on each custard.

274. Baked Custard Pudding

One egg.	Half-pint milk.
Half-ounce castor sugar.	A little grated nutmeg.

Beat up the egg lightly with the sugar, add the milk, and strain into a greased pie-dish. Grate a little nutmeg on top. Put the pudding into a slow oven, and bake till the custard is firm to the touch (about three-quarters of an hour). The pudding must not boil or the egg will curdle.

275. Bread and Butter Pudding

Two thin slices of white bread and butter (two ounces).	One tablespoonful currants. One egg. Half-ounce castor sugar.
Half-pint milk.	

Cut the bread and butter into small pieces, and put them into a pie-dish in layers with the currants, previously cleansed. Beat the egg and sugar together, add the milk, and strain over the bread. Allow the pudding to stand for fifteen minutes so that the bread may swell and absorb some of the milk. Bake in a moderate oven for about three-quarters of an hour.

276. General Favourite

Two sponge cakes.
A little jam.
One egg.

One dessertspoonful sugar.
Half-pint milk.
Vanilla essence.

Split the sponge cakes and spread them with jam. Cut them into neat pieces, and put them into a greased pie-dish. Beat up the yolk of the egg with the sugar, and pour over it the hot milk. Strain the custard over the sponge cakes. Bake the pudding in a cool oven until the custard is set (about thirty minutes) ; then take the pudding out of the oven. Whip up the white of the egg stiffly, add very lightly one table-spoonful of castor sugar, place the meringue on the pudding, dredge with sugar, and put the pudding into a cool oven to set the white of egg. It will take about thirty minutes.

277. Steamed Ginger Pudding

Half-pound flour.
Pinch of salt.
Quarter-pound suet.
Half-teaspoonful bicarbon-
   ate of soda.

Half - teaspoonful ground
   ginger.
One ounce moist brown
   sugar.
One tablespoonful syrup.

Milk to mix.

Sieve the flour and salt ; shred and chop the suet finely. Mix all the dry ingredients in a bowl. Add the syrup and sufficient milk to make the mixture of a soft dropping consistency. Turn into a greased bowl, making it about two-thirds full. Cover with a greased paper. Put the pudding into a pan with enough boiling water to come half-way up the bowl, and steam for two hours. Turn out the pudding on to a hot dish, and pour round it a cornflour sauce sweetened with syrup (see Recipe 238).

278. Syrup Sponge Pudding

Half-pound flour.
Pinch of salt.
Quarter-pound suet.
Half-teaspoonful bicarbon-
ate of soda.

Two teaspoonfuls ground
ginger.
One gill syrup.
One egg.
One gill milk.

Sieve the flour and salt ; shred and chop the suet finely. Mix all the dry ingredients in a bowl. Add the beaten egg, syrup, and milk, and mix well. Turn into a greased bowl, making it about two-thirds full. Cover with a greased paper. Put the pudding into a pan with enough boiling water to come half-way up the bowl, and steam for two hours. Turn out the pudding on to a hot dish, and pour round it three tablespoonfuls of golden syrup made hot and flavoured with a few drops of lemon juice.

279. Treacle Pudding

Four ounces flour.
Two ounces bread crumbs.
Three ounces suet.
Half-teaspoonful bicarbon-
ate of soda.
Half - teaspoonful ground
ginger.

One ounce moist brown
sugar.
One tablespoonful treacle.
One egg.
About one gill milk.

Shred and chop the suet, and mix it with all the other dry ingredients. Beat the egg in a bowl, add the milk, and mix in the treacle. Pour this into the centre of the dry ingredients, and beat the mixture well. Steam and serve as for Syrup Sponge (Recipe 278). Turn out and pour custard powder sauce (Recipe 239) round.

280. Gingerbread Pudding

Four ounces bread crumbs.
Two ounces flour.
Three ounces suet.
Half-teaspoonful bicarbon-
ate of soda.

One large teaspoonful ground ginger.
Two ounces sugar.
One tablespoonful syrup.
One or two eggs.

Three-quarters gill milk.

Sieve the flour into a bowl ; shred and chop the suet finely. Mix all the dry ingredients. Add the beaten egg, the syrup and milk, and mix well. Turn the mixture into a greased bowl ; cover with a greased paper. Put into a pan with enough boiling water to come half-way up the bowl, and steam for two hours. Turn the pudding on to a hot dish, and pour round it sweet melted butter sauce (see Recipe 226).

281. Rothesay Pudding

Four ounces flour.
Two ounces bread crumbs.
Three ounces suet.
Half-ounce sugar.
Two tablespoonfuls rasp-
berry jam.

Half-teaspoonful bicarbon-
ate of soda.
Half-teaspoonful vinegar.
About one gill milk.

Make the bread crumbs ; shred and chop the suet finely. Mix all the dry ingredients, with the exception of the soda, in a bowl. Stir in the jam ; add sufficient milk to make the mixture of a soft dropping consistency.

Moisten the bicarbonate of soda with the vinegar, and stir thoroughly through the mixture. Turn into a greased bowl, cover with a greased paper, and steam steadily for two hours. Turn the pudding on to a hot dish, and pour a sweet sauce round.

282. Fig Pudding

Four ounces bread crumbs.
One ounce flour.
Three ounces suet.
Half-teaspoonful bicarbonate of soda.

Two ounces sugar.
Three ounces figs.
One tablespoonful syrup.
One or two eggs.
Half-gill milk.

Wash the figs, remove stalks, and soak in a little water, then chop them finely ; shred and chop the suet finely. Mix all the dry ingredients in a bowl ; add the figs, beaten eggs, syrup, and milk. Turn into a well-greased bowl, cover with a greased paper, and steam steadily for two hours. Turn the pudding on to a hot dish, and pour a sweet sauce round.

Note.—Date pudding may be made by the above recipe, substituting half a pound dates for the figs.

283. Plain Suet Pudding

Six ounces flour.
Two ounces bread crumbs.
Half-teaspoonful salt.
Four ounces suet.

One teaspoonful baking-powder.
Two ounces sugar.
About one gill milk.

Sieve the flour, salt, and baking-powder into a bowl ; make the bread crumbs ; shred and chop the suet finely. Mix all the dry ingredients together, add the milk, and mix well : the mixture should drop easily from a spoon. Turn it into a greased bowl, cover with a greased paper and steam for two hours. Turn out and serve with a sweet sauce.

Note.—Two ounces of currants may be added.

284. Lemon Pudding

Six ounces bread crumbs.	Four ounces sugar.
Two ounces flour.	Two lemons (grated rind).
Quarter-pound suet.	One or two eggs.
One teaspoonful baking-powder.	One and a half gills milk.

Make the bread crumbs ; shred and chop the suet finely. Mix all the dry ingredients in a bowl, and add the grated lemon rind. Beat up the eggs, and add with the milk to the dry ingredients. Mix well. Turn the mixture into a greased bowl, cover with a greased paper, and steam for about one and a half hours. Turn the pudding on to a hot dish, and pour round it a sweet melted butter sauce flavoured with lemon juice (Recipe 226).

285. Baroness Pudding

Six ounces flour.	Quarter-pound raisins.
Two ounces bread crumbs.	Three ounces sugar.
Quarter-pound suet.	One egg.
One teaspoonful baking-powder.	One and a half gills milk.
	Pinch of salt.

Chop the suet finely ; stone the raisins, cut them in half, and mix them with the dry ingredients. Beat the egg, and add with the milk to the dry ingredients. Mix well. Turn into a greased bowl, cover with greased paper, and steam from two to three hours. When cooked, turn out, and pour round it sweet melted butter sauce (see Recipe 226).

286. Plain Plum Pudding

Four ounces bread crumbs.
Two ounces flour.
Three ounces suet.
Three ounces sugar.
Two ounces raisins.
Two ounces sultanas.
Two ounces currants.

One ounce mixed peel.
Half - teaspoonful mixed spice.
One teaspoonful baking-powder.
One or two eggs.
About one gill milk.

Salt.

Clean the fruit and stone the raisins ; shred and chop the peel finely ; shred and chop the suet finely. Mix all dry ingredients in a bowl. Beat the eggs, add the milk, and stir into the dry ingredients. Pour the mixture into a greased bowl, tie over a floured cloth, put into a pan of boiling water, and boil from three to four hours. This pudding may be boiled in a floured cloth. When cooked, turn the pudding out, and serve with melted butter sauce.

287. Snowdon Pudding

Four ounces bread crumbs.
Three-quarters ounce ground rice.
Two ounces suet.
Two ounces raisins.

Two tablespoonfuls marmalade.
Three ounces castor sugar.
One lemon (grated rind).
One egg.

Half a gill milk.

Decorate a greased pudding-bowl with the raisins, stoned and cut in half, but not divided, pressing the cut sides on the bowl. Make the bread crumbs, and shred and chop the suet finely. Mix all the dry ingredients in a basin. Beat up the egg, and add with the marmalade and milk to the other ingredients. Pour the mixture into the prepared bowl, cover with a greased paper,

and steam for two hours. Turn on to a hot dish, and
serve with marmalade sauce (see Recipe 242).

288. Sir Watkin Wynne Pudding

Six ounces bread crumbs. | Two eggs.
Three ounces suet. | One and a half tablespoon-
Three ounces sugar. | fuls marmalade.
A little milk.

Make the bread crumbs ; shred and chop the suet
finely. Mix all the dry ingredients in a bowl. Beat up
the eggs and add with the marmalade to the dry ingredients. The mixture should be rather moist, as the
bread crumbs swell : add milk, therefore, as required.
Turn into a greased bowl, cover with a greased paper,
and steam for two hours. Turn the pudding on to a
hot dish, and pour round either marmalade or sweet
melted butter sauce.   (Recipes 242 and 226.)

289. French Rice Pudding

Three ounces rice. | One ounce candied orange
Two ounces suet. | or lemon peel.
Two ounces castor sugar. | Two eggs.
Two ounces raisins. | One pint milk.

Wash the rice well, put it into a stewpan with the
milk, and cook gently until all the milk is absorbed.
Stone and chop the raisins ; chop the suet and peel.
Beat all these ingredients with the sugar into the rice.
Beat the eggs well, and add them.   Pour this mixture
into a greased pudding-bowl, cover with a greased
paper, and steam for two hours.   Turn out the pudding,
and pour marmalade sauce round.

290. Boiled Fruit Dumpling

One pound fresh fruit. | Suet pastry (six ounces
Sugar to sweeten. | flour, etc.).

Prepare the fruit as for a fruit tart. Grease a strong basin thoroughly, line with the pastry, pressing out the air between pastry and basin, and trim. Put in half of the prepared fruit, add the sugar, then the rest of the fruit. Press it well down, and have the basin quite full. Knead the trimmings and roll into a round ; wet the edges of the pastry, and put on the round to form a cover. Cover with a floured pudding-cloth, and tie the cloth firmly on with a string. Gather up the ends of the cloth, and drop the pudding gently into a pan of fast-boiling water. Have sufficient water to cover the pudding during the whole process of cooking, and boil steadily from two to two and a half hours. To dish the pudding, remove string and cloth. Dish on a deep ashet. Serve hot.

Note.—This pudding may be covered with a greased paper and steamed.

291. Roly-poly

Suet pastry.   Jam.

Roll the pastry into an oblong shape. Spread with jam to within one inch of the edge. Wet the edge of the pastry with water, and roll it up firmly, pressing the edges together. Flour a pudding-cloth, and roll the roly-poly in it. Tie firmly at each end, leaving a little room for swelling. Boil steadily for two to three hours according to the size. Drain well, undo the string at each end, and unroll carefully on to a hot dish. Serve hot.

Note.—Instead of tying in a cloth, this pudding may be placed in a greased basin and boiled or steamed.

292. Syrup Pudding

Suet pastry (six ounces flour, etc.).
Three tablespoonfuls syrup.

Pinch of ground ginger, or a little grated lemon rind.

Two tablespoonfuls bread crumbs.

Mix the syrup, bread crumbs, and ginger together. Roll the pastry out one-quarter inch in thickness. Cut into rounds of various sizes. Place a small round at the bottom of a greased bowl, and place on it a teaspoonful of the mixture. Wet the edge of the round, and place another a size larger on the top. Repeat till the basin is quite full. Cover with a floured cloth, and boil steadily for two and a half to three hours. Remove the cloth, and turn out on a hot dish. A little melted syrup may be poured round as a sauce if desired. Serve hot.

293. Delaware Pudding

Suet pastry (six ounces flour, etc.).

FILLING

Two tablespoonfuls chopped apple.
One tablespoonful currants.

Half-ounce shredded mixed peel.
Pinch of spice.
One tablespoonful moist sugar.
One tablespoonful syrup.
A little water.

Mix all the ingredients for the filling together, and use as for Syrup Pudding (see Recipe 292).

294. Sultana Pudding

Four ounces flour.
Two ounces butter.
Two ounces sugar.
Two ounces sultanas.

Half - teaspoonful baking-powder.
One egg.
About half a gill of milk.

Decorate a greased bowl with the cleaned sultanas. Cream the butter and sugar well, then add the egg and a little flour, and beat thoroughly. Add the rest of the flour, the sultanas, and the baking-powder, and mix well. Add a little milk. The pudding mixture should drop easily from a spoon. Turn it into the prepared bowl, cover with greased paper, and steam steadily for one and a half hours. Turn out, and pour round it a custard or jam sauce.

295. Newcastle Pudding

Three ounces flour.
Two ounces butter.
Two ounces sugar.

Half - teaspoonful baking-powder.
One egg.

A little milk.

Grease a bowl, and decorate with one or two cherries cut in slices. Cream the butter and sugar thoroughly ; add the egg and a little flour, and beat well. Then add the rest of the flour, the baking-powder, and a little milk if necessary. Turn into the greased bowl; cover with a greased paper ; steam for about one and a quarter hours. Turn the pudding out, and pour jam sauce round.

296. Pineapple Pudding

Use the ingredients and method given for Newcastle Pudding (Recipe 295), and add one and a half ounces of chopped pineapple to the pudding mixture. When the pudding is turned out mask it with an arrowroot sauce

(Recipe 238), using half-ounce arrowroot to half-pint pineapple juice.

297. Orange Pudding

Use the ingredients and method given for Newcastle Pudding (Recipe 295), and add the grated rind of one orange. When the pudding is turned out, pour round it an arrowroot sauce (Recipe 238), using quarter-ounce arrowroot to half-pint orange juice and water. Decorate with liths of tangerine orange heated in a little fruit juice or sherry.

298. Coffee Pudding

Three ounces flour.	Half to one tablespoonful
One ounce ground rice.	coffee essence.
Two ounces butter.	One egg.
Two ounces sugar.	Milk if necessary.
One teaspoonful baking-powder.	

Cream the butter and sugar thoroughly ; add the egg and a little flour, beat well. Add the rest of the flour, the ground rice, and baking-powder. Add the coffee essence and milk if necessary. Turn the mixture into a greased bowl, cover with a greased paper, and steam steadily for one and a half hours. Turn out the pudding and pour round a melted butter sauce flavoured with a teaspoonful of coffee essence.

299. Brown Bread Pudding

Four ounces brown bread crumbs.	Pinches of nutmeg and cinnamon.
One and a half ounces butter.	Half - teaspoonful baking-powder.
Two ounces castor sugar.	One or two eggs.
Grated rind of half a lemon.	One gill milk.

Cream the butter and sugar, add the yolks of the eggs, and beat well.   Add the cinnamon, nutmeg, bread crumbs, lemon rind, and milk.   Soak for a short time; add the baking-powder, and mix in lightly the stiffly-whipped whites of the eggs.   Turn into a greased tin or bowl; steam gently from one to one and a quarter hours. Turn the pudding out, and pour a sweet sauce round.

300. Prince Albert Pudding

Six ounces prunes.
Three ounces brown bread crumbs.
Grated lemon rind.
One and a half ounces butter.

One and a half ounces sugar.
Half-teaspoonful baking-powder.
One egg.
Half-gill milk.

Stew the prunes (Recipe 338) and remove the stones. Reserve the juice for the sauce.   Grease a basin and line it with the prunes.   Cream the butter and sugar.   Add the bread crumbs, baking-powder, lemon rind, yolk of egg, and milk.   Beat the white of egg stiffly, mix lightly into the mixture, and pour into the prepared basin. Steam for one and a quarter hours.   Turn out on to a hot dish and mask the pudding with an arrowroot sauce (Recipe 238), using half-ounce arrowroot to half-pint prune juice.

301. Coconut Pudding

One ounce coconut.
One and a half gills milk.
Three ounces bread crumbs.
One ounce butter.
One ounce sugar.

One or two eggs.
A little vanilla essence.
Half-teaspoonful baking-powder.

Put the coconut and milk into a saucepan, bring to the boil, then simmer for about ten minutes until the milk is absorbed. Cream the butter and sugar, and add the bread crumbs, the coconut, and the yolks of the eggs. Mix well, flavour with vanilla essence, and add the baking-powder. Beat up the whites of the eggs stiffly, then mix lightly with the other ingredients. Turn the mixture into a greased bowl, cover with greased paper, and steam gently from one to one and a quarter hours. Turn the pudding on to a hot dish, and pour jam sauce round.

302. Chocolate Pudding

Two ounces sweetened, or one ounce unsweetened chocolate.
One gill milk.
Three and a half ounces bread crumbs.
One and a half ounces butter.
One and a half ounces sugar.
One egg.
Vanilla essence.
Half-teaspoonful baking-powder.

Put the milk and chocolate into a saucepan, and dissolve the chocolate. Cream the butter and sugar, break the egg, and separate the yolk from the white. Whip the white stiffly. Add the yolk and a few crumbs to the butter and sugar, and mix thoroughly. Add the chocolate and the rest of the crumbs, and mix these ingredients well together. Add the baking-powder and white of egg, and mix lightly and well. Pour the mixture into a greased basin or china mould ; cover with a greased paper ; steam steadily about one hour. Turn the pudding on to a hot dish, and pour custard sauce round.

303. Marmalade and Vermicelli Pudding

Three ounces vermicelli.
Three-quarters pint milk.
Two small eggs.
One tablespoonful marmalade.
One ounce raisins.
One ounce sugar.

Cook the vermicelli in the milk until tender (about twenty minutes); add the stoned raisins, beaten eggs, sugar, and marmalade. Turn into a greased bowl; cover with greased paper; steam gently for about one and a half hours. Turn out the pudding, and pour marmalade sauce over it.

304. Plain Cabinet Pudding

Two thin slices white bread and butter (two ounces).
One tablespoonful raisins or sultanas.

Two gills hot milk.
Two eggs.
One dessertspoonful sugar.
Vanilla essence.

Grease a pudding-bowl, and decorate with a few of the prepared sultanas or raisins. Cut the bread and butter into small pieces, and put them into the prepared bowl in layers with the rest of the sultanas. Beat up the eggs with the sugar; add the hot milk and a few drops of vanilla. Strain over the bread. Cover the pudding-bowl with greased paper, and let it stand for fifteen minutes, so that the bread may swell and absorb some of the milk. Then steam the pudding very gently until firm to the touch (about an hour). The water in the pan must not boil or the custard will curdle. When cooked, turn the pudding on to a hot dish, and pour jam sauce round.

305. Vanilla Soufflé

One ounce butter.
One ounce flour.
One gill milk.

One tablespoonful castor sugar.
A little vanilla essence.

Three yolks and four whites of eggs.

Tie a fourfold band of paper round the outside of a plain soufflé tin. The paper should be about three inches wide, and should be about two inches above the top of the soufflé tin. Then grease both the tin and the paper with clarified butter. Separate the yolks from the whites of the eggs, and whip the whites very stiffly. Melt the butter in a saucepan. Add the flour and cook for a minute, add the milk, and stir briskly until the mixture is thick and leaves the sides of the pan clean. This sauce is called a panada. Add the sugar and vanilla to the panada and the yolks one by one and beat well, then fold in the stiffly-beaten whites. Pour into the tin ; cover with greased paper ; steam *very* gently for about forty to fifty minutes, or until the soufflé feels firm to the touch. When cooked, lift the tin from the pan, take off the band of paper, let the soufflé stand for a few seconds, then turn it carefully on to a hot dish. Pour round a custard or jam sauce. Serve at once.

Note.—This soufflé may also be baked.

306. Apple Balls

Short crust pastry (four ounces flour, two ounces butter, etc.).	Three teaspoonfuls sugar.
	Three cloves.
	Beaten white of egg.
Three small apples.	Castor sugar.

Wipe, peel, and core the apples without breaking them. Make the pastry, and roll it out a quarter of an inch in thickness. Cut it into rounds large enough to surround the apple. Place the apple in the centre of the round, and fill up the centre with sugar and one clove. Wet the edges of the pastry, and fold it up neatly round the apple, joining it at the top. Roll the ball between the hands, and place it on a greased baking sheet, rough side down. Brush over with beaten white of egg, dredge with castor sugar, and bake first in a hot oven till the

pastry is a light brown colour, then in a cooler shelf till
the apple is soft. Before dishing, dredge with castor
sugar, and serve either hot or cold.

307. Fruit Tart

One pound fruit.
Two to four ounces moist
  or granulated sugar.

Short crust pastry (four
  ounces flour, etc.).

Prepare the fruit first. If rhubarb is used, wipe
thoroughly with a damp cloth, remove the coarse skin,
and cut the rhubarb into lengths of one inch ; if apples,
peel, quarter, and core ; if gooseberries or other fruits,
remove the stalks and tops and wash thoroughly. In
filling the pie-dish, put in half of the fruit, then add the
sugar in the centre, piling the rest of the fruit on the top.
Add water if required. Prepare the pastry, and roll it
out about one inch larger than the rim of the pie-dish.
Cut a strip from the pastry, wet the edge of the pie-dish,
and place the strip on without stretching it. Join the
cut ends by wetting them. Brush the strip of pastry
with water and lay on the cover, pressing it down to the
strip. Trim off any rough edges, knock up the edge
of the pastry with the back of a knife, and decorate
the edge with tiny flutes. Brush the pastry over with
a little beaten white of an egg, dredge with castor sugar,
and make two small holes with a skewer to allow escape
of steam. Place the tart in a hot oven for the first five
or ten minutes till the pastry is slightly browned, then
remove the tart to a lower shelf till the fruit is quite
soft. (Average time about three-quarters to one hour,
depending on the kind of fruit and size of pie.) On
removing the tart from the oven dust over with castor
sugar. It may be served hot or cold.

308. Fruit Turnovers

Short crust or rough puff | Jam, or stewed fruit.
   pastry.

Roll the pastry out thinly, and cut it into rounds ; damp round the edges of each round ; place a little jam or fruit in the centre ; fold the pastry over, pressing the edges together. Glaze over, and bake in a hot oven for about thirty minutes. Dredge with sugar, and dish.

309. Syrup Tart

Short crust pastry (four | Two to three tablespoonfuls
   ounces flour, etc.). | of syrup.
One ounce bread crumbs. | A little lemon juice.

Line a greased Yorkshire tin with the pastry. Trim the edges. Prick the pastry at the bottom of the tin all over. Mix the syrup, bread crumbs, and lemon juice together, and spread this mixture over the pastry. Roll and cut the trimmings into strips. Twist them and lay them across the syrup mixture. Bake the tart in a steady oven till golden brown.

310. Treacle Pastry

Use the ingredients given in above Recipe 309, substituting treacle for syrup.

Roll the pastry thinly and divide in two squares. Lay the first square on a greased tin. Spread the treacle mixture over it to within one inch from the edge. Damp the edge and place the second square on top. Join the edges and turn them over. Mark the pastry into small squares. Bake. Cut into squares and dust with sugar.

311. Open Tart

Short crust pastry (six | Beaten white of egg.
ounces flour, three | Castor sugar.
ounces butter, etc.). | Jam, or stewed fruit.

Grease an old plate or ashet, and damp the edge with cold water. Roll out the pastry a little larger than the plate. Lay it on, and trim off the rough edges. Prick the centre with a fork to prevent it rising from the plate. Roll out the scraps and cut into small fancy shapes. Brush the rim of the pastry with beaten white of egg, and decorate it with the small shapes of pastry, pressing them well down in the centre. Brush over again with the white of egg, and dredge with castor sugar. Cut a round of greased paper to fit the centre of the tart ; lay it on, and place in it some haricot beans or crusts of bread to prevent the pastry rising in the centre. Put the tart into a hot oven. Reduce the heat when the pastry has begun to brown. About ten minutes before removing from the oven remove the paper and beans, and allow the pastry in the centre to dry off. When dishing, dredge the edge with castor sugar, and fill up the centre with jam, which should be heated if the tart is to be served hot.

312. Open Fruit Tart (1)

Short crust pastry (six | Arrowroot or cornflour in
ounces flour, etc.). | the proportion of one
One pound stewed or tinned | teaspoonful to half-pint
fruit. | fruit syrup.

Stew the fruit carefully so that it is not broken (Recipe 337). Then strain off the syrup. If tinned fruit is to be used, strain off the syrup and cut the fruit into neat pieces. Measure the syrup, bring it to boiling-point, and thicken it with arrowroot or cornflour, or reduce it by boiling. Let the syrup cool.

Make an open tart according to directions given in Recipe 311. Roll and shape the trimmings into long strips about half an inch broad. Twist and bake them beside the tart. Arrange the fruit neatly on the tart. Place the strips of pastry across, and pour the syrup over the top.

313. Open Fruit Tart (2)

Short crust pastry (six ounces flour, etc.).
One pound fresh fruit such as strawberries, raspberries, etc.
Two eggs.
Two ounces castor sugar.

Make an open tart according to directions given in Recipe 311. Prepare the fruit and arrange it neatly on the tart. Sprinkle it with sugar. Whip the whites of eggs stiffly and mix in the sugar lightly. Pile on top of the fruit. Dredge with sugar and place in a cool oven to set the white of egg. Use the yolks of eggs for a custard sauce (Recipe 240), and serve this with the tart.

314. Custard Tarts

Short crust pastry (four ounces flour, etc.).

CONFECTIONER'S CUSTARD
One ounce flour.
Two ounces butter.
One and a half gills milk.
One yolk of egg.
Sugar to sweeten.
Vanilla essence.

Make a thick sauce with the butter, flour, and milk according to directions given in Recipe 215. Cook thoroughly. Cool the mixture slightly and add the

sugar and yolk of the egg.   Cook gently to thicken the
yolk.   Add flavouring.   Line six or eight greased patty
tins or a greased pyrex dish with thin short crust.   Pour
the custard into the pastry cases.   Bake in a moderate
oven for twenty-five to thirty minutes until the pastry
is quite cooked and the custard slightly coloured.

315. Spiced Apple Tart

THE PASTRY	FOR FILLING
Six ounces flour.	One and a half pounds apples, or one pound apples and half-pound prunes.
Three ounces butter.	
Half - teaspoonful baking-powder.	
One teaspoonful castor sugar.	Half-ounce butter.
	A little water.
One teaspoonful cinnamon.	One teaspoonful cinna-mon.
Pinch of salt.	
Yolk of egg and water to bind.	Two ounces sugar.

Cut the apples in slices and stew till tender with the
butter and a very little water.   Stew the prunes, remove
the stones, and chop the prunes roughly.   Mix the apples
and the prunes, adding cinnamon and sugar.

Sieve the flour, salt, and baking-powder.   Rub in the
butter.   Add cinnamon and sugar.   Mix with yolk of
egg and water.   Knead the pastry, and cut off one-
third for the lid.   Roll out the larger piece of pastry,
turn it, and with it line a greased sandwich tin or
cake tin or a pyrex dish.   Trim edges.   Put the apple
mixture into the pastry case.   Roll out the remaining
third of pastry, and cover the tart, pressing the edges
well together.   Trim the edges with scissors.   Make a
small hole in the lid to allow the steam to escape.   Place
in a hot oven from five to ten minutes.   Then reduce

the heat and allow the tart to cook more slowly till the pastry is quite crisp, from thirty to forty-five minutes. Serve hot or cold, and sprinkle the top with castor sugar mixed with cinnamon.

316. Blakemore Pudding

One ounce bread crumbs or one sponge cake. | Rind and juice of half a lemon.

Two tablespoonfuls jam.

PASTRY

Three ounces cornflour. | One ounce castor sugar.
Four ounces flour. | One yolk of egg.
Three ounces butter. | A little milk.

Rub the sponge cake through a wire sieve, then mix the crumbs with the grated lemon rind, strained lemon juice, and the jam. Sieve the flour and the cornflour; rub in the butter until like fine bread crumbs; add the castor sugar. Beat up the yolk of egg with a little milk, and with this mix the dry ingredients to a stiff dough. Turn on to a floured board; knead lightly; divide in two portions; roll the pastry about a quarter-inch in thickness. Line a greased plate with the pastry, then spread the mixture over. Wet round the edges of the plate with water. Cover with the second round of pastry. Beat up the edges of the pastry, and decorate with four leaves of pastry. Brush with white of egg, sift with sugar, and bake in a quick oven for about thirty minutes.

317. Apple Amber

Short crust or rough puff pastry (two ounces flour, etc.).
One pound apples weighed after peeling.

One lemon.
Two ounces butter.
One or two eggs.
Two preserved cherries.
Three ounces sugar.

Peel, core, and slice the apples. Melt the butter in a pan, put in the apples, sugar, and a few strips of lemon rind, and cook until tender ; then beat till smooth or rub through a hair sieve. Add the yolks of the eggs to the apples, and mix well. Line a pie-dish with a thin strip of pastry, then decorate the edge of the dish with fancy shapes of pastry. Pour the apple mixture into the prepared dish, and bake in a moderate oven for about thirty minutes ; then remove from the oven. Whip the whites very stiffly, add to them about two tablespoonfuls of castor sugar. Place this meringue over the apples, dredge with castor sugar, decorate with cherries, and place the pudding in a cool oven to set the white of egg. It will take about thirty minutes.

318. Baked Lemon Pudding

Short crust or rough puff pastry (two ounces flour, etc.).
One ounce castor sugar.

One ounce butter.
Two eggs.
One lemon.
One ounce cake crumbs.

Line and decorate the edges of a pie-dish with the pastry. Cream the butter and sugar together, then add the yolks of eggs, sieved cake crumbs, the grated lemon rind, and the strained lemon juice. Whip the whites of the eggs very stiffly, and mix lightly with the other ingredients. Pour the mixture into the prepared pie-dish, and bake in a moderate oven for about forty minutes.

319. Bakewell Pudding

Short crust or rough puff pastry (two ounces flour, etc.).	Two ounces butter.
	Two ounces sugar.
	Four ounces cake crumbs.
Two tablespoonfuls raspberry jam.	Two ounces ground almonds.
	Two eggs.
Two tablespoonfuls lemon curd.	Rind of half a lemon.

Line and decorate a pie-dish with pastry ; spread the bottom of the dish with jam and lemon curd. Cream the butter and the sugar well ; add the yolks of eggs, the almonds, crumbs, grated rind, and a little milk. Mix all the ingredients well. Fold in stiffly-beaten whites. Spread the mixture over the jam ; bake in a moderate oven for about an hour.

320. West Riding Pudding

Short crust or rough puff pastry (four ounces of flour, etc.).	in butter, in sugar, and in flour.
Two tablespoonfuls jam.	Grated rind of half a lemon.
Two eggs, and their weight	Half-teaspoonful baking-powder.

Line the sides of a pie-dish with a thin strip of pastry, then decorate the edge of the dish with fancily cut shapes of pastry. Spread the jam at the bottom of the dish. Cream the butter and sugar well ; add the eggs and flour by degrees ; beat all the ingredients well ; add the baking-powder with the last tablespoonful of flour. Pour the mixture into the pie-dish, and bake in a moderate oven for about one and a quarter hours.

321. Cheese Cakes

Short crust pastry (two ounces flour, etc.).

Filling

One egg ; its weight in butter, in sugar, and in flour.
Little grated lemon rind.

Quarter - teaspoonful baking-powder.
A little jam.

Roll the pastry out thinly, cut into rounds, line greased patty-tins, and put half a teaspoonful of jam at the bottom of each tin. Cream the butter and sugar ; beat in the egg with a little flour, then add rest of flour, baking-powder, and lemon rind ; mix well, and half fill each tin with the mixture. Bake in a moderately hot oven till risen and firm (about twenty to thirty minutes).

322. Mince Pies

Short crust or rough puff pastry (four ounces of flour, etc., for six or eight mince pies).
Mincemeat (Recipe 323).

Roll pastry out to quarter-inch in thickness. Grease shallow patty-tins and line them with rounds of pastry. Cut rounds of pastry one size larger for the top. Pile the mincemeat in the centre. Damp the edges of the pastry. Cover with the larger round. Join and decorate the edges. Cut across the pie, and bake in a hot oven from twenty to thirty minutes.

It is not necessary to use patty-tins. Lay the rounds of pastry on a greased baking sheet, pile the mincemeat in the centre, and cover over with the larger rounds.

323. Mincemeat

Four ounces suet.
Four ounces Valencia raisins.
Four ounces sultanas.
Four ounces currants.
Four ounces figs.
Four ounces apples.
Four ounces Demerara sugar.
Three ounces almonds.
One and a half ounces citron peel.
One and a half ounces orange peel.
Rind and juice of one lemon.
Half-teaspoonful nutmeg.
Pinches of ginger and cinnamon.
Half-gill rum or sherry.

Wash the fruit and allow it to dry. Chop the suet. Cut the Valencia raisins in halves, and remove stones. Leave the sultanas and currants whole. Chop the figs and apples. Shred and chop the peel. Blanch and chop the almonds. Grate the lemon rind. Mix all the ingredients together. Put the mincemeat into jars. Cover.

Note.—Make the mincemeat at least a fortnight before it is required.

324. Eve's Pudding

One pound apples.
Two ounces sugar.
Half-gill water.
Two eggs ; their weight in
butter, in sugar, and in flour.
Grated rind of half a lemon.
Half-teaspoonful baking-powder.

Peel, quarter, core, and slice apples. Put into a basin with the sugar and water, and steam till tender. Turn the apples into a pie-dish.

Make the West Riding mixture (Recipe 320). Pour the mixture over the apples. Bake in a moderate oven for one and a quarter hours.

Note.—This pudding may be varied by using tinned fruit instead of stewed fruit, or by using a plainer sponge mixture.

When using tinned fruit strain off the syrup. Cut the fruit in neat pieces and place the fruit in the pie-dish. Pour the sponge mixture over, and bake. Thicken the syrup with cornflour, and serve with the pudding as a sauce.

For a plainer sponge mixture use the proportions given for Sultana Pudding (Recipe 294).

325. Railway Pudding

Half-pound flour.
Three ounces butter.
Three ounces sugar.

One large teaspoonful baking-powder.
One egg.
Jam.

Mix the flour and baking-powder in a basin ; rub in the butter ; add the sugar ; beat the egg, and mix into the dry ingredients. Beat the mixture well, and, if necessary, add a little milk to make the mixture of a soft dropping consistency. Pour into a greased tin, and bake in a hot oven for about three-quarters of an hour till firm to the touch. Turn out and allow to cool. When cold, split in half and spread with jam. Dredge the top with sugar, and cut into fingers.

326. Baked Apples

Wipe the apples ; remove the core ; cut a line through the skin round each apple ; place on a greased tray ; fill the holes with sugar ; add a clove to each; put a small pat of butter on top, and bake in a moderate oven until quite tender. Dish on a hot flat ashet, and pour the juice over the apples.

327. Baked Apple Soufflé

One pound apples.	Half-ounce butter.
Two ounces castor sugar.	Two yolks and three whites
Grated rind of one lemon.	of eggs.

Tie a double band of paper, four inches deep, round a china soufflé case. Grease the case and paper, and place on a baking sheet. Wipe the apples, and bake in a moderate oven in a Yorkshire tin covered with greased paper. When soft pass through a hair sieve, and add the sugar, yolks, lemon rind, and butter. Then beat the mixture thoroughly until it becomes lighter in colour. Whip the whites of egg and fold them into the mixture. Pour the mixture into the prepared case. Bake in a moderate oven till well risen and firm in centre, from twenty to thirty minutes. Remove the paper carefully, and place the soufflé on a fancy dish paper on a dish.

Note.—Pears may be used instead of apples. Rhubarb may be steamed and used. Bananas may be used uncooked.

328. Apple Charlotte (1)

Two or three slices stale bread.	Two ounces sugar.
Two ounces clarified butter.	Grated rind and juice of half a lemon.
One pound apples weighed after peeling.	Two yolks, or one ounce bread crumbs and one
One ounce butter.	yolk.

Cut one large round, one medium-sized round, and a number of small rounds of bread quarter-inch thick, and soak these in the clarified butter. Arrange a circle of small rounds in the bottom of a round tin or fireproof dish, and fit the medium-sized round in the centre.

Arrange another circle of small rounds overlapping those already in. Repeat until the sides of the tin are lined.

Peel, core, and weigh the apples. Put into a pan with the butter, sugar, lemon rind and juice, and stew until soft and tender, then rub through a hair sieve. Heat the apple mixture, add the bread crumbs, cool, and add the yolk of egg. Cook gently to thicken the egg.

Pour the apple mixture into the dish and place the larger round of bread over the top. Place a saucer and weight on top of the bread. Bake in a moderate oven for one hour. Turn out on to a hot dish. Add a drop of carmine to any apple-mixture which may have been left over, reheat, and pour this round the pudding. If the pudding is baked in a pyrex dish it may be served in the dish in which it is cooked.

329. Apple Charlotte (2)

One pound apples.
Two to three ounces sugar.
Three ounces freshly made bread crumbs.

One and a half ounces finely chopped suet.
A little water if apples are dry.

Wipe and peel apples, cut in quarters and core. Cut in thin slices. Mix crumbs, suet, and sugar together, and fill up pie-dish with alternate layers of apple and bread-crumb mixture, finishing with crumbs. Sprinkle with a little melted butter or margarine, and bake in a moderate oven for about an hour.

330. Pancakes

Four ounces flour.
Pinch of salt.

One egg.
Half a pint of milk.

For frying the pancakes, about two tablespoonfuls of clarified fat.

Sieve the flour and salt into a bowl. Make a well in the centre ; drop in the egg and stir in half the milk. Stir until smooth, then beat the batter well until air bubbles rise. Stir in the rest of the milk, cover, and let it stand for an hour, then pour into a jug or cup.

Pour a little of the hot clarified fat into a frying-pan. Place the pan over a good heat and make it hot, then pour into the pan just enough batter to cover the bottom thinly. Fry quickly until of a golden brown. While the pancake is frying shake the pan gently, and loosen round the edges with a knife ; then slip the knife under the pancake and turn it over. Fry until golden brown, turn the pancake on to sugared paper, sprinkle with sugar, and squeeze over it a little lemon juice. Roll up and keep hot. When all the pancakes are fried pile neatly on a hot dish, and dust with sugar.

Note.—Pancake batter may be made richer by using two eggs instead of one with the above ingredients, or, if half quantity is desired, use

Two ounces flour.	One egg.
Pinch of salt.	One gill milk.

331. Hasty Pudding

Prepare a batter as in Recipe 330, but use one dessert-spoonful sugar instead of salt. Pour the batter into greased cups, and steam for half an hour. Turn out on to a hot ashet.

332. Black Cap Pudding

Prepare in the same way as for Hasty Pudding, adding one ounce of well-cleansed currants. Place the currants in the greased cups and pour in the batter. Turn out on to a hot ashet.

333. Apple Fritters

Two apples.

BATTER

Two ounces flour.
Pinch of salt.
One dessertspoonful salad oil.

About half a gill tepid water.
Stiffly-beaten white of one egg.

Fat for frying the fritters.

Sieve the flour and salt into a bowl. Make a well in the centre, and put in the salad oil ; then with a wooden spoon stir in tepid water till a rather stiff batter is made. Beat well, and let it stand for about an hour.

Peel the apples thinly, then cut them into slices, cutting across the core of the apple ; remove the core from the slices of apple with a small cutter.

Whip up the white of egg stiffly ; mix it lightly into the prepared batter. Dip each slice of apple into the batter, then put them carefully into a pan of hot clarified fat. Fry the fritters to a golden brown, drain well, dust with castor sugar, and serve at once. The fat for frying batter should just be beginning to smoke, but should not be so hot as for frying fish, etc.

334. Poor Knight's Pudding

Two thick slices of bread.
One egg.
One teaspoonful sugar.

Pinch of cinnamon.
One gill milk.
Frying fat.

Beat the egg with the sugar and cinnamon, and add the milk. Remove the crusts from the bread, cut it in neat fingers, and soak thoroughly in the egg and milk. Make the fat hot in a frying-pan, carefully put in the pieces of bread, and fry till a golden brown colour on both sides. Lift it on to kitchen paper to drain off the fat. Dish on a hot ashet and sprinkle with sugar, and if liked a little more cinnamon.

335. Sweet Rice Croquettes

Two ounces rice.
Half-pint milk.
Quarter-ounce butter.

One teaspoonful sugar.
Vanilla essence.
Half an egg or one yolk.

FOR COATING

Beaten egg and desiccated coconut or ratafia crumbs.

Steam the rice with the milk and butter till quite soft and thick. Add the sugar and flavouring. Beat well. Add the egg, and cook till thick. Spread mixture on a plate to cool. Form into croquettes. Coat with beaten egg, and roll in coconut or ratafia crumbs. Fry in deep fat. Serve with a fruit sauce (see Sauces).

336. Sweet Omelet

Two fresh eggs.
One dessertspoonful castor sugar.

One tablespoonful heated jam.

Have an omelet pan " proved " and well greased with clarified butter. Break the eggs and separate the yolks from the whites. Beat the yolks and sugar together till creamy. Beat the whites stiffly, and fold them lightly into the yolks and sugar. Pour this mixture into the omelet pan, and shake the pan over a gentle heat until the omelet is beginning to set and rise ; then place the pan in a steady oven, and cook until the omelet is well risen and of a light brown colour. When ready, turn the omelet out on to a piece of sugared paper, put the jam in the centre, fold the omelet over, and serve at once.

Note.—To prove a pan, place a very small piece of clarified dripping in the pan and heat so that the fat smokes thoroughly.   Pour away the burnt dripping and rub the pan with paper.   Thus a good surface with no moisture is assured.

337. Stewed Apples

One pound apples. | Four ounces sugar.
Half-pint cold water.

Put the sugar and water into a lined pan, and when dissolved bring to the boil, and boil briskly for about five minutes ; skim thoroughly.   Wipe, peel, quarter, and core the apples, and put them at once into the syrup and simmer gently till tender ; then dish up, and pour the syrup over.

Note.—This method is employed for stewing fresh fruits.

338. Stewed Figs

Half-pound dried figs. | Two ounces brown sugar.
Half-pint cold water.

Wash the figs, remove the stalks, put them into a basin with the water, and soak overnight if possible (this soaking softens the figs).   Then cook with the sugar till tender (about thirty minutes).

Note.—This method is employed for stewing dried fruits—prunes, etc.

339. Cold Fruit Charlotte or Summer Pudding

Three or four slices stale| raspberries, red cur-
    bread. | rants, rhubarb, goose-
One pound fresh fruit (*e.g.*| berries).

Syrup

Half-pint water, quarter-pound sugar.

Prepare the fruit, and stew in the syrup; line a basin with stale bread cut in fingers ; pour in the hot fruit and cover with bread ; set aside till cold with a plate and weight on top.   Turn out and serve with custard, or pour round some of the syrup thickened with arrow-root.

340. Gooseberry Fool

One pound gooseberries. | cream and half-gill cus-
Quarter-pound sugar. | tard.
One gill water. | Ratafias.
One gill cream, or half-gill

Top and tail the gooseberries, and cook with the sugar and water till soft.   Rub through a hair sieve to obtain one pint of sieved purée.   Half whip the cream and mix lightly with the purée.   Sweeten and flavour if necessary. Pour into a glass dish and decorate with ratafias and whipped cream, or serve in glasses with a little whipped cream on top.

341. Apple Snow

Two apples. | One white of egg.
   Sugar.

Bake apples.   Remove pulp.   Beat it smooth.   Whisk stiffly-beaten white into the apple pulp.   Sweeten and serve with Cup Custard (Recipe 273).

342. Curds

One pint milk. | One teaspoonful rennet.

Heat one pint of milk to 98.4° Fahrenheit (or about the temperature of the blood).   Pour it into a glass dish, and stir into it one teaspoonful of rennet. Let it remain till set in a room of ordinary temperature. Serve with cream and sugar.

Note.—A tablespoonful of coffee essence may be added to the milk.

343. Lemon Jelly

One and a half pints cold water.

Juice of four lemons made up to half a pint with water.

Rind of two lemons.

Six ounces loaf sugar.

One inch of cinnamon stick.

Two cloves.

One and a half ounces powdered gelatine.

Two whites and shells of eggs.

For making jelly choose a strong, deep pan. Rinse the pan ; put in the water, wash lemons, peel rind very thinly, and add with the strained lemon juice, sugar, cloves, gelatine, and the whites and well-washed shells of eggs. Place the pan over a strong heat. Stir till gelatine is dissolved, and whisk the jelly until almost boiling ; then draw out the whisk, and boil up once or twice. Draw the pan to the side of the stove, cover the jelly with a plate, and let it stand for eight or ten minutes. Tie a clean coarse linen cloth firmly over the legs of a kitchen chair, resting the seat of the chair on the table. Place a bowl underneath the jelly cloth, and pour through the cloth a little boiling water : this is to warm the cloth to ensure the jelly running through. Empty the water from the bowl, place it again under the cloth, and pour the jelly on to the top of the cloth. When a little jelly has run into the bowl, lift it out, and slip a clean bowl in its place. Pour the jelly gently through the cloth again. Do this until the jelly in the bowl looks quite clear. If there is a danger of draught cover the chair over with a blanket. Let all the jelly drip through the cloth. When cold, but still liquid, pour the jelly into a mould first rinsed with cold water, and allow it to set. When firm, pass the mould quickly through warm water, and turn out the jelly.

Note 1.—If preferred, one quarter-pint of lemon juice and one quarter-pint sherry can be used.

Note 2.—The agents used for clearing a jelly are the white and shell of egg. Strong whisking breaks up the cells of the white of egg. When heated the albumin hardens, and it has the power of collecting all the insoluble matter in the jelly. The force of boiling causes this collection of insoluble matter to rise in the form of a thick froth which is afterwards turned into the straining cloth, and acts further as a filter when the jelly, in the process of being cleared, is poured through it.

Note 3.—If the jelly is whisked after it comes to boiling-point, the insoluble matter is driven down again.

Note 4.—The jelly should be strained in a warm place and out of a draught. If it should stiffen in the cloth before all has run through, place a basin on the jelly in the cloth and fill the basin with boiling water.

344. Coffee Jelly

Half-pint coffee.
Light half-ounce powdered gelatine.
One dessertspoonful castor sugar.

A few drops vanilla essence.
Half-gill cream.
Cherries to decorate.

Make the coffee, and strain through muslin into a basin. Dissolve the gelatine in half a gill of water, and stir it into the coffee ; add the sugar and flavouring, and set aside till almost cold. Pour into a wet border mould and leave till firm. Turn out. Whip the cream, and pile it in the centre of the mould. Decorate with one or two cherries cut in quarters.

Note.—When dissolving gelatine put the water into a pan, add the gelatine, and heat gently, stirring with a metal spoon until gelatine is dissolved. Do not let it boil.

345. Apple Jelly

One pound apples. | Strip of lemon rind.
Two ounces sugar. | Half-pint water.
Powdered gelatine to stiffen.

Wipe, peel, and slice the apples into a lined pan ; add the sugar, lemon rind, and half a pint of water, and stew till tender ; then rub through a hair sieve. Measure the purée, and allow gelatine in the proportion of half an ounce of gelatine to one pint of purée. Dissolve the gelatine in water, allowing half a gill of water to half an ounce of gelatine, and stir it into the purée. A few drops of carmine may be added. When the mixture is cold, pour it into a china mould. When set, turn out.

Note.—Rhubarb jelly is prepared in the same way, but use only one gill of water for stewing the rhubarb.

346. Banana Jelly

Three bananas. | Half-ounce powdered gela-
Two ounces sugar. | tine.
A little lemon juice. | One pint water.

Pass the bananas through a hair sieve. Put the other ingredients into a saucepan and stir over the fire until the gelatine and sugar are dissolved, then strain and mix with the banana pulp. Put the mixture into a pan and stir until boiling. Turn into a wetted mould. When cold turn out and serve.

347. Casserole of Prunes

Six ounces prunes.
Half-pint water.
Quarter - ounce powdered gelatine.

One ounce sugar.
Rind and juice of half a lemon.
Half-gill cream.

Wash the prunes and soak in half a pint of water overnight. Put into a pan, with the lemon rind and sugar, and stew till tender. Strain the prunes from the liquid, remove the stones, and chop the prunes roughly. Measure the liquid, and, if reduced, add water to make up the half-pint. Dissolve the gelatine in a quarter-gill of the prune juice. Add the remainder of the liquid to the prunes with the lemon juice and gelatine. When almost cold, put it into a wet casserole mould; and when firm, turn out. Fill up the centre with whipped cream, and decorate with one or two glacé cherries.

348. Lemon Sponge

Two lemons.
Light half-ounce powdered gelatine.

Two to three ounces sugar.
Two whites of eggs.
Half-pint water.

Wipe the lemons, and peel off the rind very thinly; put it, with the water, sugar, and gelatine, into a saucepan, and stir over the fire until the sugar and gelatine are dissolved; then strain into a basin and leave till cold. Add to this the strained juice of the lemons and the whites of eggs, and whip until stiff; then pile roughly into a glass dish.

Note.—If desired, the lemon sponge can be moulded, in which case it must not be so stiffly beaten.

349. Dutch Flummery

Three yolks of eggs.
Two lemons, rind and juice.
Six ounces sugar.
Half-ounce powdered gelatine.
One gill sherry.

Three gills water.

Put all the ingredients except the yolks of eggs into a saucepan, stir till the gelatine is dissolved, and allow to infuse for about ten minutes ; then pour on to the yolks. Strain back into the pan, which must be rinsed, and stir over the fire until the yolks are cooked. Pour into a basin ; mould when cold. When set, turn out.

350. Blancmange

Half-pint milk.
One gill cream.
One ounce castor sugar.
Light half-ounce powdered gelatine.
Flavouring.

Half whip the cream, add the milk, sugar, and flavouring. Dissolve gelatine in half a gill of water and stir in carefully. When cool, pour into a wet mould. When firm, turn out.

351. Rice Cream

One pint milk.
Two ounces ground rice.
One gill cream.
Two ounces castor sugar.
Quarter - ounce powdered gelatine.

Vanilla essence.

Cook the rice in the milk. Half whip the cream ; add the rice, sugar, and flavouring, and the gelatine dissolved in a quarter-gill of water. Mould when beginning to thicken, and turn out when set.

352. Honeycomb Mould

Two or three eggs.
One pint milk.
Two ounces sugar.

Half-ounce powdered gelatine.
Flavouring.

Make a custard with the yolks of eggs, sugar, and milk ; sweeten and flavour. Add gelatine dissolved in half a gill of water. Allow all to cool. Beat whites of eggs stiffly and stir in lightly. Pour into wet mould. Set in cool place. Turn out.

353. Fig Custard

Quarter-pound figs.
Two yolks or one egg.
Half-pint milk.

One dessertspoonful sugar.
Quarter - ounce powdered gelatine.

A little vanilla essence.

Wash the figs, remove stalks, and stew in a little water until tender, then chop them finely. Heat the milk in a saucepan. Mix the sugar and eggs well together, and pour over them the hot milk ; strain into the rinsed pan and stir until thick, but do not boil. Pour the custard into a bowl, add the figs and the gelatine dissolved in a quarter-gill of water, and the flavouring. When cool, pour the mixture into a mould, which should first be rinsed in cold water. Put it into a cool place. When firm, turn out.

354. Chocolate Shape

Two ounces of sweetened chocolate or one ounce unsweetened.
Three gills milk.
Two yolks or one egg.

Sugar to sweeten.
A few drops vanilla essence.
Half-ounce gelatine (light weight).

Break the chocolate in pieces and dissolve it in a little of the milk; add the rest of the milk, and heat. Put the yolks into a basin and beat them slightly, and pour on to them the chocolate and milk ; then strain this back into the pan, which must be rinsed, and cook over a gentle heat until the yolks thicken. Care must be taken not to allow this to boil, or it will curdle. When cooked, pour into a basin ; add the sugar and vanilla. Add gelatine dissolved in half a gill of water. When cold, pour into a china mould ; and when set, turn out.

SAVOURIES ; & CHEESE, NUT, EGG, AND VEGETARIAN DISHES

SAVOURIES

SAVOURIES should be small, dainty, highly seasoned, and prettily decorated. Hot savouries should be served very hot.

355. Cheese Biscuits

Four ounces flour.
Two ounces butter.
Two ounces grated Cheddar cheese.

Pepper, salt, cayenne.
Yolk of egg and water.

Sieve the flour ; rub in the butter ; add the grated cheese and seasonings. Mix to a stiff paste with the yolk and water. Knead lightly, roll out thinly, prick well, and cut into rounds. Place on a tin, and bake in a quick oven from seven to ten minutes.

356. Rice and Cheese Turnovers

Cheese pastry (two ounces flour, etc., Recipe 256).

Pepper and salt.
Made mustard.

FOR FILLING

Half-ounce rice.
One gill milk.
Half-ounce grated cheese.

FOR COATING

Beaten egg and dried bread crumbs or vermicelli.

Wash the rice, put into a pan with the milk, cover with a lid, and cook very slowly till the rice is soft and creamy. Add the cheese and seasonings, and leave the mixture till cold.

Make the cheese pastry, roll out, cut in rounds or squares. Place a spoonful of the cheese mixture in the centre of each, damp the edges, and fold over. Coat with beaten egg and bread crumbs or crushed vermicelli, and fry in hot fat until a golden brown colour. Drain on paper, and serve very hot.

357. Cheese Savoury

Eight or ten cheese biscuits.
Quarter-gill cream.
One dessertspoonful grated cheese.

Pinches of salt and cayenne.

FOR DECORATION
A little cress and red pepper.

Half-whip the cream. Stir in the cheese, salt, and cayenne. Pile neatly on top of the biscuits. Decorate with a little cress and red pepper.

Note.—Finely-chopped celery may be added to the mixture, and the savoury may be decorated with curled celery.

358. Finnan Haddock Savoury

Two ounces cooked finnan haddock.
Half-ounce butter.
One gherkin.
Salt, pepper, cayenne.
One tablespoonful cream.

FOR DISHING
Six small rounds of fried bread.or six cheese biscuits.
A little finely-chopped parsley.

Remove skin and bone from fish and chop finely. Chop gherkin finely. Melt butter, add all the other ingredients. Season and add the cream. Pile this

mixture on rounds of fried bread, or rounds of hot
buttered toast, or hot cheese biscuits.   Fork up neatly,
and sprinkle with parsley.

359. Herring Savoury

Six round cheese biscuits. | One ounce herring (kip-
Six thin slices of beetroot. | pered or fresh).
One hard-boiled egg. | Salt, pepper, cayenne.
One ounce butter. | One dessertspoonful cream.

Shred fish, removing all skin and bone.   Pound fish,
butter, hard-boiled egg, and seasonings together.   Rub
through a wire sieve.   Add the cream.   Cut rounds of
beetroot and lay each on top of a biscuit.   Pile the
mixture on the beetroot, and decorate with parsley and
tiny shapes of beetroot.   Dish neatly.   Serve cold.
   Note.—If it is desired to serve this savoury hot, heat
the mixture and biscuits, omit the beetroot, and decorate
with red pepper instead of parsley.

360. Sardine Savoury

Six round cheese biscuits. | One tablespoonful cream.
Six slices of tomato. |
Vinegar and seasonings. | FOR DECORATION
Six sardines. | Chopped gherkin, red pep-
Pepper, salt, cayenne. | per, capers.

Pass sardines through hot water to remove oil.   Remove skin and bone from sardines.   Chop or pass
through a wire sieve.   Mix with cream and seasonings.
Prepare tomato, season, and place on biscuits.   Pile
sardine mixture on this.   Decorate with chopped gherkin
and red pepper.

361. Sardine Rolls

Six sardines.
Vinegar and seasonings.
Cheese Pastry (one and a
   half ounces flour, etc.,
   Recipe 256).

FOR GLAZING

Beaten egg and grated
   cheese.
Parsley to garnish.

Prepare sardines as in Recipe 360. Bone, season, and fold together again. Make the pastry and divide in six. Put one sardine on each piece of pastry. Fold over, seal, glaze, mark, and sprinkle with cheese. Bake in good steady oven.

Note.—These savouries may be coated with egg and crumbs, and fried in deep fat.

362. Ham Savoury

Six small rounds of fried
   bread.
Two ounces cooked ham.

Quarter-ounce butter.
One tablespoonful sauce or
   cream to moisten.

Pepper and salt if required.

Melt the butter in a pan; add the ham, chopped finely; bind with sauce, cream, or tomato ketchup, and season well. When hot, pile the mixture on the rounds of fried bread, and serve hot.

CHEESE DISHES

Cheese is one of the best of foods. It is rich in nourishment, and can therefore be used to great advantage as a partial substitute for meat.

When cheese is cooked it is usually grated, and mixed with other food, especially starchy food, such as macaroni, bread, rice, potatoes, or served with vegetables, as cauliflower, peas, tomatoes, etc. Cheese must not be overcooked, or it becomes stringy, tough, and indigestible. Cheese dishes should be well seasoned with mustard, pepper, and salt, as this helps in making the cheese easier to digest. Dry cheese is best for grating, and hard pieces can often be used up in this way.

363. Vegetables au Gratin

Many vegetables may be served *au gratin*.

Cook them carefully according to the directions given for each in "Vegetables and Salads" section, pages 116 to 136. Drain them well. Lay on a fireproof dish. Make a cheese sauce (Recipe 218). Coat the vegetables with the sauce; sprinkle the remainder of the cheese over, and brown in a hot oven.

Suitable vegetables are :

Jerusalem artichokes	see Recipe		164.
Haricot and butter beans	,,	,,	168.
Cauliflower	,,	,,	177.
Chestnuts	,,	,,	390.
Onions	,,	,,	186.
Parsnips	,,	,,	187.
Turnips	,,	,,	208.
Vegetable marrow	,,	,,	209.

364. Rice and Cheese

Two ounces rice.
One ounce grated cheese.
Pinch of salt.

Pinch of pepper.
About one and a half gills milk.

Wash the rice. Place the milk, pepper, and salt in the pan with the rice. Simmer for thirty minutes till the rice is tender. The mixture should not be so moist as for a pudding. Cool slightly, add the cheese, reserving a little. Turn into greased pie-dish, sprinkle the rest of the cheese on top, and brown in oven or in front of fire. Serve hot.

365. Risotto

Four ounces rice.	Pepper and salt.
One sliced onion.	One or two tomatoes.
Two ounces butter.	Two tablespoonfuls grated
One pint vegetable stock.	cheese.

Wash the rice, melt the butter, stir in the rice and onion, add the stock and seasonings. Milk and water may be used instead of stock. Put on the lid and cook gently till quite soft (three-quarters to one hour). Add the tomatoes, skinned and cut up, and cook for five to ten minutes longer. The mixture should be of a creamy consistency. Lastly, stir in the grated cheese, and serve very hot.

366. Cheese Soufflé

PANADA	One ounce grated Cheddar cheese.
Half-ounce butter.	Cayenne and salt.
Quarter-ounce flour.	One and a half yolks and
Half-gill milk.	two whites of eggs.

Make panada (see p. 137). Cool slightly, and beat in the yolks, cheese, and seasonings. Fold in stiffly-beaten whites. Turn into a greased fireproof dish and bake in a moderately hot oven till well risen, and brown for about thirty minutes.

367. Potatoes and Cheese

Half-pound mashed pota- | Half-teaspoonful made mus-
toes. | tard.
Two to three tablespoonfuls | Pepper and salt.
grated cheese. | A little milk.

Put all the ingredients into a pan, beat well over the fire, and heat thoroughly. Pile in a pie-dish and serve at once, or brown in the oven or under the grill.

368. Cheese Potatoes

Two large potatoes. | One dessertspoonful cream.
One and a half ounces | Pepper and salt.
grated cheese. |

Bake the potatoes until soft. Cut in two lengthways. Remove the soft potato and mash. Add two-thirds of the cheese, the cream, and seasonings. Mix, and return the mixture to the potato cases. Sprinkle the remainder of the cheese on the top, and brown in oven.

369. Potato and Cheese Cakes

Half-pound cooked pota- | Cayenne and salt.
toes. |
Half-ounce butter. | FOR COATING
One ounce grated cheese. | Beaten egg and dried bread
One teaspoonful chopped | crumbs.
parsley. |
A little beaten egg. | FOR FRYING
| Pan of deep fat.

Mash or sieve the potatoes. Melt butter, add all other ingredients, and bind with the egg. Form the mixture into round cakes. Coat with beaten egg and bread crumbs. Fry in smoking hot fat, drain, and dish neatly.

370. Cheese Cutlets

Three ounces grated cheese.
Two ounces bread crumbs.
One teaspoonful mashed potatoes.
Half-teaspoonful made mustard.
Salt and pepper.

Half an egg.

FOR COATING

Beaten egg and dried bread crumbs.

FOR FRYING

Pan of deep fat.

Mix ingredients, season well, and bind with beaten egg. Divide in equal sections, and form into cutlets or balls. Coat with beaten egg and bread crumbs. Fry in smoking hot fat till a golden brown colour. Drain well, serve on a hot dish, and garnish with parsley.

371. Cheese Pudding (1)

Two ounces bread crumbs.
Half-pint milk.
Two ounces grated cheese.
One egg.

Pepper and salt.
Pinch of cayenne pepper.
Quarter-teaspoonful made mustard.

Heat the milk, add the crumbs, and cook for a few minutes. Take the pan off the fire; add the yolk of egg, cheese, and seasonings. Beat up the white very stiffly, and fold lightly into the mixture. Pour into a greased pie-dish, and bake in a moderate oven for about forty minutes till risen and brown.

372. Cheese Pudding (2)

Two thin slices of bread and butter.
Two ounces cheese.

One egg.
Half-pint milk.
Made mustard.

Pepper and salt.

Grate the cheese ; cut the bread and butter into small squares ; fill up a greased pie-dish with alternate layers of each. Beat the egg ; add the milk and seasonings to it and pour the custard over the bread. Allow the pudding to stand for half an hour. Then bake in a moderate oven twenty to thirty minutes, until the custard has set.

373. Cheese Batter Pudding

Four ounces flour.
Half-pint milk.
One egg.

Pinch of salt.
One and a half ounces grated cheese.

Measure the flour and salt into a basin, make a well in the centre, and drop in the egg. Add a little milk, and draw in the flour gradually, adding enough milk by degrees to make a smooth thick batter. Beat thoroughly till covered with air bubbles. Stir in the cheese and the remainder of the milk. Cover, and leave to soak for one hour if possible. Pour into a greased pie-dish or Yorkshire pudding tin, and bake in a hot oven for thirty to forty minutes till well risen and brown. Serve in the same dish, or cut in pieces and serve on a hot ashet.

374. Cheese Pancakes

Ingredients same as for Cheese Batter Pudding. Make a batter with the flour, milk, egg, and salt ; fry mixture as for ordinary pancakes. Sprinkle with grated cheese and roll up. Garnish with fried parsley.

375. Macaroni and Cheese

Two ounces macaroni.
Two ounces grated cheese.
Half-ounce butter.
Half-ounce flour.

About half-pint milk.
Half teaspoonful made mustard.
Cayenne pepper and salt.

Cook the macaroni in boiling salted water for forty to fifty minutes till soft, drain and cut it in pieces half an inch long. Make a white sauce. Boil for five minutes, then add the macaroni. Cool the mixture slightly, then add two-thirds of the cheese and the seasonings. Turn this into a greased dish, sprinkle the remainder of the cheese on the top, and brown in a hot oven.

376. Macaroni and Cheese Croquettes

One ounce macaroni.	Half-gill milk.
Half-ounce butter.	A little beaten egg.
Half-ounce flour.	Pepper, salt, cayenne.
One and a half ounces grated cheese.	Beaten egg.
	Dried white bread crumbs.

Cook the macaroni and chop it finely. Melt the butter ; add the flour, then the milk. Stir over the fire till the mixture leaves the sides of the pan. Add the macaroni to this sauce ; bind with the egg, then add the grated cheese and seasonings. Mix all together, and turn on to a plate to cool. Form into croquettes ; egg and crumb, and fry in deep fat till of a golden brown colour. Drain well, dish, and garnish with fried parsley.

377. Rice and Cheese Balls

Prepare as for Macaroni and Cheese Croquettes, substituting two ounces rice for one ounce macaroni, and shape into balls.

378. Italian Polenta

One quart milk.	Six ounces semolina.
One ounce butter.	Pepper and salt.

Boil milk and butter together, then sprinkle in semo-lina. Cook about fifteen minutes, stirring constantly, until mixture is of a thick consistency. Add seasonings. Pour into a buttered baking tin, and allow to cool. Cut up in neat pieces, and arrange in a baking dish in a pile. Pour melted butter over, sprinkle thinly with grated cheese, and bake till golden brown.

379. Gniocchi

One pint water.	Eight ounces flour.
One ounce butter.	One egg.

Boil water and butter together. Add the flour. Cook till it forms a ball. Season and beat in an egg. Roll on a floured board till one-eighth of an inch in thickness. Cut into pieces. Allow the paste to dry for a few hours. Poach or boil for ten minutes till floating. Coat with a cheese sauce.

380. Toasted Cheese

Make slices of buttered toast. Cut thin slices of cheese. Toast the cheese and lay one slice on each piece of toast. Spread a very little mustard on the cheese, and sprinkle with pepper and salt. Serve very hot.

381. Welsh Rarebit

Three ounces grated cheese.	Half-teaspoonful flour.
One teaspoonful made mus- tard.	About one tablespoonful milk.
One ounce butter.	Pinch of pepper.

Melt the butter, add the flour, then add the milk, and cook thoroughly. Add cheese, mustard, and seasonings.

Stir over the fire till these are melted, then pour the mixture over a piece of hot buttered toast.

382. Tomato Rarebit

One ounce butter.
One ounce flour.
One gill milk.
One gill tomato purée.

Three ounces grated cheese.
Cayenne.
One egg.

Make a sauce with butter, flour, milk, and tomato purée. Add the grated cheese and cayenne. Then add the beaten egg. Cook together without boiling. Pour over neat pieces of hot buttered toast. Sprinkle with chopped parsley, and serve hot.

383. Cheese Custard

Two eggs.
Half-pint milk.
Two ounces grated cheese.

Pepper, salt, cayenne.
A little made mustard.

Heat the milk and add to the beaten eggs. Strain into grated cheese. Add seasonings, and pour into a greased pie-dish and bake in a moderate oven until custard is set.

Note.—One gill of tomato purée may be added.

DISHES WITH NUTS

Nut Butters.—Of vegetarian fats there is now a large variety on the market. These, both for cooking and table use, are of excellent quality and flavour. They are made from nuts, and contain all the valuable properties of the nut, proteid as well as fat. For cooking purposes, the hard white fat is to be recommended, as it flakes down easily, or may be grated. It also makes a splendid frying medium for frying such food as fritters, cutlets, etc. Nut margarine is now procurable in a very tempting form for table use. Another variety of nut table butter is known as the "Nut Cream Butter." This has the distinct flavour of the nut from which it is prepared (walnut, almond, hazel, coconut, etc.), and thus supplies both fat and flavour.

Nut butters or nut margarines take the place of butter in almost all forms of cooking. They may be added to soups to enrich them, and be used in puddings of all descriptions, cakes, buns, scones, and biscuits, and in salad dressings.

Frying nutter is used in place of clarified dripping for frying.

384. Nut and Macaroni Cutlets

Two ounces macaroni.
Two ounces finely-chopped or milled nuts.
One ounce nut butter.
One ounce flour.
One gill milk or macaroni boilings.
One yolk of egg, or a little beaten egg.

Pepper and salt.

For Coating
Beaten egg and dried bread crumbs.

For Frying
Pan of frying nutter.

Cook the macaroni and chop finely. Make a thick sauce with the butter, flour, and milk. Add the macaroni, nuts, seasoning, yolk of egg. Cook over a fire for a few seconds. Turn on to a plate. Divide into twelve pieces, and form into cutlet shapes. Coat with beaten egg, toss in crumbs, and fry in hot fat till crisp and brown. Drain and serve.

Small nut mills can be procured, and by chopping or milling nuts their digestibility is much increased.

385. Potato and Nut Scallops

Six potatoes.
Half-pint white sauce.
Two ounces chopped or milled nuts (walnuts, hazelnuts, etc.).
One dessertspoonful grated cheese.
Pepper and salt.
One tablespoonful bread crumbs.
A little margarine.

Cook, but do not over-boil the potatoes. Cut into dice. Chop nuts roughly. Make the sauce. Add the potatoes, nuts, and cheese. Season well. Put the mixture into scallop shells or pie-dish, sprinkle bread crumbs and margarine on the top, and brown in the oven.

386. Nut and Lentil Roast

Two ounces lentils.
One ounce cooked macaroni.
Two ounces bread crumbs.
Two ounces mixed nuts.
Mace.
Pepper and salt.
Half-teaspoonful grated onion.
One egg.

FOR COATING
Dried bread crumbs.

FOR BASTING
Two ounces nut butter.

Grind or chop nuts finely. Cook the lentils, strain, and render very dry. Chop the macaroni finely, put all into a pan and cook till crumbs swell. Bind with beaten egg. Cool slightly, and form into a neat roll ; roll in bread crumbs. Roast for one hour ; baste with the butter. It may be baked in a mould. Dish and serve with any good vegetable sauce.

387. Walnut Mince

Two ounces chopped nuts.
Three ounces bread crumbs.
Quarter-ounce nut butter.
One chopped onion.

Powdered herbs.
Pepper and salt.
One tablespoonful ketchup.
One gill water.

Make butter hot in saucepan ; add nuts and chopped onion, and stir till lightly browned. Add the bread crumbs and seasonings, and the ketchup with one gill of boiling water. If a dry consistency is preferred, add less water. Simmer slowly for fifteen minutes ; serve with sippets of toast.

Note.—Brazil, peccan, or hazel nuts may be used instead of walnuts.

388. Mock Chicken Cutlets

Half-ounce flour.
One gill milk.
Four ounces shelled wal-
    nuts (chopped).
Eight ounces bread crumbs.
One tablespoonful chopped
    onion.
One beaten egg.

Mace.
Pepper and salt.

FOR COATING

Beaten egg and dried bread
    crumbs.

FOR FRYING

Pan of frying nutter.

Make a sauce with flour and the gill of milk. When it thickens, add the other ingredients and mix well over the fire ; remove, and stir in a beaten egg and a squeeze of lemon juice. Mix thoroughly and turn out to cool. Form into cutlets. Egg, crumb, and fry. Serve with bread or tomato sauce.

CHESTNUTS

Of all nuts the chestnut is probably of the greatest general value as an article of diet. From it can be made excellent soups and puddings, and served as a vegetable it is highly favoured.

389. Chestnut Purée

One pound chestnuts.   One ounce butter.
One Spanish onion.   One quart stock.
One cupful milk.

Blanch the chestnuts, and remove the outer shell and inner brown skin. Skin and dice the onion. Toss the chestnuts and the onion in the butter. Add the stock. Simmer for about one and a half hours till chestnuts are quite soft, then sieve the soup and return it to the pan. Bring it to the boil, add milk, and serve at once.

Note.—When blanching chestnuts, wash them and make a small slit in the rounded side of each with the point of a knife. Put them into an old saucepan with cold water to cover them. Bring to boiling-point, and boil for two to three minutes.

390. Boiled Chestnuts

Wash and make a slit with a knife in the shell. Place in a saucepan of boiling salted water. Boil quickly from twenty to thirty minutes until quite tender. Drain. Remove outside shell and inner brown skin. Toss in a little butter, pepper, and salt. Serve hot.

391. Chestnut Pudding

Quarter-pound chestnuts.
Quarter-pound nut cream butter.
Quarter-pound sugar.

Quarter-pound glacé cherries.
Quarter-pint milk.

Cook chestnuts until quite tender, drain, and remove shell and inner brown skin. Then put through a wire sieve. Cream the butter and the sugar together. Add the other ingredients, and mix well. Place in buttered pudding-dish and bake one hour. This pudding may be put in a basin and steamed for two hours.

392. Chestnut Stew

Half-pound chestnuts.
One tomato.
One small onion.
Two ounces mushrooms.
One ounce nut butter.

Pepper and salt.
Stock or water.
FOR SERVING
Two ounces boiled rice.
One baked or fried tomato.

Score, boil, and peel chestnuts. Fry mushrooms, onion, and tomato in butter; add chestnuts to vegetables with stock and seasonings. Simmer one hour. Dish in a border of rice, and garnish with tomato.

393. Chestnut Croquettes

Half-pound chestnuts.
Quarter-ounce nut butter.
Egg to bind.
Pepper and salt.

FOR COATING
Egg or batter and dried bread crumbs.
FOR FRYING
Pan of frying nutter.

Score, and boil chestnuts until soft. Skin, pound in a mortar with fat and seasonings; bind with beaten egg. Put into a saucepan, and cook for a few minutes over the fire. When cool, form into croquettes. Coat twice, and fry in deep fat. Serve with a suitable sauce.

394. Macaroni with Chestnuts

Four ounces macaroni.
Half-pound chestnuts.
One gill milk.
One onion.

One and a half ounces grated cheese.
Two ounces butter.
Pepper and salt.

Boil the macaroni until tender, drain, and cut into inch lengths. Parboil the chestnuts, drain, and skin. Then stew with the milk until tender for about an hour. Put through a wire sieve. Melt the butter in a pan. Add the macaroni and chestnut purée, and cook for a few minutes, adding a little milk if the mixture is too thick. Season well. Turn into a greased fireproof dish. Sprinkle the cheese on top, and brown in a hot oven.

Note.—Instead of cheese, bread crumbs may be used, with a few pats of butter.

EGG DISHES

A usual test for the freshness of eggs.—Hold the egg between a bright light and the eye. The air chamber should be small and there should be no dark spots, but instead a rather uniform rose colour.

The use of water-glass is an easy and reliable method of preserving eggs. It can be bought from a grocer or from a chemist, with full directions for its use on each tin.

To boil an egg.—Place an egg gently with a spoon in water almost, but not quite, boiling. Let it simmer steadily for three and a half minutes. A small egg is sufficiently cooked in three minutes ; a new-laid egg takes four minutes.

To boil a preserved egg.—Prick the egg and place in cold water, bring slowly to boiling-point, and boil gently for one and a half minutes.

To boil an egg for an invalid.—Place a new-laid egg in boiling water. Cover and keep hot, under simmering point, for seven minutes.

To hard-boil an egg.—Place an egg in cold water, bring slowly to boiling-point. Let it simmer for thirteen minutes, turning it occasionally to keep the yolk in centre. Lift it into cold water to prevent the white discolouring. When sufficiently cool remove the shell, and if not for immediate use keep the shelled egg in cold water.

395. Poached Egg

One fresh egg.
One piece buttered toast.
Quarter-teaspoonful salt.
Few drops vinegar.
Water.

Put water, salt, and vinegar into a saucepan, and bring to boiling-point. Break each egg separately into a wet cup, and slip it into the water. Bring to boiling-point again, remove from fire, cover, and leave for two minutes, till the white is set. Drain on a fish slice, and dish on buttered toast.

396. Scrambled Egg

One egg.
One large tablespoonful milk.
Half-ounce butter.
Pepper and salt.
One piece buttered toast.
Parsley.

Beat the egg and milk together, and add the seasonings. Melt the butter in a pan, and pour in the egg and milk. Stir gently with a spoon over a moderate fire till the egg is creamy, then pile on buttered toast. Garnish with parsley.

397. Baked Egg

One egg.   Half-ounce butter.

Melt the butter in a small round fireproof dish. Break the egg into a cup, and slip it from the cup into the dish. Bake in a moderate oven until the white is set.

398. Swiss Eggs

Three eggs. | Two ounces grated cheese.
One ounce butter. | One tablespoonful cream.
Salt and cayenne.

Sprinkle half the grated cheese into a greased fireproof dish. Break the eggs on top of the cheese, keeping them whole. Pour the cream over the eggs, and sprinkle the remainder of the cheese on top. Season with salt and cayenne. Bake in a moderate oven until eggs are set.

399. Egg in Spinach

One egg. | Quarter-ounce butter.
Two tablespoonfuls cooked | Salt.
spinach (Recipe 204). |

Put the spinach into a small greased fireproof dish. Make a hollow in the centre. Drop in a fresh egg. Sprinkle with salt, and put a small pat of butter on the top. Cook in a moderate oven until the white of the egg is set.

Note.—Two tablespoonfuls of tomato sauce may be

used instead of the spinach, and grated cheese may be sprinkled on top of the egg.

400. Savoury Omelet

Two eggs. | One ounce butter.
Pepper and salt.

Beat eggs till sufficiently mixed but not frothed, and add pepper and salt.   Melt the butter in an omelet pan, and when beginning to colour, pour in the eggs, and keep moving mixture with a spoon till creamy throughout.   Fold over to one side of the pan in a neat shape, using a broad-bladed knife.   Turn on to a hot dish, garnish with a sprig of parsley, and serve at once.

Note.—One tablespoonful tepid water may be added to the eggs in order to make a softer omelet.

Variations.—Half-teaspoonful chopped parsley and a pinch of powdered herbs may be added to the eggs.

One tablespoonful grated cheese and a pinch of cayenne may be added to the eggs.

Some chopped cooked ham or meat may be sprinkled on the omelet before folding.

401. Fried Bacon and Eggs

Quarter-pound sliced bacon.   Two eggs.

Remove rind and rust from the bacon.   Place in a frying-pan and fry until the fat becomes transparent; turn the bacon and fry on the other side till it is just beginning to brown slightly.   Lift on to a hot dish. Break the eggs first into a cup, then slip them gently into the frying-pan.   Fry gently, basting with the hot fat, until lightly set, and dish on the top of the bacon.

402. Curried Eggs

Two hard-boiled eggs. | Curry sauce.
Two ounces Patna rice.

Hard-boil eggs according to direction given on page 222. Make the curry sauce (for quantities and method see Recipe 231). Add the eggs cut in neat pieces. Reheat without boiling, and dish in a border of rice, or serve curry and rice in separate dishes.

Note.—Eggs may be left whole and coated with the sauce.

403. Eggs with Cheese Sauce

Three eggs. | Half a pint of cheese sauce (Recipe 218).

Boil eggs for four minutes, shell very carefully, and lay on a fireproof dish. Make the sauce and pour over the eggs. Sprinkle them with cheese. Brown under grill.

404. Scotch Woodcock

Two slices of toast. | One dessertspoonful of anchovy essence.
One hard-boiled egg. | Pinches of cayenne and white pepper.
One ounce butter. |

CUSTARD

One yolk of egg. | One dessertspoonful chopped parsley.
One gill milk. |
Pepper and salt.

Chop egg. Pound with the butter, anchovy essence, and seasonings, and work all together till quite smooth. Sandwich this between the slices of hot buttered toast.

cut in fingers. Arrange these on a dish and keep hot. Mix yolk and seasonings, add hot milk, strain into pan, and cook till it thickens without boiling; then pour the custard over the toast.

405. Scotch Eggs

Two hard-boiled eggs.
Two sausages or three ounces sausage meat.

For Coating
Beaten egg and dried bread crumbs.

For Dishing
Four rounds of fried bread.

Shell eggs; cover with sausage meat; coat with egg and bread crumbs. Fry in deep fat (faintly smoking) until golden brown. Drain and cut in halves. Place each half on a round of fried bread. Garnish with parsley. Serve with tomato sauce.

406. Egg Cutlets

Two hard-boiled eggs.

Panada
Half-ounce butter.
Half-ounce flour.
Half-gill milk.

One or two mushrooms.
Pepper and salt.
Yolk of egg to bind.
For Coating
Beaten egg and dried bread crumbs.

Prepare and fry mushrooms, drain and chop. Chop eggs roughly. Make panada; add the mushrooms, eggs, and seasonings. Bind with the yolk. Spread mixture on plate to cool. Then divide into sections. Form into cutlets. Coat with egg and bread crumbs. Fry in deep fat. Serve with a suitable sauce.

407. Celery and Egg Croquettes

One ounce butter.
One ounce flour.
One gill celery purée.
One hard-boiled egg.
Pepper and salt.
One yolk of egg.

FOR COATING
Beaten egg and dried bread crumbs.

FOR FRYING
Pan of deep fat.

Stew pieces of celery in one gill of milk for one hour. Rub through a hair sieve. Chop the hard-boiled egg roughly. Make panada ; add the egg and seasonings, and bind with yolk of egg. Turn the mixture on to a plate to cool. Divide into sections. Shape into croquettes. Coat with egg and bread crumbs. Fry in deep fat to a golden brown colour. Drain, dish, and garnish with fried parsley.

408. Stuffed Eggs

Three hard-boiled eggs.
Mustard and cress—watercress.
One tablespoonful finely-chopped cooked ham.
Two ounces butter.
One teaspoonful chopped parsley.
Seasonings.

Shell eggs, and cut lengthways. Remove yolks. Cut small piece from backs. Sprinkle with pepper and salt. Pound yolks in basin with butter. Add chopped ham, seasoning, parsley, and mix well. Arrange four watercress leaves in each of the whites. Fill with mixture. Set on brown bread and butter, and decorate with small cress.

Note.—Four to five mushrooms cooked in a little butter, and chopped, may be added to the mixture as well as the ham.

VEGETARIAN DISHES

409. Fricassée of Vegetables

A variety of cooked vege-
tables, *e.g.*,
Two cooked artichokes or
new turnips.
Half a cooked cauliflower.
One tablespoonful cooked
haricot or butter beans.
Two raw tomatoes.
Two ounces cooked French
beans or green peas.

SAUCE

One ounce nut butter.
One ounce flour.
Three gills vegetable stock
or milk.
Pepper and salt.

FOR GARNISH

Chopped parsley.
Sippets of fried bread.

Cook the haricot beans for one hour. Add artichokes and turnips cut in neat pieces, and cook for
twenty minutes. Then add the sprigs of cauliflower,
the peas and shredded French beans, and cook till all the
vegetables are tender. Strain off the stock, reserving
it for the sauce. Make the sauce, add the cooked vegetables, the tomatoes and seasonings. Reheat gently.
Serve in a hot vegetable dish garnished with chopped
parsley and fried sippets of bread.

Note.—Other suitable vegetables are carrots, parsnips,
mushrooms, etc.

410. Vegetable Pie

A variety of cooked vege-
tables as indicated in
Recipe 409.
Half a pint of cheese sauce
(Recipe 218) or other
suitable sauce.

FOR THE TOP OF PIE

One pound cooked sieved
potato.
Pepper and salt.
One ounce butter.
Milk or beaten egg.

Cook the vegetables as in Recipe 409. Make the sauce. Put the vegetables and sauce in layers in a fire-proof dish. Spread the creamy potato on top. Sprinkle with cheese, and bake.

411. Curry of Vegetables

A variety of cooked vegetables as indicated in Recipe 409.

Half-pint curry sauce.

Cook the vegetables as in Recipe 409. Make the curry sauce (Recipe 231). Reheat the vegetables for fifteen minutes in the sauce. Pour into a hot vegetable dish, and serve with boiled rice.

Note.—The vegetable stock may be used for the curry sauce, and the curry is improved by the addition of one tablespoonful cream.

412. Curried Lentils

Half-pound lentils.
One pint water.
One or two chopped onions.
Half-ounce nut butter.

One tablespoonful curry powder.
Salt to season.
Few drops vinegar.

Wash lentils. Toss lentils, onion, and curry powder in melted butter ; add water, salt, and vinegar. Cook for one to one and a quarter hours till tender.

Note.—The mixture should be a soft thick consistency when ready. Serve with quarter-pound boiled rice.

413. Vegetable Hot-Pot

Raw vegetables (for variety see Recipe 409).
Four potatoes.
One ounce nut butter.

Seasonings.
Vegetable stock (sufficient to cover the vegetables).

Prepare vegetables, and slice them thickly or cut in suitable pieces. Melt the butter in a hot-pot. Toss the vegetables and seasonings in the butter, keeping back two potatoes. Cover with stock. Place sliced potato on top. Cover with the lid and cook in the oven for about two hours till the vegetables are soft. Remove the lid and brown the potatoes.

414. Roman Pie

One ounce macaroni.
Pieces of cooked carrot and turnip.
One cooked onion.
Two cooked potatoes.
One tomato.
Two mushrooms.

Pepper and salt.
One teaspoonful curry powder, or one table-spoonful grated cheese.
One gill vegetable stock.
Short-crust pastry (six ounces flour, etc.).

Cook the macaroni (see Recipe 375), drain, and cut in pieces. Cut the vegetables in small pieces. Grease a basin, and coat with brown crumbs. Make the pastry, and line the basin. (See Boiled Meat Pudding.) Fill up with layers of macaroni and vegetables. Season well, and moisten thoroughly. Cover with pastry. Prick the top to prevent rising. Twist a greased paper on top, and bake in a moderately hot oven for one to one and a half hours. Turn out, and serve with a good sauce.

Note.—Other suitable vegetables are cauliflower, French beans, parsnips, artichokes.

415. Lentil Cutlets

Two ounces lentils.
One and a half gills water.
Piece of chopped onion.
One teaspoonful ketchup.
Pinch of mace.

Pepper and salt.
Quarter-ounce butter.
One tablespoonful ground rice.

Wash lentils. Melt butter in a saucepan, and toss the vegetables in this until fat is absorbed. Add the water and seasonings. Simmer about one hour till soft. Add ground rice and cook for ten minutes. Turn on to a plate. Shape into cutlets. Coat and fry in deep fat. Drain. Place on hot ashet. Serve with sauce.

416. Fillets of Mock Sole

Two ounces ground rice.
Little chopped onion.
One mashed potato.
Pepper and salt.
Half-pint milk.
Pinch mace.

FOR COATING
Beaten egg and dried bread crumbs.

FOR FRYING
Pan of frying nutter.

Cook rice in milk ; add mashed potato and seasonings ; make the mixture fairly stiff. Spread on plate to cool. Cut in slices, coat with egg and crumbs, and fry in hot fat. Drain, and serve with a good sauce.

417. Macaroni and Tomatoes

Half a pint tomato sauce (Recipe 230).

Two ounces macaroni.
Sippets of fried bread.

Cook the macaroni, and cut it in pieces half an inch long. Heat the sauce thoroughly ; add the macaroni. Simmer for a few minutes. Turn into a hot dish, and garnish with sippets of fried bread.

Note.—Spaghetti or vermicelli may be used instead of macaroni. Cooked beans (quarter-pound) may also be used instead of macaroni.

418. Macaroni and Mushrooms

Two ounces macaroni.
Half-pint sauce.
Four mushrooms.
Pepper and salt.

One tablespoonful grated cheese.
One tablespoonful bread crumbs.

Cook the macaroni, peel the mushrooms, and cut in pieces. Infuse mushroom trimmings in milk. Make sauce, and cook mushrooms in it for ten minutes. Add the macaroni chopped, turn into pie-dish. Sprinkle with bread crumbs and cheese. Bake in a hot oven.

419. Macaroni Viennoise

Four ounces cooked macaroni.
Quarter-ounce nut butter.
One tablespoonful chopped parsley.
Pepper and salt.

One yolk of egg.
Half-gill cream.

GARNISH

Chopped capers.
Potato straws (Recipe 199).

Cut the macaroni into half-inch lengths. Melt butter, add macaroni, and heat thoroughly. Add parsley; then mix cream and yolk of egg together, and add to macaroni; make very hot. Season with pepper and salt, and pile in hot dish. Garnish with potato straws and capers heated in basin.

420. Tomato Soufflé

PANADA
Three-quarters ounce of butter.
Three-quarters ounce of flour.
One gill tomato purée.

One dessertspoonful grated cheese.
Pepper and salt.
Two yolks and three whites of eggs.

Make panada with tomato purée, etc. Cool slightly, and beat in yolks of eggs, cheese and seasonings. Fold in stiffly-beaten whites of eggs. Turn into a greased fireproof dish, and bake in a moderately hot oven till well risen and firm to touch, from thirty to forty minutes.

BREAD, CAKES, BISCUITS, AND SHORTBREAD

BREAD

Notes on Yeast.

Yeast is composed of numerous little cells which, under favourable conditions, grow and multiply very rapidly. Yeast cells grow by budding. Conditions favourable to growth of yeast are the same as for ordinary plants :

(1) Warmth ; (2) moisture ; (3) suitable soil, viz., sugar.

Action.—The action of yeast is to set up fermentation in the flour. This changes some of the starch of the flour into sugar, and as the yeast grows it acts on the sugar, splitting some of it up into alcohol and carbon dioxide gas. The alcohol evaporates, and the gas expands and is driven off by the heat, after forming little cavities in the dough which makes it light and spongy.

Compressed yeast is used for home baking. It is produced in the rye distilleries. It can be obtained from grocers and flour dealers. Yeast must be used fresh. It should have a fresh fruity smell, and should be cool and moist to the touch. It should be in a block, not dry and crumbly. It should cream easily with sugar.

Proportions.—For bread, one ounce of yeast will raise three and a half pounds of flour (quartern or four-pound loaf).

For larger quantities of flour less yeast in proportion is used, viz., one and a half ounces yeast will raise seven pounds flour. For smaller quantities a larger proportion of yeast is required, viz. for tea-cakes, buns, etc., use one and a half ounces yeast to two pounds flour.

TERMS USED IN BREAD-MAKING

1. Setting the Sponge. (For method, see Recipe 421.)

This is done to increase the yeast when dealing with large quantities or rich mixtures.

2. Raising the Dough.

This allows the yeast to grow, and therefore carbon dioxide gas is formed in the dough. If bread is over-risen it will fall, due to over-stretching of the dough.

3. Kneading.

When sufficiently risen the dough is again kneaded, to distribute the gas evenly throughout, and to make the dough of an even texture. Too much kneading makes it close.

4. Proving.

The loaves, buns, etc., are again set to rise until the dough regains the bulk lost in the process of kneading, and until a smooth surface is produced.

5. Baking.

Very hot oven is necessary : (1) to kill the yeast ; (2) to expand the gas formed ; (3) to cook bread thoroughly.

When using the Oven of a Coal Range.

1. Have clean flues and adjust the damper so that flame circulates round oven.

2. Make up the fire so that it will not need further attention for one hour at least; but if a cake requires several hours' cooking put a little coal on the fire from time to time so that a uniform heat may be maintained.

3. Avoid sending any draughts of air into the oven while bread or cake is rising by any incautious opening or closing of oven door.

4. Make good use of oven space by baking pastry, small cakes, or scones on the top shelf, while a large cake is cooking in the more moderate heat of the lower shelf.

When using a Gas Oven.

1. See that burners are lit for fifteen minutes before using. Leave the oven door open for the first few minutes after lighting to let any steam escape. Lower the gas slightly when cakes are put in.

2. The hottest part is usually under the reflector, but some of the newest types maintain an even temperature throughout by being provided with a space for hot air at the back of the oven. Another recent improvement is the regulator at the tap, the use of which ensures that the gas flame in the oven will be automatically reduced when the heat rises above the point at which the index finger is set.

3. Place cakes in the middle of the shelf, not directly over the gas flame, and remove the reflector when baking large cakes in a comparatively small gas oven.

When using an Electric Oven.

1. Switch on twenty to thirty-five minutes before using—moderately hot, twenty minutes; hot, thirty minutes; very hot, thirty-five minutes.

2. Make good use of oven space.

3. Use residual heat after switching off for baked custards, biscuits, meringues, etc. When cooking with residual heat do not open oven door until the food is ready to come out.

4. Heat plates on top of oven when the oven is in use.

421. Bread

To make a quartern loaf—

Three and a half pounds flour.	One ounce yeast.
One and a quarter teaspoonfuls salt to each pound of flour.	One teaspoonful castor sugar.
	One and a half pints tepid water.

Sieve the flour and salt into a large warm bowl. Cream the yeast and sugar together with a wooden spoon until liquid, and add the tepid water. Make a well in the centre of the flour, and strain in the yeast and water. Sprinkle a little of the flour over, cover the basin with a cloth, and set to rise in a warm place for twenty minutes till the surface is covered with bubbles. This is called " setting the sponge." Work in all the flour with the hand, adding more tepid water if necessary to make a firm, elastic dough, and knead thoroughly. Cover again with a cloth, and set to rise in a warm place for two hours. When well risen, knead the dough lightly on a floured board, and form into loaves. The dough may be put into warm greased tins. Place loaves in a warm place to prove for fifteen minutes ; then bake in a hot oven for thirty minutes to one hour, according to size of loaf. When ready, the bread will be well risen, will feel light, and when tapped underneath will sound hollow. If in a tin, turn out and place

loaf on tray in oven in order to brown the sides. Then
cool rapidly on a wire tray.

422. Brown Bread

Two pounds whole wheaten flour.
One and a half pounds household flour.
One and a quarter teaspoon-fuls salt to each pound of flour.
One ounce yeast.
One teaspoonful castor sugar.
One and a half pints tepid water.

Prepare and bake as for white bread, but do not sieve
the wheaten flour.

423. Currant Bread

One and a quarter pounds flour.
One teaspoonful salt.
One ounce butter.
Half-pound currants.
Half-ounce yeast.
One teaspoonful castor sugar.
Two and a half gills tepid milk.

Sieve flour and salt; rub in butter. Clean currants
and add; mix all dry ingredients. Cream yeast and
sugar; add tepid milk. Strain into centre of flour,
and set the sponge for three-quarters of an hour. Mix
to soft dough. Turn out and knead well on board; put
into greased tins, and set to rise one and a half to two
hours. Bake in hot oven—time according to size of
loaves.

424. Breakfast or Dinner Rolls

One pound flour.
One small teaspoonful salt.
Two ounces butter.
One ounce yeast.
One teaspoonful sugar.
About half-pint tepid milk.

Sieve the flour and salt, and rub in the butter. Cream
the yeast and sugar, add the tepid milk, and strain into

the flour. Make into a soft dough, cover, and set to rise for one hour. Knead lightly, and divide into equal-sized pieces. Form into rolls, place on a greased and floured tin, and prove for fifteen minutes. Brush with milk or beaten egg (to give a glaze), and bake in a hot oven for fifteen to twenty minutes.

Note.—This quantity is sufficient to make sixteen rolls.

425. Yeast Cookies

Half-pound flour.
Half-teaspoonful salt.
One ounce butter.

Half-ounce yeast.
Half-ounce castor sugar.
About one gill milk.

Rub butter into flour; add salt. Cream yeast and sugar, add the tepid milk, and strain into the flour. Mix to soft dough and set to rise for one hour. Form into rounds. Prove fifteen to twenty minutes. Bake for fifteen minutes. Brush with melted butter.

426. Vienna Bread

One pound flour.
One teaspoonful salt.
Half-ounce yeast.
One teaspoonful castor sugar.

One ounce butter.
Half-pint milk (short measure).
One egg.

Sieve flour and salt into a bowl. Melt the butter, add the milk, and make tepid. Cream the yeast and sugar until liquid. Pour the tepid milk over the beaten egg. Add this to the yeast and strain it into the middle of the flour. Mix together to a smooth dough and beat well. Cover with a cloth, and put in a warm place till well risen (about one hour). Form into shapes, place on a greased baking-sheet, and prove for about fifteen minutes. Brush with beaten egg. Bake in a quick oven for about twenty to thirty minutes.

Note.—Instead of brushing with beaten egg before baking, the bread may be brushed with melted butter after baking.

427. Buns

Half-pound flour.	One teaspoonful castor
One ounce yeast.	sugar.

Three gills milk.

Sieve the flour into a warm bowl. Cream the yeast and sugar, and add the milk lukewarm. Strain and add to the flour gradually, stirring with a wooden spoon to make a smooth batter. Cover with a cloth, and set to rise in a warm place for an hour.

Have ready also—

One and a quarter pounds flour.	Quarter-pound castor sugar.
Quarter-pound butter.	Two ounces candied peel.
Quarter-pound sultanas.	Two eggs.

Rub the butter into the flour, prepare the fruit, and mix all the dry ingredients. When the sponge in the first bowl has risen, beat in the dry ingredients from the second basin with the beaten eggs. Mix thoroughly, and beat with the hand for about five minutes. Cover, and set to rise again in a warm place for one and a half hours. Form into small buns, and place on a greased and floured baking-tray. Put in a warm place to prove for ten to fifteen minutes. Bake in a hot oven from twenty to thirty minutes. When ready, brush with milk and sugar to glaze.

Note.—CLEAR GLAZE FOR BUNS. Two ounces sugar, small half-gill water. Dissolve sugar in water. Bring to boiling-point and boil for five minutes. Use while hot.

428. Yorkshire Tea Cake

Three - quarters pound flour.
One teaspoonful salt.
Half-ounce yeast.

One teaspoonful castor sugar.
One ounce butter.
One and a half gills milk.

One egg.

Sieve the flour and salt into a warm bowl. Cream the yeast and sugar; melt the butter, add it to the milk, and make it tepid. Beat the egg, add the tepid milk, and mix it with the yeast. Strain into the flour, and mix to a dough with the hand; turn it on to a floured board, and divide it into two or three pieces. Knead slightly, and make each piece smooth on the top, and drop into a greased ring on a baking-sheet. Cover, and set in a warm place for one hour till the mixture has risen to the top of the tins. Bake in a hot oven for fifteen minutes. While hot, glaze with milk and sugar.

429. Sally Lunns

Three-quarters pound flour.
Pinch of salt.
Half-ounce yeast.
One teaspoonful castor sugar.

Two ounces butter.
One and a half to two gills milk.
One egg.

Sieve the flour and salt into a warm bowl. Cream the yeast and sugar; melt the butter, add to it the milk, pour over the beaten egg and mix it with the yeast. Strain into the flour, and mix to a dough with the hand; beat well. Cover with a cloth, and put to rise for three-quarters to one hour. Turn out on to a floured board, knead lightly, and form into round cakes. Place on a

greased and floured tray. Prove and bake. Brush with
milk and sugar. Split and butter hot.

430. Doughnuts

Six ounces flour.
Pinch of salt.
Quarter-ounce yeast.
Half - teaspoonful castor
  sugar.
Half-gill milk.

Three-quarters ounce
  butter.
One yolk of egg.
One white of egg (stiffly
  beaten).
Jam.

Warm and sieve flour, add salt. Cream yeast and
sugar. Melt butter, add milk, and make it tepid. Pour
milk on beaten yolk, add to yeast, and strain into flour.
Add beaten white. Beat well. Set to rise for one hour.
Roll out. Cut in rounds, quarter-inch thick. Put a
little jam between two, joining edges well with white
of egg. Prove for fifteen minutes. Fry in deep fat.
Dredge with sugar.

431. Dough Cake

Half-quartern of dough (see
  Recipe 421).
Quarter-pound castor sugar.
Quarter-pound sultanas.

Two ounces candied peel.
Two ounces butter.
Two eggs.

Put the dough into a bowl, and add to it the sultanas,
shredded peel, sugar, eggs, and the butter in small pieces.
Beat well together with the hand until the ingredients
are well mixed. Turn into a greased and floured tin.
Put in a warm place to prove for thirty to forty minutes.
Bake in a hot oven from thirty to forty minutes. When
ready, glaze with milk and sugar.

432. Galettes

Quarter-pound flour. | Half-ounce castor sugar.
Half-ounce yeast. | One gill milk.

Sieve the flour, cream the yeast and sugar, add the tepid milk, strain it into the flour, and beat this mixture till smooth. Cover it with a cloth, and put in a warm place till well risen (about thirty minutes). Have ready—

Three-quarters pound flour. | One teaspoonful salt.
Four ounces butter. | Three eggs.

Sieve flour and salt, rub in the butter, and beat this and the eggs into the risen sponge. Let it rise for one and a half hours. Form into oval-shaped cakes ; prove for above fifteen minutes. Bake in a quick oven for twenty minutes. Brush with a little clarified butter, or sugar and milk.

433. Savarin

Quarter-pound flour. | Two eggs.
Quarter-ounce yeast. | Two and a half ounces
Quarter-teaspoonful sugar. | butter.
Half-gill milk. |

Sieve the flour into a bowl. Cream the yeast and sugar till liquid, add the tepid milk, and strain it into the flour. Cover with a cloth ; put the bowl in a warm place to allow the sponge to rise (about thirty minutes). When risen, work in the flour, and beat in the eggs and the butter broken in small pieces. Beat until the mixture drops from the fingers. Grease a mould with clarified butter, dust it with rice flour, and put in the mixture. The mould should be three-quarters full.

Prove in a warm place until the mixture has risen to the top of the tin. Bake in a hot oven for about thirty minutes. Turn out, and pour over the following syrup:

SYRUP FOR SAVARIN

Four ounces sugar.	One tablespoonful sherry
Half-pint water.	or rum.

Juice of half a lemon.

Boil the water and sugar about seven minutes until it forms a syrup. Add the sherry and lemon juice, and it is ready for use.

Note.—BABA. Use savarin mixture, with the addition of one ounce of currants, and bake in small tins. When cooked, soak in syrup.

BREAD AND SCONES MADE WITHOUT YEAST

Raising Agents.

(*a*) Bicarbonate of soda combined with cream of tartar or some other acid. For example:

When really *good* buttermilk is used no additional acid is necessary.

A teaspoonful of vinegar has the same action with bicarbonate of soda as cream of tartar, and may be used successfully for cakes and puddings.

Proportions for Bread and Scones.

To one pound flour:

When using buttermilk or sour milk:

One teaspoonful cream of tartar.	One teaspoonful bicarbonate of soda.

When using sweet milk :

Two teaspoonfuls cream of tartar. | One teaspoonful bicarbonate of soda.

Note.—Be careful to remove lumps in the bicarbonate of soda before use.

(*b*) Baking-powder is greatly used as a raising agent for various kinds of bread and cakes.   It can be made at home.

Recipe for Home-made Baking-powder.

Two ounces bicarbonate of soda. | Four ounces cream of tartar. Six ounces rice flour.

Sieve these ingredients together, mix *very thoroughly,* and store in covered tins.

Proportions for Bread, Scones, and Plain Cakes.

Two teaspoonfuls baking-powder to one pound flour.

434. Soda Bread

One pound flour.
One teaspoonful salt.
One teaspoonful bicarbonate of soda. | One teaspoonful cream of tartar.
One ounce butter.
About half-pint buttermilk.

Mix the flour, salt, soda, and cream of tartar together. Rub in the butter.   Add the buttermilk, and mix to a soft dough.   Knead up very quickly and lightly.   Form into loaves and place on a floured tin.   Bake in a hot oven from thirty to forty minutes till well risen, lightly browned, and firm in the centre.

435. Brown Bread

Twelve ounces whole wheaten flour.
Four ounces flour.
One teaspoonful salt.
One teaspoonful bicarbonate of soda.

One teaspoonful cream of tartar.
One ounce butter.
About half-pint buttermilk.

Method.—Same as Recipe 434.

436. Oatmeal Bread

Half-pound flour.
Half-pound oatmeal.
One teaspoonful salt.
One teaspoonful bicarbonate of soda.

One teaspoonful cream of tartar.
One breakfast-cup buttermilk.

Soak the oatmeal in the buttermilk for one to two hours. Then add the flour mixed with the other dry ingredients. Knead lightly, form into a loaf, or rolls, and bake in a hot oven from thirty to forty minutes.

437. Milk or Baking-powder Rolls

Half-pound flour, or quarter-pound flour and quarter-pound wheaten flour.
Two teaspoonfuls baking-powder.

Half-teaspoonful salt.
One and a half ounces butter.
About one gill milk or water.

Mix the dry ingredients; rub in the butter. Stir in enough milk or water to make a fairly soft dough. Place in rough heaps on a floured tin, or form quickly into twists or rolls. Brush with milk to give a glaze, and bake in a quick oven from fifteen to twenty minutes.

438. Soda Scones

Half-pound flour.
Half-teaspoonful bicarbon-
  ate of soda.
Half-teaspoonful cream of
  tartar.
Half-teaspoonful salt.

About one gill buttermilk.

Sieve the flour, soda, cream of tartar, and salt ; add enough buttermilk to make a soft dough. Turn on to a floured board ; knead very lightly, and roll out half an inch in thickness. Cut across in four. Place on a warm girdle, and bake steadily till well risen and of a light-brown colour underneath. Turn and bake on the other side till quite dry in the centre.

439. Oatmeal Scones

Quarter-pound oatmeal.
Quarter-pound flour.
Half-teaspoonful bicarbon-
  ate of soda.
One teaspoonful cream of
  tartar.
Half-teaspoonful salt.
One ounce butter.

Milk to mix.

Mix dry ingredients ; rub in the butter. Mix to a soft dough with the milk. Roll out and cut in four or eight. Bake on a hot girdle, first on one side till risen and brown, then more slowly on the other side till quite dry in the centre. If preferred, place scones on a floured tray and bake in a hot oven for about twenty minutes.

Note.—Wheaten flour, barley flour, etc., may be substituted for the oatmeal.

440. Afternoon Tea Scones

Half-pound flour.

Half-teaspoonful bicarbonate of soda.

Half-teaspoonful cream of
tartar.

Pinch of salt.

One   teaspoonful   castor
sugar.

One and a half ounces
butter.

Buttermilk.

Sieve the dry ingredients, and rub in the butter ; add
enough buttermilk to make a soft, elastic dough.   Turn
on to a floured board, knead very lightly, and roll out.
Cut in rounds, place on a warm girdle, and bake steadily
till well risen and of a light-brown colour underneath.
Turn and bake on the other side till quite cooked.

Note.—These scones may be placed on a floured tray
and baked in a quick oven from ten to fifteen minutes.
In this case make scones a little thicker.   One tablespoonful currants may be added.

441. Luncheon Scones

One pound flour.

One small teaspoonful bicarbonate of soda.

Two teaspoonfuls cream of
tartar.

One ounce castor sugar.

Three ounces butter.

Half-pint milk.

Sieve the flour, sugar, cream of tartar, and bicarbonate of soda into a basin ; rub in the butter, and mix
to a soft dough with the milk.   Turn on to a floured
board, and knead very lightly.   Roll out into a round
about half an inch in thickness.   Cut in eight sections,
brush with beaten egg or milk, and bake in a hot oven
for thirty minutes.

Note.—One ounce sultanas or currants may be added.

442. Treacle Scones

Half-pound flour.
One and a half ounces butter.
One ounce sugar.
Half-teaspoonful bicarbonate of soda.
Quarter-teaspoonful cream of tartar.

Half-teaspoonful ground ginger.
Half-teaspoonful cinnamon and spice.
Pinch of salt.
One tablespoonful treacle (melted).
Buttermilk to mix.

Rub the butter into the flour and mix all the dry ingredients. Warm the treacle and mix with a little milk. Add to the dry ingredients to make a stiff dough. Turn on to a floured board, knead lightly, roll in a round shape, and cut in four or eight, but do not completely separate the scones. Glaze with beaten egg ; place on a floured tin, and bake in a steady moderate oven for about twenty minutes.

Note.—If sweet milk is used take half a teaspoonful cream of tartar.

443. Dropped Scones

Half-pound flour.
One teaspoonful bicarbonate of soda.
One and a half teaspoonfuls cream of tartar.
Pinch of salt.

Two tablespoonfuls castor sugar, or one tablespoonful sugar and one dessertspoonful syrup.
Milk.
One egg.

Sieve the dry ingredients into a basin ; make a well in the centre, and drop in the egg and a little milk. Stir with the back of a wooden spoon, and add enough milk to make a thick creamy batter. Grease a hot girdle, and drop on the mixture in small rounds. When the surface rises in bubbles, turn the scones over with a knife and brown the other side.

Cool on a clean towel.

444. Potato Scones

Half-pound cooked pota-　About half-gill sweet milk.
　toes.　　　　　　　　　Pinch of salt.
About two ounces flour.

Mash or sieve the potatoes, and add the salt ; knead as much flour into this as it will take up, and add enough milk to make a stiff dough. Roll out very thinly on a floured board. Cut into rounds, and prick with a fork. Bake on a hot girdle for about five minutes, turning when half cooked. When baked, butter the scones, roll up, and serve very hot.

445. Oatcakes

Four ounces fine oatmeal.　Pinch of bicarbonate of
One dessertspoonful melted　　soda.
　dripping or bacon fat.　Hot water.
Quarter-teaspoonful salt.

Mix the oatmeal, soda, and salt. Make a well in the centre ; add the melted dripping and enough hot water to make a soft mixture. Rub plenty of meal on to the baking-board ; turn out the mixture and form into a smooth ball ; knead and roll out thinly. Rub well with meal to make the cakes white, and cut across in four or in eight pieces. Place on a hot girdle, and bake steadily till the cakes curl up at the edges. Toast in a moderate oven till slightly brown.

446. Thick Oatcakes

Half-pound oatmeal.	One teaspoonful baking-powder.
Quarter-pound flour.	
Half-teaspoonful salt.	Three ounces butter or lard.
One teaspoonful sugar.	Cold water.

Mix dry ingredients; rub in the butter, and add enough cold water to make a stiff dough. Sprinkle a little oatmeal on the board; turn out the dough, knead lightly, and roll out to quarter-inch in thickness. Cut in shapes; place on a greased tin, and bake in a moderate oven for about twenty to thirty minutes.

CAKES

Four Principal Methods of making Cakes.

1. *The Rubbing-in Method.*—The fat is rubbed into the flour, and is equal to half, or less than half, the amount of flour. The baking-powder is in the proportion of two teaspoonfuls to one pound flour.

2. *The Creaming Method.*—The butter and sugar are worked to a cream. They are in equal proportions, and the weight of each is equal to half, or more than half, the weight of flour. The baking-powder is usually in the proportion of two teaspoonfuls to one pound flour, but if many eggs are used this proportion is reduced.

3. *The Sponge Cake Method.*—The eggs and sugar are whisked till creamy, and the flour is lightly folded in.

4. *The Melting Method.*—The fat is melted, and as this is the method often used for gingerbread, the syrup, treacle, and sugar are usually melted with the fat. Bi-carbonate of soda, in the proportion of one teaspoonful

to one pound flour, is used instead of baking-powder when treacle or syrup is in the recipe.

Note.—Cakes should be turned out on to wire trays and cooled gradually, not in a draught. When cooled they should be kept in tins, and different kinds of cakes should not occupy the same tin.

Rules for the Preparation of Ingredients.

Almonds.—Blanch, remove skins, shred, and chop.

Currants and Sultanas (Alternative Methods).—(1) Wash and dry thoroughly.

(2) Place on a wire sieve; sprinkle with flour; rub with palm of hand.

(3) Lay in corner of a towel; sprinkle with flour; rub well; look over carefully to see that stalks are removed.

Raisins.—Wash and remove stones, dipping fingers in hot water.

Candied Lemon and Orange Peel.—Wash off the sugar before weighing; dry and shred.

Lemon Rind.—Wash and dry lemon; grate thinly; never going beyond the thin yellow skin.

White Flour.—Dry before sieving. Sieve to introduce air and to free from any lumps.

Treacle or Syrup.—Melt before measuring.

THE RUBBING-IN METHOD

447. Plain Cake

Six ounces flour.	Half-ounce peel.
Quarter-teaspoonful salt.	Half-teaspoonful baking-
Three ounces butter.	powder.
Two ounces castor sugar.	One egg.
Two ounces currants.	A little milk.

Sieve the flour and salt together, and rub in the butter. Clean the currants, shred the peel, and mix all the dry ingredients. Beat the egg, and add a little milk. Mix into the dry ingredients to form a dropping consistency. Turn into a greased Yorkshire tin, and bake in a steady oven for thirty minutes till risen, firm, and lightly browned.

448. Luncheon Cake

Six ounces flour.
Two ounces rice flour.
Three ounces butter.
Four ounces castor sugar.
Two ounces currants.

Half-ounce candied peel.
Pinch of nutmeg.
One or two eggs.
One teaspoonful baking-powder.

About half-gill milk.

Sieve the flour and rub in the butter. Clean the currants, shred the peel, and mix all the dry ingredients. Beat the eggs and add to the dry ingredients with the milk, and mix well. Turn into a prepared cake-tin, and bake in a steady oven from one and a half to two hours.

Note.—When cake is tested with a heated skewer the skewer should come out bright and clean.

449. Currant Cake

Half-pound flour.
Three ounces butter.
Four ounces castor sugar.
Four ounces currants.

Two eggs.
One teaspoonful baking-powder.
About half-gill milk.

Prepare and bake as for Luncheon Cake.

450. Soda Cake

One pound flour.
Six ounces butter.
Eight ounces moist sugar.
Eight ounces sultanas.
Half-ounce ground ginger.

Half-ounce ground cinnamon.
Two eggs.
One teaspoonful bicarbonate of soda.

A little milk.

Sieve the flour ; rub in the butter, and mix all the dry ingredients together. Beat the eggs, and pour them into the middle of the dry ingredients. Dissolve the soda with a little milk, pour it into the eggs, and beat all together. Turn the mixture into a prepared tin and bake in a steady oven for about one and a half hours.

451. Buttermilk Cake

Three-quarters pound flour.
Quarter-pound butter.
Quarter-pound sugar.
Three ounces raisins.
Three ounces currants.
Pinch of spice.

Three-quarters teaspoonful bicarbonate of soda.
Three-quarters teaspoonful cream of tartar.
About three gills buttermilk.

Prepare and bake as for Soda Cake.

452. Oatmeal Gingerbread

Six ounces flour.
Two ounces oatmeal.
Two ounces butter.
Two ounces moist sugar.
One teaspoonful ground ginger.
Three-quarters teaspoonful bicarbonate of soda.

One tablespoonful syrup and one tablespoonful treacle, or two tablespoonfuls treacle.
One egg.
Buttermilk.

Measure the flour, rub in the butter, and mix in all the other dry ingredients. Add the syrup and treacle melted, the egg beaten, and enough buttermilk to make a soft dropping consistency. Turn into a well-greased tin and bake in a moderate oven from one to one and a half hours, till well risen and firm in the centre.

453. Gingerbread

(For other methods, see Recipes 476 and 482.)

One pound flour.
Four ounces butter.
Three ounces sugar.
Half-teaspoonful salt.
One teaspoonful ginger.
Half-teaspoonful cinnamon.
Half-teaspoonful nutmeg.
Half-teaspoonful cloves.
One teaspoonful bicarbonate of soda.
Three ounces sultanas.
Two ounces almonds.
Two ounces preserved ginger.
Three eggs.
Four tablespoonfuls treacle.
Buttermilk.

Mix all dry ingredients and rub in butter. Add the sultanas cleaned, the almonds blanched and shredded, and the ginger cut into small pieces. Melt treacle, add to dry ingredients, also eggs beaten, and enough milk to make the mixture of a dropping consistency. Bake from two to two and a half hours.

454. Small Gingerbread Cakes

Four ounces flour.
One ounce butter.
One ounce sugar (light weight).
Half-teaspoonful ground ginger.
Pinch of mixed spice.
Half an egg.
Small half-teaspoonful bicarbonate of soda.
One large tablespoonful treacle or syrup.
About quarter-gill milk.
Four or five blanched almonds.

Grease some small patty tins, and place half an almond at the bottom of each. Sieve the flour and baking-soda, rub in the butter. Add the sugar and spices and mix well. Add treacle melted, the beaten egg, and enough milk to make a soft consistency. Half fill the prepared tins. Bake in a moderate oven for about twenty minutes till well risen and firm to the touch.

455. Rock Buns

Half-pound flour.
Three ounces butter.
Four ounces sugar.
Two ounces currants.
Half-ounce candied peel.

One teaspoonful baking-powder.
Pinch of ginger or spice.
One egg.
A little milk.

Sieve the flour, and rub in the butter ; add the currants cleaned, the peel shredded, the baking-powder, sugar, and spice. Mix all the dry ingredients thoroughly. Beat the egg, and add to it a little milk. Add it to the flour, and mix to a stiff dough. Place in rough heaps on a greased baking-tray, and bake in a hot oven for about fifteen minutes.

456. Seed Buns

Half-pound flour.
Three ounces butter.
Four ounces sugar.
One teaspoonful baking-powder.

One teaspoonful carraway seeds.
One egg.
A little milk.

Sieve the flour, and rub in the butter ; add the sugar, baking-powder, and carraway seeds. Beat the egg, and add to it about one tablespoonful of milk. Mix the dry ingredients to a firm dough, form into small buns, place on a greased tray, and bake them in a hot oven for about fifteen minutes.

457. Lemon Jumbles

Eight ounces flour.
Two ounces butter.
Three ounces castor sugar.
Half-teaspoonful bicarbonate of soda.
Half-teaspoonful cream of tartar.
Rind and juice of one lemon.
One egg.
A little milk.

Rub the butter into the flour, and mix all the dry ingredients. Make into a dough with the egg beaten, the lemon juice, and a little milk. Knead lightly. Divide the dough into small pieces, and roll each piece under the hand into a long strip, then twist up into a round. Place on a greased tin, and bake in a moderate oven from fifteen to twenty minutes.

458. Raspberry Buns

Six ounces flour.
Pinch of salt.
Two ounces butter.
Two ounces castor sugar.
One teaspoonful baking-powder.
One egg.
A little milk.
About one tablespoonful raspberry jam.

Sieve the flour and salt. Rub the butter into the flour. Add the sugar and baking-powder. Beat the egg, and add to it a little milk. Mix the dry ingredients with the egg and milk to form a stiffish dough. Divide the dough into equal portions and roll into balls, using a little flour. Lay them on a greased tray and make a hole in the top of each. Fill with a small quantity of raspberry jam and pinch the dough together again. Flatten the buns slightly; brush with a little milk and egg, and sprinkle with sugar; bake in a good oven for about fifteen minutes. When ready, the buns will crack on top and show the jam.

459. Coffee Buns

Eight ounces flour.
Two ounces butter.
Two ounces moist sugar.
Two ounces currants or sultanas.
One teaspoonful baking-powder.

Pinch of salt.
One egg.
A little milk.
One small teaspoonful coffee essence.
Few drops of vanilla.

Rub the butter into flour. Mix all the dry ingredients ; add the vanilla, coffee essence, egg, and milk, and mix to a stiff paste. Put on a greased tray in rough lumps. Bake from fifteen to twenty minutes.

460. Ginger Buns

Five ounces flour.
Two ounces butter.
Two ounces sugar.
One ounce preserved ginger (finely chopped).

One small teaspoonful ground ginger.
Half-teaspoonful baking-powder.
One egg.

A little milk if necessary.

Sieve the flour and rub in the butter. Add all the dry ingredients. Mix with beaten egg and milk to make a stiff dough. Place on a greased tray in rough heaps. Bake in a moderately hot oven till firm and brown.

461. Doughnuts

(For another method with baking-powder, see Recipe 478.)

Four ounces flour.
One ounce butter.
One ounce sugar.

Half-teaspoonful baking-powder.
One egg.

Sieve flour and baking-powder together. Rub in the butter, add the sugar. Mix with beaten egg to a fairly stiff consistency. Knead lightly. Roll out to about quarter-inch in thickness, cut into rounds, and sandwich two together with jam. Fry in deep fat, just beginning to smoke, till well risen and of a nice brown colour. Drain well and dredge with sugar.

THE CREAMING METHOD

462. Plain Plum Cake

Half-pound flour.	Two ounces currants.
Quarter-pound butter.	Two ounces candied peel.
Quarter-pound sugar.	One teaspoonful baking-powder.
Half-teaspoonful mixed spice.	Two eggs.
Two ounces Valencia raisins.	A little milk.

Sieve the flour. Clean and prepare the fruit, and mix with it the spice and one teaspoonful of flour. Cream the butter and sugar; add the flour and the eggs by degrees, beating thoroughly. Add the fruit and the baking-powder mixed with the last spoonful of flour. The mixture should be of a consistency to drop easily from the spoon, so if necessary add a little milk. Turn into a prepared cake-tin. Place in a hot oven till risen. Moderate the heat, and bake steadily for about one and a half hours.

463. Sultana Cake

Half-pound flour.	Two ounces candied peel.
Quarter-pound butter.	One teaspoonful baking-powder.
Quarter-pound castor sugar.	
Quarter-pound sultanas.	Two eggs.
Grated rind of half a lemon.	A little milk.

Prepare and bake as for Plum Cake.

464. German Pound Cake

Ten ounces flour.
Eight ounces butter.
Eight ounces castor sugar.
Eight ounces sultanas.

Four ounces candied peel.
Grated rind of one lemon.
One teaspoonful baking-powder.

Five eggs.

Prepare and bake as for Plum Cake.

465. Scotch Seed Cake

Fourteen ounces flour.
Eight ounces butter.
Eight ounces sugar.
Eight ounces mixed peel (lemon, orange, citron).

Four ounces almonds.
One dessertspoonful baking-powder.
Six eggs.

Prepare and bake as for Plum Cake.

466. Madeira Cake

Eight ounces flour.
Five ounces butter.
Five ounces castor sugar.
Grated lemon rind.

One teaspoonful baking-powder.
Three or four eggs.
Citron peel.

Sieve the flour, cream the butter and sugar, and add the grated lemon rind. Add the flour and eggs by degrees, and beat well. Add the baking-powder with the last spoonful of flour. Turn into a greased and papered tin ; place the citron peel on the top. Place in a moderate oven, and bake steadily for one and a half hours.

Note.—For Cherry Cake add four ounces glacé cherries, cut in quarters, and omit citron peel and lemon rind.

467. Carraway Seed Cake

Half-pound flour.
Quarter-pound butter.
Quarter-pound castor sugar.
One dessertspoonful carraway seeds.

One teaspoonful baking-powder.
Two eggs.
A little milk.

Prepare and bake as for Madeira Cake.

468. Rice Cake

Four ounces rice flour.
Four ounces flour.
Four ounces butter.

Four ounces sugar.
One large teaspoonful baking-powder.

Two eggs.

Prepare and bake as for Madeira Cake.

469. Spice Cake

Half-pound flour.
Four ounces butter.
Four ounces sugar.
One and a half teaspoonfuls

of cloves, cinnamon, and nutmeg mixed together.
One teaspoonful baking-powder.

Two eggs.

Prepare and bake as for Madeira Cake.

470. Coconut Cake

Six ounces flour.
Three ounces butter.
Four ounces castor sugar.
Three ounces coconut.

One large teaspoonful baking-powder.
Two small eggs.
A little milk.

Prepare and bake as for Madeira Cake.

471. Cornflour Cake

Four ounces cornflour
Four ounces flour.
Six ounces butter.
Six ounces castor sugar.

One teaspoonful baking-powder.
Three eggs.
A little vanilla essence.

Prepare and bake as for Madeira Cake.

472. Swiss Roll

(For another method, see Recipe 480.)

Three eggs ; their weight in flour, in butter, and in castor sugar.
A little milk.
Half - teaspoonful baking-powder.
Two tablespoonfuls jam.

Sieve the flour, cream the butter and sugar, add the flour and eggs by degrees, and beat well. Mix the baking-powder with the last spoonful of flour. Turn the mixture on to a baking-tray which is well greased and lined with paper. Spread evenly with a knife, and bake in a quick oven from seven to ten minutes. Heat the jam. When the cake is ready, turn it out on to a sugared paper. Spread the jam over, and roll up.

473. Sandwich Cake

Six ounces flour.
Four ounces butter.
Four ounces castor sugar.

One large teaspoonful baking-powder.
Three eggs.

Sieve flour. Cream butter and sugar. Add flour and eggs by degrees and beat well. Add baking-powder mixed with last spoonful of flour. Turn mixture into two greased sandwich tins, with round of greased paper in the bottom. Bake in a hot oven from ten to fifteen minutes. Turn out, and when the rounds are cold spread them with jam, and sandwich them together.

474. Queen Cakes

Six ounces flour.
Four ounces butter.
Four ounces castor sugar.
Two ounces sultanas or currants.

One teaspoonful baking-powder.
Two eggs.
Milk if necessary.

Sieve the flour ; clean the sultanas or currants, and mix a teaspoonful of flour with the fruit. Cream the butter and sugar ; add the flour and eggs by degrees, and beat well ; then stir in the fruit. Add the baking-powder with the last spoonful of flour, and a little milk if necessary to make the mixture of a dropping consistency. Half fill some small well-greased tins. Bake in a hot oven from fifteen to twenty minutes.

Note.—(1) For small Spice Cakes add one teaspoonful ground cloves, cinnamon, and nutmeg mixed together to the above mixture and omit the fruit.

(2) Three ounces sweet chocolate dissolved in a little milk may be added with a few drops of vanilla to make Chocolate Queen Cakes. Omit the fruit.

475. Chocolate Sandwich Cake

Six ounces flour.
Three ounces sweetened chocolate.
Four ounces butter.
Four ounces castor sugar.
Half-gill milk.

One large teaspoonful baking-powder.
Few drops of vanilla essence.
Three eggs.

Dissolve the chocolate in the milk. Cream the butter and sugar. Separate the eggs ; add the yolks and dry ingredients by degrees to the creamed butter and sugar ; mix well, and add the dissolved chocolate and vanilla essence. Lastly, fold in the stiffly-beaten whites of eggs. Turn the mixture into two greased and papered sandwich tins. Bake in a hot oven from twelve to fifteen minutes. Turn out, and when the rounds are cold spread them with whipped and sweetened cream, and sandwich them together.

476. Damp Gingerbread

(For other methods, see Recipes 453 and 482.)

Ten ounces flour.
Six ounces butter.
Six ounces moist sugar.
Three ounces almonds.
Six ounces sultanas.
Three-quarters teaspoonful bicarbonate of soda.
One and a half teaspoonfuls ground ginger.
One and a half teaspoonfuls cinnamon.
Quarter-pound treacle.
Two eggs.
Warm milk.

Sieve the flour ; clean the sultanas ; blanch and shred the almonds, and mix a teaspoonful of flour with the fruit. Cream the butter and sugar ; add dry ingredients ; then add treacle, beaten eggs, and a little milk if necessary. Turn mixture into prepared tin and bake in a moderate oven for about two hours.

477. Coconut Buns

Three-quarters pound flour.
Two small teaspoonfuls cream of tartar.
One small teaspoonful bicarbonate of soda.
Quarter-pound desiccated coconut.
Quarter-pound castor sugar.
Three ounces butter.
One egg.
One gill milk.

Sieve the flour, the cream of tartar, and the baking-soda through a wire sieve. Beat the egg. Cream the butter and sugar, and add the liquid, coconut, and flour by degrees to make a rather stiff mixture. Place this in rough heaps on a greased tray, and bake in a hot oven for about twenty minutes.

478. Doughnuts

(*For another method with baking-powder, see Recipe 461.*)

Three-quarters pound flour.
Pinch of salt.
Three ounces butter.
Three ounces sugar.
Two heaped teaspoonfuls baking-powder.

One egg.
Three-quarters to one gill milk.

FOR FRYING

Pan of deep fat.

Sieve the flour, salt, and baking-powder together. Cream the butter and sugar. Add the flour, egg, and milk by degrees to make a fairly stiff dough. Knead and roll out the dough to quarter-inch in thickness. Cut into rounds, and then cut out small holes in the centre of each round. Fry the rings in deep fat, faintly smoking. Drain and dredge with sugar.

THE SPONGE CAKE METHOD

479. Sponge Cake

Four eggs.
Four ounces castor sugar.

Three and a half ounces flour, dried and sieved.

Grease a cake-tin, and dust it with one teaspoonful of castor sugar mixed with one teaspoonful of rice flour. Beat the eggs and sugar over hot water till creamy ; then quickly mix in the flour. Half fill the prepared tin, and bake the cake in a moderate oven for about thirty minutes.

480. Swiss Roll

(For another method, see Recipe 472.)

Three eggs.	Three ounces flour.
Three and a half ounces castor sugar.	Quarter - teaspoonful baking-powder.
Two tablespoonfuls jam.	

Heat and sieve the flour. Beat the eggs and sugar over hot water until thick and frothy. Then remove from heat and whisk until cool. Stir in the flour, adding baking-powder with last spoonful. Pour into greased and papered tin, and bake in a hot oven from seven to ten minutes. Turn on to sugared paper, spread with hot jam, and roll up.

481. Rice Biscuits

Two yolks of eggs.	One teaspoonful ground rice.
Two whites of eggs.	
One and a half ounces castor sugar.	Pinch of cream of tartar.
One and a half ounces flour.	Pinch of bicarbonate of soda.

Beat yolks and sugar till thick. Add whites and beat again till very thick. Add dry ingredients. Drop in spoonfuls on to greased tray. Bake in a steady oven from ten to fifteen minutes.

THE MELTING METHOD

482. Gingerbread

(For other methods, see Recipes 453 and 476.)

One pound flour.
Four ounces butter.
Five ounces syrup.
Five ounces treacle.
Two ounces sultanas.
One gill milk.

Two and a half ounces sugar.
One dessertspoonful ground ginger.
One teaspoonful bicarbonate of soda.

Two eggs.

Sieve the flour and bicarbonate of soda, add the ginger and sultanas. Put the syrup, treacle, butter, and sugar into a pan, and melt them, but do not boil, and add to the flour. Add beaten eggs and milk to make a soft consistency, and beat very thoroughly. Pour into a prepared tin, and bake in a moderate oven for two hours or longer.

483. Parkins

Quarter-pound flour.
Quarter-pound fine oatmeal.
Pinch of salt.
Two ounces lard or butter.
Three ounces sugar.
Three-quarters teaspoonful bicarbonate of soda.

Half-teaspoonful ground cinnamon.
Half-teaspoonful ground ginger.
Quarter-teaspoonful spice.
Three ounces syrup.
Half a beaten egg.

Eight almonds.

Rub the butter into the flour. Add all the dry ingredients and mix to a firm dough with egg and syrup. Divide into pieces the size of a walnut; place on a greased baking-tray and flatten a little into biscuits. Blanch, skin, and split the almonds, and put one half on the top of each biscuit. Bake in a moderate oven till set and crisp.

484. Brandy Wafers

Two ounces syrup.	Half - teaspoonful ground ginger.
One and three - quarter ounces flour.	Two ounces butter.
One and three - quarter ounces castor sugar.	Half - teaspoonful grated lemon rind.
Half-teaspoonful lemon juice.	

Melt the syrup, sugar, and butter in a saucepan ; then stir in the flour, ginger, lemon rind, and lemon juice. Mix the ingredients well together, and drop the mixture in small teaspoonfuls on to a greased baking-sheet about three inches apart. Bake in a cool oven from seven to ten minutes. When baked and slightly set, remove carefully from the tray with a broad-bladed knife and immediately roll each wafer round the greased handle of a wooden spoon. Then slip off carefully. When quite cold fill the wafers with whipped and sweetened cream.

SHORTBREAD AND BISCUITS

485. Scotch Shortbread

Four ounces flour.	Four ounces butter.
Two ounces rice flour.	Two ounces castor sugar.

Sieve the flour, rice flour, and sugar into a basin ; add the butter, and work all together with the hand until of the consistency of short crust. Form into a round cake either with the hand on a pastry-board or in a shortbread mould. Place the cake on a greased and papered tin, prick it well, and bake it in a good steady oven till beginning to colour ; then moderate the heat, and allow it to crisp off slowly for about one hour.

486. Pitcaithly Bannock

Six ounces flour.
One ounce rice flour.
Four ounces butter.
Three ounces castor sugar.

One ounce almonds.
One ounce candied orange
 or citron peel.

Blanch and chop almonds finely. Shred and chop peel finely. Sieve the flour, rice flour, and sugar into a basin ; add the butter, and work in all the ingredients. Finish as for Scotch Shortbread.

487. Ayrshire Shortbread

Four ounces flour.
Four ounces rice flour.
Four ounces castor sugar.

Four ounces butter.
Half an egg beaten.
Two tablespoonfuls cream.

Sieve the flour and rice flour into a basin, and rub in the butter ; mix in the sugar, and bind the mixture to a stiff consistency with the egg and cream. Roll out thinly, prick with a fork, and cut out in fancy shapes. Place the biscuits on a tin, and bake in a steady oven for about fifteen minutes until of a pale brown colour. Cool the biscuits on a wire sieve.

488. Oatmeal Biscuits

Three ounces flour.
Four ounces oatmeal.
Three ounces butter.
A little beaten egg.

Quarter - teaspoonful bak-
 ing-powder.
One teaspoonful sugar.
Half-teaspoonful salt.

Rub the butter into the flour, and mix all the dry ingredients. Add the beaten egg mixed with a little water, and mix to a stiff paste. Turn on to a floured

board, roll out thinly, and prick. Cut into rounds or
squares, place on a greased tin, and bake in a moderate
oven from fifteen to twenty minutes.

489. Butter Biscuits

Quarter-pound flour. | Two ounces butter.
Quarter-teaspoonful salt. | A little water.

Sieve the flour into a basin, and rub in the butter.
Mix this to a stiff paste with a little water ; turn it on to
a floured board, and roll it out thinly. Prick, and cut
it into rounds. Place the biscuits on a tin, and bake in
a moderate oven till crisp (about ten minutes).

490. Shrewsbury Biscuits

Four ounces flour. | One teaspoonful grated
Two ounces butter. | lemon rind.
Two ounces castor sugar. | A little beaten egg.

Cream the butter and sugar, and add the grated lemon
rind. Add the flour and sufficient egg to bind to a
stiff paste. Turn on to a floured board, and roll it out
thinly. Prick, and cut it into rounds. Place these on a
greased baking-tin, and bake in a hot oven for about ten
minutes till of a pale brown colour.

491. Milk Biscuits

Quarter-pound flour. | Half-teaspoonful baking-
Half-ounce butter. | powder.
Half-gill milk.

Sieve the flour and baking-powder into a basin ; put
the milk and butter into a pan, and when the butter
has melted pour it into the flour, and mix together to a

smooth paste. Turn on to a floured board, roll out thinly, and prick well. Cut into rounds, place them on a greased tin, and bake in a moderate oven from fifteen to twenty minutes.

492. Cinnamon Biscuits

Three and a half ounces flour.
Half-teaspoonful ground cinnamon.
Quarter-teaspoonful baking-powder.

Two ounces sugar.
Two ounces butter.
Half an egg.
Milk if necessary.
Jam.

Mix the dry ingredients together ; rub in the butter, and mix to a firm paste with the egg. Roll out thinly, cut into rounds, and bake till firm, for about fifteen minutes. When cool, sandwich two together with jam and sprinkle with a little icing sugar.

493. Napoleon Biscuits

Four ounces flour.
Three ounces butter.
One ounce ground almonds.
One and a half ounces castor sugar.

Egg and milk to bind.
Sieved jam.
Icing sugar.

Rub the butter into the flour, and mix all dry ingredients together. Mix to a firm paste with the egg and milk. Roll out thinly, cut into rounds and rings, matching in size. Place on a greased tray and bake till firm, for about fifteen minutes. When cool, sandwich a round and a ring together with the sieved jam. Sprinkle with a little icing sugar.

PRESERVES

JAMS AND JELLIES

Notes—

1. The fruit must be dry and in good condition ; just ripe, but not over-ripe.

2. The sugar used must be pure.

3. The preserving pan must be absolutely clean, and should be rinsed before use.

4. A wooden spoon should be used for stirring, and a plated spoon for skimming.

5. The jars must be free from cracks, well washed, scalded, and heated before use.

To Cover Jam and Jelly

Wax circles should be put on immediately, while the jam is hot. They must fit exactly over the top of the preserve. Further covering may be done at once, or when the jam is quite cold.

Cover with a round of gummed paper, or tie on a round of parchment damped on the uppermost side only, or cover while hot with wet cellophane. Label with name and date. Store in a cool, dry, airy cupboard.

494. Strawberry Jam

Six pounds strawberries (for jam Scotch strawberries are best).

Half-pint red currant or gooseberry juice.

Six and a half pounds preserving sugar.

Carefully wipe and pick the strawberries. Put into a preserving pan with the fruit juice and bring slowly to boiling-point. Add the sugar, and stir over the fire until the sugar is dissolved. Bring again to boiling-point, and boil from twenty to thirty minutes. When tested on a plate, it should run unevenly. Skim, and allow to cool before pouring into jars.

495. Raspberry Jam

To each pound of raspberries allow one pound of sugar.

Heat fruit gently in preserving pan, bring to boiling-point, add the sugar, stir until sugar is dissolved, and boil the jam rapidly for three minutes. Skim, and pour at once into jars.

496. Greengage Jam

Six pounds greengages. | Six and a half pounds pre-
Half-pint water. | serving sugar.

Wipe and stone the fruit. Break half of the stones, and remove the kernels ; blanch and skin them. Tie the rest of the stones in muslin. Put into preserving pan with fruit and water, and cook gently for fifteen minutes. Add sugar, and stir over the fire until the sugar is dissolved. Bring to boiling-point and boil for twenty minutes. Add kernels. Test as for strawberry jam. Skim, and pour into jars.

Note.—(1) The kernels may be left out if desired. (2) All "stone" fruits, such as mussel plums, damsons, Victoria plums, etc., are prepared in this way.

497. Rhubarb Jam (1)

Six pounds rhubarb. | Six pounds sugar.
Six ounces whole ginger.

Wash and dry the rhubarb, and cut in pieces one inch long. Crush the ginger, and tie it up in a piece of muslin. Put rhubarb, sugar, and ginger into the preserving pan, and stir till it boils. Test after twenty minutes' boiling. If firming, remove ginger, skim, and pour into jars.

498. Rhubarb Jam (2)

Six pounds rhubarb (weighed after preparing). | Six pounds preserving sugar. Six ounces preserved ginger.

Half-pint water.

Wash and dry the rhubarb, and cut in pieces one and a half inches long. Put it into a strong basin, with the sugar and ginger in alternate layers. Pour on the water, and allow this to stand covered for twenty-four hours. Pour off the liquid. Put it into the pan, bring to boiling-point, and add the rhubarb and the ginger cut in small pieces. Boil steadily for forty minutes, stirring from time to time. Test, and, if firming, put a lid on the pan, draw it to the side of the fire, and allow it to stand for fifteen minutes : this swells out the rhubarb. Skim. Put into jars.

Note.—Red Victoria rhubarb is best for this preserve. For storing for winter use it should be preserved in early autumn.

499. Black Currant Jam

Four pounds black currants. | Two and a half pints water. Six pounds sugar.

Pick and wash the currants, stew in the water until tender, add the sugar, stir till the sugar is dissolved, and boil until ready. Skim, and pour into jars.

500. Vegetable Marrow Jam (1)

Four pounds marrow.	Two ounces preserved
Four pounds sugar.	ginger.
Two lemons.	Water.

Wash, dry, and peel the marrow. Cut in slices one inch thick. Remove the seeds and cut in quarter-inch blocks. Weigh and put in basin with the sugar, grated rind and juice of lemons, and ginger cut in small pieces. Put skins and seeds in a pan ; cover them with water and boil for half an hour, then strain. Allow one gill of this liquid to each pound of marrow. Put into basin. Cover and leave for twenty-four hours. Put contents of basin into a preserving pan. Bring to boiling-point, stirring constantly, and cook till marrow is transparent and will set, from three-quarters to one hour. Pour into jars.

501. Vegetable Marrow Jam (2)

Four pounds marrow.	Juice of two lemons.
Three and a half pounds	Two ounces preserved
sugar.	ginger.

Wash, dry, and peel the marrow. Cut in big cubes. Put the cubes of marrow in a colander. Place the colander over a pan of boiling water and steam the marrow until it is quite tender. Then put the marrow into a basin, add the sugar and the lemon juice, and leave overnight. Put the contents of the basin into a pan, and add the ginger cut in small pieces. Bring to boiling-point and cook the jam for about one hour, stirring frequently, until the syrup is thick and the cubes of marrow are quite clear. Put into jars.

502. Dried Apricot Jam

Two pounds dried apricots.　Seven pounds preserving
Five pints cold water.　　　　sugar.
Two to four lemons.　　　　One ounce almonds.

Wash and cut up apricots in small pieces ; pare rind
from lemons and chop it finely ; squeeze the juice from
the lemons and strain it. Put apricots, lemon rind and
juice into a large basin ; add the water and soak for
twenty-four hours. Measure this pulp, and to each pint
allow one pound of sugar. Put all into a preserving pan.
Boil for half an hour, stirring carefully all the time, till
it sets. Skim. Add almonds blanched and shredded.
Pour into jars.

503. Black Currant Jelly

Wash the currants. Put them in a preserving pan,
and cover well with cold water. Bring to boiling-point,
and boil gently until the fruit is reduced to a pulp, then
strain it through a jelly-bag.

Proportions.—To each pint of juice allow one pound of
sugar.

Put the juice into the pan, bring to boiling-point, and
add the sugar. Stir till boiling, and boil from ten to
fifteen minutes. Test, and, if firming, skim, and pour
into small pots.

Note.—This method applies to nearly all kinds of
jellies, such as green gooseberry, raspberry, apple, etc.

504. Red Currant Jelly (1)

Wash the currants. Put them in a preserving pan
with just enough cold water to cover the currants.

Bring to boiling-point, and boil gently from fifteen to twenty minutes until the fruit is reduced to a pulp, then strain it through a jelly-bag.

Proportions.—To each pint of juice allow one pound of sugar.

Put the juice into the pan, bring to boiling-point, and add the sugar. Stir till boiling, and boil from seven to ten minutes. Test, and, if firming, skim, and pour into small pots.

505. Red Currant Jelly (2)

Wash the currants, squeeze them in a coarse cloth with the hands till all the juice is extracted. Measure this into a preserving pan, and add one pound of sugar to each pint of juice. Stir until the sugar is dissolved. Bring to boiling-point, and boil for exactly three minutes. Skim, and pour into small pots.

506. Rowan Jelly

Wash the berries. Put into a preserving pan. Cover with cold water and cook to a pulp. Strain. To each pint of warm juice allow one pound of sugar. Bring to boiling-point. Cook for about twenty minutes. Test, skim, and pour into small pots.

507. Bramble Jelly

Four pounds brambles.
One pound apples.
Water.

One pound sugar to one pint juice.

Look over brambles and wash apples. Cut apples in pieces without paring or coring, and put with the brambles into a preserving pan. Barely cover with water, and boil to a pulp. Strain through a jelly cloth.

To each pint of juice allow one pound of sugar. Dissolve sugar, and boil from ten to fifteen minutes until the jelly sets when tested on a cold plate. Skim; pour into small pots.

508. Apple and Cranberry Jelly

Four pounds apples.
One pound cranberries.
Water.

One pound sugar to one pint juice.

Wash apples and cranberries. Cut apples in pieces without paring or coring, and put with cranberries into a preserving pan. Cover with water, and boil to a pulp. Strain through a jelly cloth. To each pint of juice allow one pound of sugar. Dissolve sugar and boil from twenty to thirty minutes until the jelly sets when tested on a cold plate. Skim; pour into small pots.

509. Crab-Apple Jelly

Four pounds crab-apples.
Two quarts water.

One pound sugar to each pint juice.

Wash the apples, cut in pieces, and put into a preserving pan with the water. Boil to a pulp. Strain through a jelly cloth. To each pint of juice allow one pound of sugar. Put juice and sugar into a preserving pan, stir till the sugar is dissolved, and boil until the jelly sets. Pour into small pots.

510. Marmalade

To each pound of marmalade oranges allow three pints water.

Wash the oranges, remove skin, and cut it in fine shreds. Slice the oranges, removing pips. Put all into a large basin, and cover with the water. (Soak the pips separately in a little of the water.) Leave to soak overnight. Strain the water from the pips, and put it into the preserving pan with the soaked orange pulp. Bring to boiling-point, and boil until the rind is soft. Measure the pulp, and allow one pound of sugar to each pint of pulp. Return to clean pan, and boil for thirty minutes, or until it sets. Pour into jars.

Note.—(1) A mixture of sweet and bitter oranges may be used, and lemons may be added if liked. (2) Mixed Marmalade may be made in the same way, using two grape-fruit, two sweet oranges, and two lemons. For the preparation of the grape-fruit see Recipe 511.

511. Grape-fruit Marmalade

Four grape-fruit. | Water (three pints to one
Four lemons. | pound).
Sugar (one pound to one pint pulp).

Wash the grape-fruit ; remove the yellow rind and cut it in fine shreds. Take off the pith ; cut it up roughly. Slice the grape-fruit, removing pips and centre core. Tie pith, pips, and core together in muslin. Wash the lemons, remove skin, and cut in fine shreds and slice the lemons (any pips may be added to the contents of muslin). Put all into a large basin, and cover with the water. Leave to soak overnight. Put the contents of the basin into a preserving pan ; bring to boiling-point, and boil until the rind is soft. Remove the muslin bag. Measure the pulp, allowing one pound of sugar to each pint of pulp, and return both to clean pan. Stir until sugar is dissolved. Boil for thirty minutes, or until the marmalade sets. Pour into hot jars.

512. Jelly Marmalade

Four pounds marmalade | Sugar.
oranges. | Water.
Two lemons. |

Wash the oranges and lemons. Pare the yellow part of the rind very thinly, and cut it up in small chips. Soak the chips with one pint of water overnight, and boil till tender. Cut the oranges and lemons into small pieces, and soak with the pips overnight in water to cover. Put all, except the chips, into a preserving pan, and boil till tender, stirring frequently. Strain through a jelly cloth. Measure the liquid. Put it into a clean preserving pan with the chips and the liquid in which chips were boiled, and the sugar, allowing one pound of sugar to each pint of liquid. Stir until the sugar is dissolved ; bring to boiling-point, and boil from fifteen to twenty minutes or until the marmalade sets. Skim ; pour into jars.

513. Lemon Curd

Three lemons. | Half-pound loaf sugar.
Quarter-pound butter. | Two eggs.

Rub the sugar over the lemon rind to take off the zest. Squeeze the juice from the lemons and strain it. Melt the butter, and add the sugar, lemon juice, and beaten eggs. Cook till the mixture thickens, pour into jars, and cover.

Note.—Orange Curd may be made in the same way, substituting oranges for lemons.

514. Damson Cheese

Two pounds damsons.

Wash damsons, put them into a jar or basin, and stand this in a pan of boiling water, and boil until the fruit is quite soft. Rub the fruit through a hair sieve. Measure the fruit pulp, and to each pint allow one pound of sugar. ↄ the pulp with the sugar in a preserving pan, and ؟ؤir over heat until th؟ sugar dissolves. Then boil from thirty to forty minutes, and longer if necessary, until the cheese sets stiffly. Pour into small moulds.

515. Pickled Damsons

Four pounds damsons.
Four pounds lump sugar.

Half-pint white wine vinegar.

Put damsons and sugar in earthenware pan, and pour the vinegar over. Let it stand two days, then bring to simmering-point, and simmer for twenty minutes. Bottle or put in jars.

516. Raspberry Vinegar

One and a half pounds raspberries.

Half a pint white vinegar.

Cover the raspberries with the vinegar. Stand for two to four days. Mash well and strain. To each pint of juice add fourteen ounces of sugar. Boil for ten minutes. Bottle when cold.

517. Lemon Syrup

One and a half pounds loaf sugar.

Two lemons.
One ounce citric acid.

One quart boiling water.

Peel the rind thinly from the lemons, and soak it for half an hour in enough boiling water to cover it. Put the sugar and citric acid in a basin, and pour the boiling water over them. When cold, add the juice of the lemons, strained, and the liquid from the rind. Put into bottles and cork tightly.

THE PICKLING OF VEGETABLES

Notes—

1. Use glazed stoneware vessels, lined pans, and glass jars when preparing, boiling, and storing pickles.
2. Trim and wash vegetables.
3. One chilli may be laid in each jar.
4. Tie a piece of wetted parchment over the jar. Label with name and date.

518. Pickle for Vegetables

One quart vinegar.
Two teaspoonfuls pepper-corns.
One teaspoonful allspice berries.
Piece of root ginger (bruised).
Blade of mace.
Cayenne and salt (tied in double muslin).

Boil all the ingredients together for five minutes. Strain through muslin. This may be used hot or cold: for a soft pickle the former, and for a hard pickle the latter.

519. Brine for Vegetables

Half-pound salt. | One quart water.

Dissolve salt in water. Strain and use cold.

520. Pickled Onions

Choose small, silver-skinned onions. Skin and scald (see Recipe 91, Note 2), and leave in brine (Recipe 519)

for two days, being careful that they are completely
covered by the brine. Rinse thoroughly. Put into
bottles. Cover with the pickle (Recipe 518). Then seal
the jar.

521. Pickled Cauliflower

Wash and break into sprigs. Put into boiling salted
water, and boil from three to four minutes ; drain. Use
the brine and the prepared pickle as for Pickled Onions.

522. Pickled French Beans

Wash, string, and cut up. Small beans may be left
whole. Blanch beans and plunge into cold water. Use
the brine and the prepared pickle as for Onions, Cauliflower, etc.

Note.—For explanation of blanching and cold-dipping,
see under Directions for the Bottling of Vegetables,
page 289.

Pickled Beetroot

See Recipe 169.

523. Pickled Red Cabbage

Remove coarse outer leaves and wash. Slice the
cabbage and lay on a dish. Sprinkle with plenty of
salt. Leave for two days, turning occasionally. Drain,
and dry on a cloth. Put into a jar and cover with the
prepared pickle. Seal the jar.

524. To Salt French Beans

String, wash, and dry the beans. Leave them whole.
Use equal weights of beans and salt. Put a layer of
salt in an earthenware crock ; then put in a layer of

beans, pressing down well. Fill up the crock with alternate layers of beans and salt, having the top layer of salt. Cover the crock with a wooden cover, and place on this heavy weights to press the vegetables down.

When using the beans soak them for twelve hours in cold water to remove the salt. Rinse and cook them in the usual way, but omit salt.

525. Apple Chutney

Nine ounces apples.
Six ounces Demerara sugar.
Four ounces sultanas.
Two ounces onions.
One ounce almonds.
Two teaspoonfuls salt.
One teaspoonful ground ginger.

One teaspoonful white peppercorns.
Half-teaspoonful coriander seed.
Two red chillies.
Cayenne.
Three-quarters pint of vinegar.

Prepare and chop the apples, sultanas, onions, and almonds. Tie peppercorns and coriander seeds in muslin. Put all the ingredients except the chillies into a lined saucepan, and simmer slowly from one and a half to two hours. Put into glass jars, place one chilli in each jar, and cover when cold.

Note.—A tomato and apple chutney may be made by using one pound ripe tomatoes (skinned) and half a pound of apples with the ingredients given above, but omitting the sultanas.

526. Tomato Chutney

Two pounds tomatoes, or a two-pound tin of tomatoes.
Two to three ounces moist sugar.
Six cloves.

Half-teaspoonful allspice berries (tied in muslin).
One teaspoonful salt.
Three-quarters to one gill white vinegar.
Three medium-sized onions.

Skin, scald, and chop onions. Add tomatoes and all other ingredients (if using fresh tomatoes skin them first). Boil, till tender, one to one and a half hours. Put into glass jars. Cover when cold.

Note.—If using tinned tomatoes do not add the liquor from the tin.

527. Gooseberry Chutney

One and a half pounds green gooseberries.
Half-ounce salt.
Four ounces chopped onion.
Half-pint vinegar.
One teaspoonful nutmeg and allspice mixed together.

Three ounces stoned raisins.
Five ounces Demerara sugar.
Half-ounce mustard seed.
Pinches of cayenne and ground ginger.

Wash, top, and tail gooseberries, and put them in a pan with half a pint of vinegar and onion. Bring to boiling-point and cook till tender (twenty minutes). Add remainder of ingredients. Boil five minutes. Put into glass jars or tumblers. Cover when cold.

528. To Dry Herbs

Pick the herbs (mint, sage, marjoram, parsley, etc.) in July. Wash well and remove stalks. Tie in muslin. Blanch (see page 20) for one minute. Then plunge into cold water. Drain; dry till crisp on trays in hot press or in cool oven. Pass through a sieve. Keep in dark bottles to preserve the colour.

529. To Dry Thyme

Pick just before flowering. Wash well. Tie in bunches, and hang in a warm place till dry. Keep hung up in a paper bag.

GENERAL DIRECTIONS FOR THE BOTTLING OF FRUIT

This is a popular and convenient method of preserving fruit when the fruit is plentiful.

The fruit must be firm, sound, and in full season.

To prepare the fruit.—Wash and prepare as for cooking, according to kind. Grade for size. If pears are hard stew in the prepared syrup till tender, and leave till cold before sterilizing.

Note.—When preparing pears, apricots, etc., have ready a basin of cold water with salt added (one tablespoonful to the quart). Cut pears in half and core before peeling. Peel pears and put them quickly into salt solution to prevent discoloration.

The Homely Method

Use earthenware or glass jam jars. They must be of equal height and be free from cracks. Use a deep pan with a false bottom, *e.g.* a fish-kettle.

Grade fruit ; rinse jar ; pack fruit tightly ; rinse the fruit after packing. Cover with water to overflowing ; place in a pan with water coming up to the shoulder of jars. Bring slowly to simmering-point in one hour's time. Keep at simmering-point for ten minutes. Lift out and seal at once.

Home-made Seals

(1) Use several pieces of parchment gummed together.

(2) Use ox-bladder previously dressed by the butcher : —Soak the bladder in several changes of boiling water till quite clean. Cut in suitable-sized pieces for covering

PRESERVES 287

the jars—fairly large pieces. Stretch tightly over the top of the jar and tie down with damp string.

(3) Use cloth and wax :—Cut a square of calico large enough to tie over the bottle. Spread with just sufficient paste to cover the top of the bottle. Cover the contents of the bottle with a grease-proof circle. Tie the calico on the bottle and cover with paste on the outside. The paste is made from four ounces of resin, half-ounce of vaseline, and half-ounce of beeswax, all melted together.

The Oven, or Dry Method

Use glass or earthenware jam jars. Pack jars with the prepared fruit. Place on a tray and put into a moderate oven (180° F.). Leave in oven until fruit is cooked, but not burst. Fill three jars at least, and when the fruit has shrunk fill up two jars from the extra jar. Remove from the oven. Fill jar to overflowing with boiling water or syrup. Seal at once.

Scientific Method

The full outfit consists of sterilizer, thermometer, and bottles. The best types of bottles are either the screw top or the spring-clip. The fittings consist of a rubber band, a glass lid, and a screw band or a spring-clip. The band or clip is for the purpose of holding the lid in position.

Note.—All bottles, lids, and rubber bands must be thoroughly tested for flaws before using. New bottles should be sterilized before use, and rubber rings should be soaked in cold water for one hour.

Method—

1. Fill the bottles with fruit of an even size, and pack tightly.

2. Rinse the fruit, after packing, with cold water to clear.

3. Pour in cold water or syrup, filling bottle to over-flowing.

4. Put on rubber ring, cap, and screw band, or place spring-clip in position.

5. Screw down firmly and give half turn back.

6. Place in sterilizer.

7. Completely cover with cold water.

8. Bring up to required temperature and then keep at that temperature for required time.

9. When sterilization is complete lift out bottles and screw down very tightly. Next day remove metal screw or spring-clip, when the glass cap and rubber should be so firm that one should be able to lift bottles right up by the lid. If the cap is not firm, re-sterilize, as the seal must be secure.

Note.—When put away, the metal screw cap may be oiled with salad oil, or it may be screwed loosely on the bottle.

Temperatures for Sterilizer—

For small fruits, *e.g.*, cranberries, mulberries, and bilberries : Raise to 165° F. in one and a half hours, and keep at that temperature for five minutes.

For plums, damsons, and soft fruit such as rasps : Raise to 165° F. in one and a half hours, and keep at that temperature for ten minutes.

For pears and apples : Raise to 190° F. in one and a half hours, and keep at that temperature for half an hour.

Strength of syrups for different fruits—

For pears and apples, use twelve ounces sugar to one pint water.

For plums and greengages, use eight ounces sugar to one pint water.

For gooseberries and rhubarb, use four ounces sugar to one pint water.

For raspberries and black currants, use two ounces sugar to one pint water.

Note.—If the syrup is too heavy the fruit will rise in the bottles, and if the heat is brought up too quickly the fruit rises and then breaks. The heat must be applied gradually.

GENERAL DIRECTIONS FOR THE BOTTLING OF VEGETABLES

The vegetables must be sound and fresh, with no discoloured parts.

To prepare the vegetables—

Wash and prepare as for cooking, according to kind. Bottle as soon as possible after preparation. Grade for colour, shape, and size.

To blanch the vegetables—

1. Have boiling water salted in the proportion of one teaspoonful salt to the quart.

2. Tie the prepared vegetables loosely in muslin, or put into a wire basket, and plunge into the fast-boiling water for one to five minutes according to age and size.

3. Then plunge into cold water. This is called cold-dipping.

Note.—When blanching white vegetables add three tablespoonfuls lemon juice to the boiling salt water.

Acidified brine—

One gallon of water.
Two and a half ounces salt.

Five to six ounces lemon juice (two tablespoonfuls equal one ounce).

Dissolve salt in water. Allow to cool and add lemon juice. Strain and use cold.

Acidified brine for peas—

Two to four ounces sugar.	Five ounces lemon juice.
Two ounces mint leaves.	One gallon boiling water.
Two and a half ounces salt.	

Put the dry ingredients in a jug. Pour on the boiling water. Infuse for thirty minutes. Strain and use.

Method—

1. Blanch and cold-dip the vegetables.
2. Fill the bottles with vegetables of an even size, and do not pack tightly.
3. Rinse the vegetables, after packing, with cold water to clear.
4. Pour in the brine, filling bottle to overflowing. Remove air bubbles.
5. Put on rubber ring, cap, and screw band or spring-clip.
6. Screw down firmly and give half turn back.
7. Place in sterilizer.
8. Completely cover with cold water.
9. Bring quickly to boiling-point, and boil for one and a half hours.
10. Lift out bottles, and, if necessary, fill up with boiling brine, and re-sterilize for half an hour.

Leave bottled carrots overnight before filling up with cold brine, and re-sterilize for one hour.

Broad beans : After sterilizing, rinse the beans in the bottle with boiling water ; re-fill with boiling brine and re-sterilize for half an hour.

530. Bottled Tomatoes

Choose small, even-sized tomatoes. Blanch and cold-dip. Remove the skins, cut in quarters or eighths. Pack tightly into a bottle, putting a layer of salt between each layer of tomato. For a pound-bottle use a tea-spoonful of salt. Put on fittings. Place bottles in a pan with sufficient cold water to come up to the shoulder of the bottles. Bring the water in the pan to 190° F. in one hour, and leave at that temperature for half an hour. Lift out bottles. If necessary, fill up from another bottle and re-sterilize for ten minutes to half an hour.

One teaspoonful of sugar may be used with the salt.

COOKERY FOR INVALIDS

Notes—

1. Consult doctor as to patient's diet.
2. Orders regarding diet must be strictly obeyed.
3. Procure the best ingredients obtainable.
4. The food must be nourishing and easily digested.
5. The food must be very carefully prepared, nicely cooked, and served punctually.
6. Give variety as far as is possible.
7. Season all foods lightly.
8. The food must not be prepared in the sick-room.
9. The food must be served in an appetizing form, and the patient should not be told beforehand what is to be served.

531. Beef-tea (Ordinary Method)

| Half-pound lean, juicy beef. | Half-pint cold water. Salt, if allowed. |

Remove all the skin and fat from the beef, and wipe thoroughly ; then shred finely, and put it into a thick jar with the cold water and a pinch of salt, if allowed. Cover tightly with a lid or greased paper ; let it stand half an hour. Stir up well, and place the jar (still covered) in a pan of cold water (to come half-way up the jar). Bring slowly to the boil, and cook gently for two

or three hours. Strain and remove any fat floating on
it by passing small pieces of kitchen paper or blotting-
paper lightly over it. If not wanted immediately, let it
cool, and warm as much as is wanted at a time, as beef-
tea spoils when kept warm. Keep with lid off jar.

Newly-killed beef is the best for beef-tea, as it con-
tains more juice than beef that has been kept. After
straining the beef-tea, the beef may be added to the
stockpot. Prepare beef-tea in small quantities, not
more than will be required for one day.

532. Quickly made Beef-tea

Use the same proportions, and prepare beef as above.
Allow to stand for as long as time permits, pressing it
frequently. Then turn it into a rinsed pan, and heat
gently until the liquid turns brown and the meat has a
white appearance. Stir all the time, and do not let it
boil. Strain through a coarse strainer, remove any fat,
and use as required.

Note.—If beef-tea is boiled the albumin is hardened
and rendered useless.

533. Raw Beef-tea

Two ounces lean, juicy beef. One gill water.

Prepare the beef as before, let it stand for half an hour,
then strain off the liquid and serve it. It should be
made fresh each time it is wanted, as it soon becomes
putrid. Raw beef-tea is sometimes given during teeth-
ing, dysentery, and typhoid fever, but should not be
given without a doctor's orders. Raw beef-tea should,
if possible, be given in a covered cup, as the appearance
is not attractive.

534. Essence of Beef

One pound lean, juicy beef.

Prepare the beef as before. Put it into a jar, omitting water, and cook as for ordinary beef-tea. If wanted weaker, add hot water to the liquor when it is to be used.

535. Mutton Broth

One pound neck or knuckle of mutton.
One dessertspoonful whole rice.

Two pints cold water.
One teaspoonful chopped parsley.
One teaspoonful salt.

Wipe the meat with a damp cloth, remove skin and fat, and cut the meat in small pieces. Remove the marrow from the bone, and put the bone with the meat, water, and salt into a clean lined pan. Bring it slowly to the boil, and remove all scum carefully. Simmer from two to three hours, skimming occasionally, then strain it through a fine strainer. When cold, remove all fat from the top, return the soup to a lined pan, and add to it the rice. Cook this for about twenty minutes and at the last add the parsley.

536. Chicken or Veal Broth

Prepare in the same way as Mutton Broth, using chicken or veal instead of mutton.

537. Chicken Jelly

One chicken.   Salt.   Cold water.

Remove the breast fillets from the chicken, and reserve these for steaming, etc. Cut the chicken into joints, and cut all flesh from the bones. Rinse the bones and wash the neck and gizzard well. Put all into a pan, cover with cold water, and add a little salt. Bring to the boil and skim well. Simmer gently from three to four hours. Strain through a hair sieve, and when cold remove all fat from the top. The stock can then be served cold in its jellied state, or heated as required.

538. Restorative Soup

One pound knuckle of veal.	One pound shin of beef.
One pound neck or knuckle of mutton.	Two quarts cold water.
	One teaspoonful salt.

Put the water and salt into a strong pan. Wipe the meat, free it from fat, and cut it into small pieces; put these at once into the water. Remove marrow, skin, and fat from the bones, wash them well, and add them to the other ingredients. Bring slowly to the boil, skim if necessary, and simmer from three to four hours. Strain the soup through a hair sieve. When cold remove any fat, and reheat the soup.

If desired, this soup may be thickened with (a) tapioca, sago, or rice, (b) arrowroot or cornflour, etc., allowing one teaspoonful of grain to half a pint of stock.

539. Fish Cream

Four ounces white fish (whiting or haddock).	Half-gill milk.
Half-ounce butter.	One tablespoonful cream.
Half-ounce bread crumbs.	A squeeze of lemon juice.
	One beaten white of egg.
Pepper and salt.	

Melt the butter in a small pan, add the crumbs and milk, cook until thick, and turn the sauce into a mortar.

Wipe and shred the fish finely, add it to the sauce, and pound them well together; then rub the mixture through a fine wire sieve. Season well. Add the cream and the stiffly-beaten white of egg. Turn the mixture into a greased basin or mould, cover with greased paper, and steam very gently from twenty to thirty minutes. When firm, turn the cream on to a hot dish. If liked, it may be coated with a white sauce.

540. Chicken or Veal Cream

Made in the same way as Fish Cream, but the meat must be passed through the mincing machine before it is pounded.

541. Fish Quenelles

Four ounces white fish.	Half an egg.
Half-ounce butter.	Pepper and salt.
One ounce bread crumbs.	Squeeze of lemon juice.
Half-gill milk.	One tablespoonful cream.

Melt the butter in a small pan, add the bread crumbs and the milk, and cook till thick. Wipe and shred the fish, and pound it with the sauce and the egg in a mortar; then rub the mixture through a fine wire sieve. Add the cream and seasonings, and shape into quenelles, using dessertspoons. Lay them on a greased frying-pan, and pour into the pan enough boiling water to nearly cover them. Put a buttered paper over, and poach slowly for about fifteen minutes, basting them occasionally. When firm, drain well on a heated cloth, dish neatly, and garnish with a sprig of parsley. If sauce is allowed, the quenelles may be coated with a white sauce.

542. Veal Quenelles

Four ounces of veal.
Quarter-ounce butter.
One ounce flour.

Half-gill stock.
Half a beaten egg.
Pepper and salt.

Remove all skin and fat from the veal, wipe thoroughly, cut it small, and pass twice through a mincing machine. Heat and sieve the flour. Melt the butter in a saucepan with the stock, and when boiling add the flour and cook until thick. Pound the veal, sauce, egg, and seasonings in a mortar ; then rub the mixture through a fine wire sieve. Shape into quenelles, using dessertspoons. Lay them on a greased frying-pan, and pour into the pan enough boiling water to nearly cover them. Put a buttered paper over, and poach slowly for about twenty minutes, basting them occasionally. When firm, drain well on a heated cloth and dish neatly. Garnish with parsley, and serve. If potato is allowed, the quenelles may be dished on mashed potato, and coated with a white sauce.

Note.—Chicken or rabbit quenelles may be made in the same way.

543. Steamed Fish

One filleted whiting, sole, or haddock.

Pepper and salt.
Lemon juice.

Trim the fillets, and wipe carefully. Season on the skinned side, and fold in two. Lay on a buttered plate, cover with a buttered paper and a lid. Put the plate over a pan of boiling water, and steam steadily from fifteen to twenty minutes, until the fish looks quite white. Serve on a hot dish with the juice poured over.

544. Mutton Chop Steamed

One mutton chop.
Pinch of salt.

One tablespoonful stock or water.

Choose a loin chop cut from well-hung mutton. Trim and wipe, beat with a cutlet bat or an iron spoon, and make it a good shape. Place the chop on a greased plate, season, add water, and cover it with a greased paper and a pan lid. Put the plate over a pan of boiling water, and steam for forty minutes. Keep the water boiling all the time, and turn the chop when half cooked. Serve on a hot dish with the juice poured over. Breasts of chicken and game are steamed in the same way. The length of time varies according to the thickness of the meat.

545. Chicken Panada

Quarter-pound breast of chicken.
One teaspoonful cold water.

One or two tablespoonfuls of cream.
Salt.

Wipe the meat and cut it in small pieces, and put it into a small basin with the water and a pinch of salt. Cover it with greased paper, and steam it slowly from one to one and a half hours. Then put the contents of the basin into a mortar, pound well, and rub through a fine sieve. Put the sieved mixture into a pan, add the cream, heat thoroughly, and pile the panada on a round of toast. Garnish with a sprig of parsley, and serve.

546. Raw Beef Sandwiches

One ounce lean beef.

Thin slices of buttered bread.

Shred the beef, pound it and rub it through a sieve, then add a little salt. Cut dainty slices of bread and butter, spread a little of the beef on one side and cover with another slice. Trim off the crusts and cut it into neat shapes.

Other Meat Dishes specially suitable for invalids are :

Stewed Sweetbread (see Recipe 108).

For invalids choose calf's or lamb's sweetbreads. The heart one is the more digestible and delicate. They must be perfectly fresh, and should be well blanched, and all fat should be removed.

Stewed Tripe (see Recipes 105, 106, 107).

Stewed Pigeon (see Recipe 109).

For the Cooking of Liver see pages 307-314.

Vegetables suitable for Invalids are :

Asparagus (see Recipe 165).

Cauliflower should be boiled for five minutes in boiling salted water, then drained and the cooking finished according to directions given in Recipe 177.

Stewed Celery (see Recipe 178).

Onions (see Recipe 186).

Spinach (see Recipe 204). It is often served with a Poached Egg.

547. Invalid Fruit Tart

One small sponge-cake.	One gill milk.
One egg.	One large apple.
One teaspoonful castor sugar.	Two tablespoonfuls water.
	One dessertspoonful sugar.

Wash, peel, and slice the apple, removing core. Put into a pan with the water and sugar, and cook till tender. Beat the apple smooth, and put it at the bottom of a greased pie-dish. Cut the sponge-cake into thin slices, and place these on the stewed apple. Beat up the egg, add the teaspoonful of castor sugar and the milk, and strain over the sponge-cake. Let the pudding stand for a few minutes, then bake in a moderate oven for about twenty minutes until the custard is set.

548. Calf's-foot Jelly

FOR THE STOCK

One ox-foot or two calf's feet. Five pints cold water.

Cut the foot into four or six pieces, and remove all marrow and fat. Wash and scrape it well in warm water, put it in a deep pan, and cover it with cold water. Bring it to the boil and rinse well, then return it to the pan with the five pints of water. Simmer slowly from six to seven hours, then strain through a hair sieve into a basin, and allow it to become cold.

TO CLEAR THE JELLY

To every pint of stock allow—

Half-gill lemon juice.
One gill sherry.
Three ounces loaf sugar.
Two cloves.
One inch of cinnamon stick.
Rind of one lemon.
One shell and white of egg.

Gelatine if stock is not very firm (for example— three-quarters ounce powdered gelatine to three pints of stock, depending on consistency when cold).

Carefully remove every particle of grease from the stock with a spoon dipped in hot water, then wipe the surface with a cloth wrung out of hot water. Rinse a well-lined deep pan, and into it put the stock, gelatine (if required), sherry, sugar, cloves, and cinnamon. Wash, dry, and peel the lemon thinly, and add peel and strained lemon juice to the other ingredients. Then add the white of egg and shell (washed and crushed). Place this over the fire and continue as for Lemon Jelly (Recipe 343).

Note.—If brandy is added, put in after straining the jelly.

549. Port Wine Jelly

Two gills port.
Two gills water.
Half a tablespoonful red currant jelly.
Two ounces loaf sugar.

One inch of cinnamon stick.
Rind and juice of one lemon.
Half-ounce powdered gelatine.

Wash and peel the lemon thinly, and strain the juice from it ; put all the ingredients except the port into a lined rinsed pan, and stir over the fire until dissolved ; then draw the pan to one side, and allow it to infuse for fifteen minutes. Add the port. Strain the jelly through muslin. When cool, pour into wine-glasses.

550. Orange Jelly

Half-pint water.
Half-pint orange juice.
Juice of two lemons.
Rind of two oranges.

Three ounces loaf sugar.
Three-quarters ounce powdered gelatine.

Put the water, sugar, orange rind, and gelatine into a saucepan and stir until dissolved ; cover, and allow to infuse for ten minutes, then strain it into a basin ; add the orange and lemon juice, also strained. Pour the jelly into a rinsed mould, and when set turn out and serve.

551. Egg Jelly

One egg.
Three ounces loaf sugar.
Quarter - ounce powdered gelatine.

One lemon, the juice made up to half-pint with cold water.

Rub sugar on to lemon rind. Squeeze juice and make up to half-pint with cold water. Rinse pan and put in water, sugar, gelatine, and egg slightly beaten. Stir till gelatine is dissolved, and the egg thickened, but do not boil. Strain and mould, when just setting, in small moulds or in custard cups.

Note.—The beaten egg may be added to the dissolved ingredients and left uncooked.

552. Milk Jelly

One pint milk.
One and a half ounces castor sugar.

Strip of lemon rind.
Half-ounce powdered gelatine.

Infuse lemon rind in the milk. Bring to boiling-point and strain the milk on to the gelatine and sugar, stirring until the gelatine is dissolved. Keep in the basin, stirring from time to time until the mixture is of the consistency of thick cream. Pour into small wetted moulds and turn out when set.

Note.—Unless the milk is allowed to thicken partly before being moulded it will separate.

553. Irish Moss Jelly

Half-ounce Irish moss.
One pint water.
Half a glass of sherry.

One dessertspoonful lemon juice.
Sugar to taste.

Wash the moss thoroughly and soak in cold water for twelve hours. Strain ; tie in muslin and simmer in the water for about five hours, adding more water as evaporation occurs, so as to keep the liquid to the pint. Strain. Sweeten to taste. Add lemon juice and sherry. Mould in small moulds. It may also be served hot as a drink.

Note.—Irish or Carrageen Moss is a seaweed. It is washed, bleached, and dried.

554. Whey

One pint milk.　　　One teaspoonful rennet.

Warm the milk to the heat of new milk, but do not let it become too hot ; stir in the rennet, keep it warm for a few minutes till the whey appears and is clear. Pour into a basin, let it cool : break up the curd and strain off the whey.

555. Wine Whey

One gill milk.　　　　| Half-gill of sherry.
One lump of sugar.

Put the milk and sugar into a rinsed saucepan and bring it to the boil, then pour in the sherry ; and when the milk is well curdled, strain through clean muslin into a glass, and serve the whey.

556. Gruel

One ounce of fine oatmeal.　　Half-pint cold water.

Break the oatmeal with the water, cover it over, and allow it to stand for one hour ; then stir it up, strain it into a saucepan, and stir over the fire until boiling. Allow the gruel to simmer for fifteen minutes. Add sugar or salt according to taste.

557. Linseed Tea

One ounce whole linseed.	Rind and juice of half a
Two or three lumps of	lemon.
sugar.	One pint boiling water.

Put the linseed, sugar, and lemon rind into a saucepan, add the boiling water, and simmer for twenty minutes ; then add the lemon juice, and strain into a glass or jug. Serve when cold.

Note.—If the drink is used for a bad cold, a small piece of liquorice or sugar candy may be boiled with it, or half a tablespoonful of honey may be used.

558. Black Currant Drink

One dessertspoonful black	Half-pint boiling water.
currant jam.	Squeeze of lemon juice.
A little sugar.	

Put all the ingredients into a jug. Stir well, cover, and stand it by the side of the fire from fifteen to twenty minutes. Strain through muslin.

559. Treacle Posset

One tablespoonful of treacle. One gill of milk.

Put the milk into a rinsed pan, bring it to boiling-point, and then add the treacle. When the milk is well curdled, strain the posset through muslin into a glass and serve.

560. Egg Drink

One egg.	One tablespoonful of
One teaspoonful castor	sherry or brandy.
sugar.	One gill warm milk.

Beat the egg in a small basin till it is well mixed, add the sugar and sherry, and pour on the warm milk, stirring all the time. Pour into a glass and serve.

561. Egg Flip

One white of egg.

Teaspoonful castor sugar.
One gill hot milk.

Beat the white of egg until frothy, but not stiff, add the sugar and hot milk to it, stir well together, and serve.

562. Cup of Arrowroot

One teaspoonful arrowroot.
Half-pint milk.

Quarter-teaspoonful of sugar.

Break the arrowroot smooth with a little cold milk; heat the rest of the milk and pour it over the arrowroot, stirring all the time; pour it back into the rinsed pan, stir till boiling, and cook from seven to ten minutes. Add sugar, and serve.

Note.—If wine is desired, add two tablespoonfuls of sherry before serving.

563. Barley Water

One ounce pearl barley.
One pint cold water.

Rind and juice of one lemon.
Sugar to taste.

Wash and blanch the barley, then put it into a well-lined pan with the pint of water and the thinly-peeled lemon rind. Simmer it slowly for two hours, then strain, and sweeten it to taste. Add the strained lemon juice, unless the barley water is to be used with milk, in which case omit the lemon juice, as it would curdle the milk. Serve hot or cold.

564. Rice Water

Half-ounce whole rice.   One pint cold water.

Wash the rice, put it into a pan with one pint of cold water, and bring to boiling-point.   Boil for half an hour, strain, and serve cold.   If permitted by the doctor, a teaspoonful of sugar may be added, and an inch of cinnamon cooked with it to give flavour.   Rice water is good for diarrhœa, dysentery, and cholera.   It is cooling and slightly nutritious.

565. Lemonade

Two lemons. | Two or three lumps of sugar.
One pint boiling water.

Wash the lemons, and peel the rind off one of them as thinly as possible, then cut them in two and squeeze out the juice.   Strain the juice into a jug, add to it the lemon rind and sugar, and pour on the boiling water. Cover the jug, and allow the lemonade to stand until cold, then strain.

Note.—Oranges can be used instead of lemons.

566. Toast Water

One slice bread.   One pint boiling water.

Toast the bread on both sides till dried through and quite brown, but not burnt.   Put it into a basin or jug, pour over it the boiling water, let it stand till cold; strain.   Toast water is cooling.

567. Apple Water

Three apples. | A piece of lemon rind.
Half-ounce sugar. | One pint boiling water.

Wash the apples ; cut them in slices (neither pare nor core them), and put them into a jug with the sugar and lemon rind. Pour the boiling water over them, cover the jug, and let it stand till cold. Strain off the liquor. Apple water is cooling, and is useful in fevers.

568. Port Wine Lozenges

One gill port.
Quarter-ounce isinglass.
One inch of stick cinnamon.
Four lumps of sugar.

One teaspoonful red currant jelly.
Strip of lemon rind.

Put all the ingredients into a pan and stir over the fire until dissolved ; put the lid on the pan, and infuse for ten minutes. Strain through muslin, and pour the mixture into a flat dish. When cold and set, cut into pieces of a neat size.

RULES AND RECIPES FOR COOKING LIVER

The following recipes and rules for cooking liver were compiled by Miss Pybus, Sister Dietitian to the Royal Infirmary, Edinburgh, for the use of patients suffering from Pernicious Anæmia.

[Reprinted by kind permission of the publishers from " Pernicious Anæmia " by Davidson and Gulland, published by Henry Kimpton, London.]

1. The best liver to use is that of ox or calf. Chicken or pig liver may be used occasionally. If liver is unobtainable use kidney.

2. The liver or kidney must be lightly cooked, and at as low a temperature as possible. It must never be fried hard, or some of it may escape digestion. Grilling

renders it hard. It is unnecessary to eat raw liver if the rules for cooking are observed.

3. The juice of the liver must not be wasted, or some of the value will be lost.

4. The liver must not be cooked with more fat than is necessary, or it will be greasy and may upset digestion.

5. Liver juice is of some use as a substitute for liver, but large amounts would have to be taken.

6. Raw liver pulp is of great value, but it is unnecessary when enough lightly-cooked liver can be taken.

7. The amount of liver should be weighed after cooking. All patients should have scales for weighing the liver.

8. Liver must never be allowed to get stale. It should be ordered fresh daily, or at most every two days.

9. Do not soak the liver. It should be wiped with a damp cloth or held under running cold water for a few seconds. All veins, etc., should be removed before cooking. If there is difficulty in removing the skin, the liver may be dashed in boiling water to facilitate this.

10. When serving liver do not remove the lid of the dish in front of the patient, as the smell is sometimes nauseating.

569. Raw Liver Pulp

Mince liver through a fine attachment of the mincer. Weigh out five ounces of the pulp. Add a little water. Beat thoroughly with an egg beater, adding more water till the liver is the consistency of thick cream. If not to be taken as a drink do not add the water.

570. Raw Liver Sandwiches

Cut very thin brown bread and butter. Spread thinly with marmite or bovril. Add some of the liver pulp flavoured with a little lemon juice, pepper and salt.

571. Cooked Liver Sandwiches

Rub cooked liver through a sieve and season.　Make into a sandwich with lettuce and brown bread and butter.

572. Liver Broiled

Broiling consists of cooking in a thoroughly hot pan *without* fat.　The pan can be lightly greased to prevent sticking.　Cut the liver into pieces, cook quickly on both sides.　Then cook more gently for not more than five minutes.　Serve with a good brown sauce.

573. Half-cooked Liver

Make small balls of the liver pulp.　Flavour with a little marmite or bovril, a pinch of herbs, chopped onion if desired, pepper and salt.　Roll the balls in browned bread crumbs, or a little fine oatmeal.　Fry for about a minute in mineral oil or clarified fat.　The liver inside the balls will be almost raw.　Serve with tomato sauce, etc.

574. Liver used for Stuffing Tomatoes

Two large firm tomatoes.	Pepper and salt.
Two ounces chopped, lightly-broiled liver.	Any seasoning liked.

Cut a small ring from the top of the tomato.　Scoop out the tomato pulp with the handle of a teaspoon. Sieve pulp to remove seeds.　Mix chopped liver with tomato pulp and seasoning.　Stuff tomato with the mixture.　Bake in a moderate oven till tomato skin begins to shrink.

Red peppers, potatoes, marrow, onions, and eggs, can

be stuffed similarly, or the mixture can be piled on the top of mushrooms, and baked.

To vary stuffing, add:

Pinch of herb.
Grating of lemon rind and squeeze of lemon juice.

A little chopped onion, mushroom, parsley, and bread crumb.

575. Liver Minced

Half-pound minced liver.
One onion.
Half a teacupful water.

Pieces of dripping about size of a walnut.

Cut onion into rings. Make dripping smoking hot in a stewpan and fry onion. Fry the minced liver very lightly. Add the water and seasoning and bring to the boil. Serve with sippets of toast.

576. Liver in Batter.

Prepare as Toad-in-the-hole (see Recipe 134), using liver instead of sausages.

577. Scalloped Liver

Cut broiled liver into small cubes. Mix with a well-cooked white sauce. Sprinkle with brown crumbs and bake in a hot oven.

578. Kromeskies of Liver

Mince some broiled liver. Season and form into cork shapes. Roll each in a strip of lean bacon. Dip into batter. Fry in deep fat till of a golden-brown colour.

579. Liver and Chicken Fricassée

Cut cooked chicken and lightly broiled liver into small cubes. Heat up in a good brown sauce.

580. Liver Quenelles

Half-pound minced, broiled liver. | Pinch of herbs.
One cupful bread crumbs. | Pepper and salt.
| Beaten egg to bind.
Tomato sauce.

Mix ingredients and form into quenelle shape (spoon-shaped). Poach in a frying-pan in a little water. Drain on a warm piece of linen. Coat with tomato sauce.

581. Liver Kedgeree

Use liver instead of fish (see Recipe 62).

582. Liver and Egg

Mince cooked liver. Beat up with egg, pepper and salt. Scramble. Serve on hot buttered toast. (Make with ox, calf, or chicken liver.)

583. Liver Soufflé

Two ounces sieved liver. | One egg.
Half a teacupful bread crumbs. | One tablespoonful cream.
| Pepper and salt.
Squeeze of lemon juice.

Rub raw liver through a wire sieve. Mix with the bread crumbs and seasoning. Pound together with yolk of egg and cream. Fold in the stiffly-beaten white of egg. Put into a small buttered soufflé mould or jam jar. Cover with buttered paper. Steam gently for fifty minutes. Turn out and serve with brown or tomato sauce.

584. Liver Soup

Made with a foundation of chicken broth, meat stock, marmite or bovril, vegetable soup such as tomato, or thin white sauce.

| Two ounces raw liver finely chopped or minced. | One breakfast cup soup or thin white sauce, etc. |

Pepper and salt.

Bring soup to the boil. Add the raw chopped liver. Cook until the liver has lost its red colour. Season and serve at once.

Note.—The raw liver may be added in cubes.

585. Liver Omelet

| One tablespoonful milk or cream. Two eggs. | One ounce broiled liver cut into small cubes. One ounce butter. |

Seasoning.

Have the pan very hot. Melt the butter, and add the eggs (very little beaten) with the milk and seasoning. Gently raise the cooked portion with a knife, letting the liquid run below. When nearly done, put the liver on one half and cover with the other. The centre of the omelette should not be solid but almost liquid.

586. Shepherd's Pie

Make with liver instead of with meat, and add a little bread crumbs to keep liver more firm.

587. Curried Liver

Half-pint curry sauce. | One ounce sultanas.
Half-pound raw liver. | Chutney.
Boiled rice.

Make curry sauce, and allow to simmer slowly for two hours to cook thoroughly and to blend flavour.   Cut the liver into slices ; add liver, raisins, and chutney to curry sauce, and simmer for five minutes.   Serve with boiled rice.

588. Liver in Casserole

Quarter-pound liver. | Carrot and turnip.
Small onions as for pickles. | A little stock or water.

Fry the small onions whole.   Cut the carrot and turnip into small pieces.   Cook them and the onions in a very little stock in the individual casserole.   When tender, add the liver cut into finger-lengths.   Cook in the oven. All the juice must be taken.

Suggestions for Liver in Pastry :

Cornish Pasties (see Recipe 129).—Use liver instead of meat.
Liver Rolls (see Sausage Rolls, Recipe 127).—Use liver instead of sausage.
Liver and Kidney Pie (see Beef-steak and Kidney Pie, Recipe 124).—Use liver instead of steak.

589. Liver Fried

Remove skin from liver.   Cut into slices half-inch thick.   Make fat in frying-pan smoking hot.   Fry liver lightly and quickly on one side, then on the other. Do not allow to become hard on outside.

590. Liver Steamed

Prepare liver as for frying. Put liver into a small basin or jam jar and cover with a saucer. Set in a pan of boiling water. Allow to steam until liver has lost its red appearance.

MISCELLANEOUS RECIPES

591. To make Porridge

| Two tablespoonfuls medium oatmeal. | One pint water. Salt. |

Bring fresh water to boiling-point in a deep pan, and add the salt. Sprinkle in the oatmeal, stirring carefully with a porridge stick or wooden spoon to prevent lumps. Boil and stir for the first five or six minutes till the meal is swollen, then put on the lid and simmer for at least half an hour, stirring frequently. If necessary, add more boiling water, as porridge should be of a good pouring consistency.

Note.—Some people find porridge more digestible if the meal is soaked overnight in the cold water.

592. To make Tea

See that the water is freshly boiled. Heat the teapot thoroughly. Put in the tea, allowing one teaspoonful for each person and one extra teaspoonful, according to the kind of tea. Pour the boiling water over the tea, and leave to infuse for five minutes.

593. To make Coffee (1)

| One heaped tablespoonful of pure coffee, freshly ground. | Half-pint of freshly-boiled water. |

See that the water is freshly boiled. Heat the coffee-jug. Put the coffee into the jug, pour in the boiling water, stir up, and infuse for ten minutes by the side of the fire. Strain, reheat, and serve as black coffee, or with hot milk.

594. To make Coffee (2)

One ounce pure coffee.   One pint boiling water.

(Use two-thirds coffee and one-third milk when serving.)

Place coffee-jug and jug containing milk in a pan with a false bottom, e.g. a fish kettle. Have enough boiling water in the pan to come half-way up the jugs. Put the coffee into the jug and pour the boiling water over it. Put the lid on the jug. Infuse from five to ten minutes. Then stir the coffee and allow the grounds to settle. Infuse further from fifteen to thirty minutes, keeping the water in the pan boiling.

595. To make Cocoa

One teaspoonful cocoa.   One cupful milk.

Break the cocoa with a little milk. Boil the milk, and pour it over the cocoa. Sugar may be added.

Note.—Cocoa may be boiled after adding milk. Half milk and half water may be used.

596. To make Chocolate

Half-pint milk.
One ounce chocolate.

One teaspoonful castor sugar.

Put the milk and chocolate into a rinsed pan, and stir over the fire till the chocolate dissolves. Add sugar if wished.

597. To make Toast

Slices of thinly-cut stale bread.

Put the slice of bread on to a toasting-fork, and hold for a few seconds before a clear red fire or under the grill. This dries the bread. Turn and dry the other side; then toast each side of the bread till of a golden brown colour. Cut it into neat pieces, place in a toast-rack, and serve hot and crisp.

If much toast has to be prepared, keep crisp and hot till required.

598. To make Toasted Dice of Bread

Cut a slice of bread quarter-inch thick. Remove the crusts and reserve for drying (see Recipe 600). Toast as above, then cut into exact dice.

Note.—When frying dice of bread, cut the bread into dice first, and then fry a golden brown and drain well.

599. To make Fairy Toast

Cut thin shavings of stale bread. Lay on a tray and bake until crisp, lightly brown and slightly curled, in a cool oven. Either use at once, or store in a tin and reheat before use.

600. To make Dried Bread Crumbs

For this use any crusts that may have been cut off bread, also scraps of cut bread. These may be kept separate, in order to have both dried brown crumbs (made from the crusts), and dried white crumbs (made from the white part only). Lay the bread on papered trays. Dry it until quite crisp in the hot press or in a cool oven. Then lay it on a double sheet of paper on a wooden board, and roll it smooth with a heavy rolling pin. (One can be made for the purpose by filling a large bottle with water, corking and sealing it securely.) Then pass the crumbs through a fine sieve and store for use. After crumbs have been used for the process of coating fried foods, those left over should be re-sieved before being put back into the jar.

601. To make Bread Crumbs

The bread should not be too hard and stale. Rub it down on a grater, or rub through a wire sieve. These crumbs may be toasted on a papered tray in a cool oven.

602. To Clarify Butter or Margarine

Place some butter in a saucepan. Melt it and let it boil gently until the salt is precipitated. Skim and strain through muslin into a pie-dish or basin.

603. To make Caramel Browning

| Half-pound brown sugar. | About half-pint boiling water. |

Heat an old iron pan on the fire ; rub it with a little dripping. Put the sugar into it, let it melt, and stir with an iron spoon till it is a dark brown. Draw the pan to the side of the fire and add the water gradually, stirring all the time. Place the pan on the fire again, and stir till all is smooth. Let it cool, and pour it into a bottle ; cork it well, and it will keep for some months.

604. To make Sandwiches

1. Cut thin slices of white or brown bread and butter. The bread should be twenty-four hours old. The butter should be beaten with a wooden spoon to make it spread more easily.

2. Spread the sandwich mixture over one slice.

3. Cover with another slice exactly matching in shape.

4. Press well together and trim off the crusts.

5. Cut the sandwich in halves or quarters.

Note.—Sandwich fingers may also be used.

605. Creamed Butter for Sandwich Mixtures

Half-pound fresh butter.	Made mustard (if desired).
One gill cream.	Salt, pepper, cayenne.

Beat the butter to a cream, half whip the cream and add it lightly to the butter. Season to taste.

606. Sandwich Mixtures

(1) EGG AND CRESS

Hard-boiled eggs.	Creamed butter.
Small cress.	

Chop eggs finely. Wash, drain, and chop cress. Mix all together with creamed butter.

(2) HAM

Remove fat from ham and mince very finely. Mix with creamed butter.

(3) Cheese

Grate cheese finely. Mix with creamed butter adding a little anchovy essence if liked.

(4) Nut and Cream

Walnuts or salted almonds. | cream, or Cream Salad
Half - whipped seasoned | Dressing (see Recipe 247).

Chop nuts finely. Mix with the cream.

(5) Nut and Horse-radish

One dozen Brazil nuts. | One dozen hazel nuts.
One large teaspoonful | A little cream.
grated horse-radish. | Pepper and salt.

Shell nuts, roast and chop finely. Mix all ingredients.
Note.—Chopped celery may be used instead of horse-radish.

(6) Sardine and Tomato

One tin of sardines. One tomato.

Drain sardines, and remove skins and bones. Scald and skin tomato. Rub both through a hair sieve. Mix and season with cayenne and salt.

(7) Banana

Cut banana in thin slices. Sprinkle with sugar and drops of lemon juice. Chopped dates may be used with the banana.

INDEX

Mutton cutlets, **105.**
— cuts of, 59, 63.
— haricot, 80.
— roast, 89.

NAPOLEON BISCUITS, 271.
Newcastle pudding, 173.
Nut and cream sandwiches, 320.
— and horse-radish sandwiches, 320.
— and lentil roast, 217.
— and macaroni cutlets, 216.
— and potato scallops, 217.
— butters, 215.
Nuts, dishes with, 215–221.

OATCAKES, 250.
— thick, 251.
Oatmeal biscuits, 269.
— bread, 246.
— gingerbread, 254.
— scones, 247.
— stuffing, 70.
Oil stoves, cleaning of, 17.
Olives, beef or veal, 82.
Omelet, liver, 312.
— savoury, 224.
— sweet, 194.
Onions, 120, 128.
— fried, 103.
— pickled, 282.
— sauce, 139.
— soup, brown, 31.
— spring, 120.
Open fruit tart, 181, 182.
— tart, 181.
Orange curd, 280.
— jelly, 301.
— pudding, 174.
Ox-tail soup, 36.
— stewed, 84.
Ox tongue, wet pickle for, 67.
Oyster sauce, 140.
Oysters, scalloped, 56.

PANADA, 137.
— chicken, 298.
Pancakes, 191.
Pantry work, 9.
Parkins, 267.
Parsley, 121.
— sauce, 138.
Parsnips, 121, 128.

Partridge, stewed, 87.
Pasties, Cornish, 99.
Pastry, 149–154.
— cheese, 150, 153.
— cornflour, 150, 153.
— potato, 149, 151, 152.
— rough puff, 150, 153.
— suet, 149, 151.
Patties, cold meat, 98.
Pear soufflé, baked, 190.
Pearl tapioca, 159.
Peas, green, 121, 128.
— soup, 29.
— — green, 33.
Pease pudding, 67.
Peccan nut mince, 218.
Peel, orange and lemon, prepara-
    tion of, 252.
Peppers, 121, 128.
Pickle for beef or ox tongue, wet,
    67.
— for spiced beef, dry, 66.
— for vegetables, 282.
Pickled beetroot, 123.
— cauliflower, 283.
— damsons, 281.
— French beans, 283.
— onions, 282.
— red cabbage, 283.
Pickling of vegetables, 282–285.
Pie, liver and kidney, 313.
— plate, 100.
— rabbit, 97.
— raised, 99.
— sea, 78.
— Roman, 230.
— shepherd's, 113, 312.
— steak and kidney, 96.
— veal and ham, 97.
— vegetable, 228.
Pies, mince, 187.
Pigeon, roast, 95.
— stewed, 86.
Pineapple pudding, 173.
Piquante, sauce, 141.
Pitcaithly bannock, 269.
Plaice, stuffed, 45.
Plain cake, 252.
Plate pies, 100.
Plum cake, plain, 259.
— jam, 273.
— pudding, plain, 169.
Polenta, Italian, 213.

INDEX

333

SCOTTISH INTEREST TITLES FROM HIPPOCRENE

THE SCOTTISH-IRISH PUB AND HEARTH COOKBOOK: RECIPES AND LORE FROM CELTIC KITCHENS

Kay Shaw Nelson

From hearty, wholesome recipes for family dinners, to more sophisticated and exotic dishes for entertaining with flair, this book is the perfect source for dining the Celtic way! In this collection of 170 recipes of the best of Scottish and Irish pub fare and home cooking, you'll find old classics like Corn Beef 'N Cabbage, Cock-A-Leekie, Avalon Apple Pie, and Fish and Chips, and new recipes as well: Tobermory Smoked Salmon Pâté, Raisin Walnut Porridge, and Skibbereen Scallop-Mushroom Pie. Each chapter begins with entertaining stories, legends, and lore about Celtic peoples, traditions, customs, and history.

260 pages • 5 ½ x 8 ½ • b/w photos/illustrations • 0-7818-0741-7 • $24.95 hc • (164)

CELTIC COOKBOOK: TRADITIONAL RECIPES FROM THE SIX CELTIC LANDS

Helen Smith-Twiddy

This collection of over 160 recipes from the Celtic world includes traditional, yet still popular dishes like Rabbit Hoggan and Gwydd y Dolig (Stuffed Goose in Red Wine).

200 pages • 5 ½ x 8 ½ • 0-7818-0579-1 • NA • $22.50hc • (679)

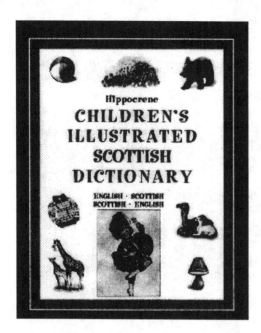

Hippocrene Children's Illustrated Scottish Dictionary

ENGLISH-SCOTTISH/ SCOTTISH-ENGLISH

Designed to be a child's very *first* foreign language dictionary for ages 5 and up, this book includes 500 entries (objects, people, colors, numbers, and activities), each accompanied by a large, full-color illustration. The words are clearly divided into syllables, and a handy pronunciation guide at the beginning of the book allows children and parents to learn the correct way to pronounce each word.

96 pages • 8 ½ x 11 • 0-7818-0721-2 • W • $14.95 hc • (224)

SCOTTISH GAELIC-ENGLISH/ENGLISH-SCOTTISH GAELIC DICTIONARY

R.W. Denton & J.A. MacDonald

In addition to its 8,500 modern entries, this dictionary features a list of abbreviations, an appendix of irregular verbs, and a grammar guide. The English-Scottish Gaelic section is expanded to facilitate conversations and composition. Geared for both students and travelers, the handy size and thorough vocabulary make it a perfect traveling companion throughout the Scottish highlands.

162 pages • 4 x 6 • 8,500 entries • 0-7818-0316-0 • NA • $8.95 pb • (285)

SCOTTISH PROVERBS

Compiled by the Editors of Hippocrene Books
Illustrated by Shona Grant

Through opinions on love, drinking, work, money, law and politics, the sharp wit and critical eye of the Scottish spirit is charmingly conveyed in this one-of-a-kind collection. The proverbs are written in the colloquial Scots-English language of the turn of the century. Twenty-five witty and playful illustrations by Glasgow artist Shona Grant bring the proverbs to life for readers.

130 pages • 6 x 9 • 25 illustrations • 0-7818-0648-8 • $14.95 hc • W • (719)

SCOTTISH LOVE POEMS

A Personal Anthology
edited by Lady Antonia Fraser

Lady Antonia Fraser has selected her favorite poets from Robert Burns to Aileen Campbell Nye and placed them together in a tender anthology of romance. Famous for her own literary talents, her critical writer's eye has allowed her to collect the best loves and passions of her fellow Scots into a book that will find a way to touch everyone's heart.

253 pages • 6 x 9 • 0-7818-0406-X • NA • $14.95pb • (482)

All prices subject to change without prior notice. To purchase Hippocrene Books contact your local bookstore, call (718) 454-2366, or write to: HIPPOCRENE BOOKS, 171 Madison Avenue, New York, NY 10016. Please enclose check or money order, adding $5.00 shipping (UPS) for the first book and $.50 for each additional book.